Another book on love. Just what we need, more cliches. That's what I thought when I started reading *Receiving Love.* How wrong I was! This is a book that will define the obscure, clarify the overused words, and give you some biblical, practical, and balanced teaching on the most important of all Christian concepts. This is one you don't want to miss.

> Rev. Steve Brown
> President, Keylife Network

Today there are billions of people walking around this planet, and each one of us is in need of love—there are no exceptions! Yet, the irony is that so many do not understand how to receive love. This book is an excellent tool for guiding us to the love that exists in our lives, even when we least feel its presence. By its encouragement, we can find the love that is waiting for each of us through a relationship with God and the people He brings into our lives.

> Paul Meier, M.D.
> Co-founder Minirth Meier New Life Clinics

Receiving LOVE

DR. JOSEPH BIUSO, M.D.
AND
DR. BRIAN NEWMAN, D.PHIL.
WITH GARY WILDE

VICTOR BOOKS

A DIVISION OF SCRIPTURE PRESS PUBLICATIONS INC.
USA CANADA ENGLAND

Unless otherwise noted, all Scripture references are from the
Holy Bible, New International Version®. Copyright ©
1973, 1978, 1984 by International Bible Society.
Used by permission of Zondervan Publishing House.
All rights reserved.

Editor: Barbara Williams
Design: Scott Rattray

ISBN: 1-56476-539-3

© 1996 by Joseph Biuso and Brian Newman.
All rights reserved.
Printed in the United States of America.

1 2 3 4 5 6 7 8 9 10 Printing/Year 00 99 98 97 96

V I C T O R   B O O K S ,
1825 College Avenue,
Wheaton, Illinois
60187.

DEDICATION

To

Jo Nell, Joseph, and Jenna Biuso
along with
Debi, Rachel, and Benjamin Newman:

God's gifts to us with whom we've
developed a much deeper understanding
about receiving love.

C O N T E N T S

PREFACE

We have a message to tell, a message about love.

It won't all flow out in step-by-step instructional form, because love cannot be so ordered. Rather, we hope to convey the message from heart to heart, as our gift of love to you. We'll simply tell you of our lives, of our human interactions, and of the signposts in the Scriptures and culture that keep pointing us to something we now recognize as crucial: *that it is better to risk openness to love than to be safe and closed off to life.*

We repeat this message in so many ways: love is there for you. We spend some time describing life's saddest dysfunction—the inability to love or be loved. We also devote time to exploring what you can do for yourself in the face of love's loss. Finally, at the end of the book, we address the culmination of the journey: reaching out to others with the love you have taken into yourself.

We do not prescribe; we can only suggest. But we hope you will take our suggestions to heart and be ready—just in case something most wonderful should happen in your life. For every work of goodness and love is ultimately a surprise. A blessed surprise that makes life worthwhile.

Since we are convinced that all truth is God's truth, we draw from every aspect of real life—stories from our medical and psychotherapy practices, books we have read, films we have seen. Life in the real world is the proving ground of God's transforming work in us.

Of course, we draw from Scripture and our response to that living, breathing Word. And when others have said a thing better than we could, we quote them. We draw from our journals and our memories the ideas and anecdotes that have moved us toward love, in hopes that just the right quotation or insight might inspire and encourage you too.

ACKNOWLEDGMENTS

When I started working on this book more than five years ago, I had no idea of the journey I was about to begin. The conception of an idea is only the beginning of growth and that has been true, not only in the creation of this idea, but also in the writing and rewriting of this book. This growth process was often exhilarating and at other times arduous, but to bring it to completion has been an unforgettable journey for Brian and me.

I cannot begin to thank all the people who have been instrumental and important to the creation of this book. But I will try to name a few. First of all, my coauthor and very dear friend Brian Newman. He not only made this project easier, but also made it fun for me. Brian has a way of bringing out the best in people, and he leaves that fingerprint through the book. We started this book for the benefit of others, but Brian and I found ourselves to be the beneficiaries. The sharing of our ideas has deepened our friendship.

Brian and I are also greatly indebted to Gary Wilde. Gary is truly a gifted, creative person. Without his hours of advice, organizational skill, and ability to bring the material together, this book could not have been written. We are also indebted to Dave Horton of Victor Books, who gave us true freedom to be creative and was always helpful and kind. We would also like to thank Dr. Robert Hemfelt for his creative ideas and suggestions.

On a more personal level, I would like to thank and acknowledge several people. This book would not have been possible if these folks had not touched my life in the ways they have. First, my brother-in-law, the Reverend Ronald Hooks, who led me to Christ and has become my close friend. This friendship has helped me learn to walk with God. I am also greatly indebted to the Reverend Gray Temple, who helped me catch my first glimpse of what it means to connect with God's love. I also wish to thank Dr. Julie Thomley for her early encouragement with this project. I hope her special brand of kindness, compassion, and love come through in these pages. I would also

11

like to thank Bob Farrar, who is truly a friend who sticks closer than a brother. He is an encouragement to me and an example of integrity that few people can better model.

Most importantly, I would like to thank my family: my wife Jo Nell, my son Joseph, and my daughter Jenna. They loved me even when I was unlovable and continue to give me unconditional love to this day. Without their support I could never have undertaken such a daunting project. I am so grateful they are in my life.

—Joseph Biuso

NOTES TO THE READER

How to use this book. Receiving Love can be both inspirational and practical for you. It should move you forward in a personal growth process toward receiving—and giving—more love in your daily life. We have filled the book with inspiring quotations. And we've included "Time Out" exercises and personal-evaluation surveys that can help you put our suggestions into practice.

So take your time going through the book. Stop at points that intersect with your experience or areas of needed growth. Do the exercises. Pray. Let ideas and insights take root in your soul. When that happens, you may wish to lay the book aside for a few days to practice the principles and suggestions we offer.

We recommend that you keep a personal journal handy as you read. Jot down favorite quotes that you can reread for inspiration in the future. Plan to expand the exercises and surveys with your journal, as well. Use its pages to make more extensive notes and responses. Go back and read through them over the weeks ahead, adding to your notes as appropriate. In other words, make this a practical, life-changing experience.

How we handled "I" and "We." Dual authorship creates a minor problem with personal pronouns. The reader may occasionally wonder: Who is speaking now? We have decided to make the book as personal as possible by using the first person singular as our standard voice. Sometimes this "I" is Joe speaking, and that will be especially evident when the action takes place in the hospital or doctor's office. At other times the "I" will be Brian speaking. Again, often this will be evident when the context is the counseling room.

But much of the time it really won't matter, for we have had similar experiences along the road to receiving more love in our lives. Our friendship has grown warm through writing this book together, and the much-used "I" simply indicates our natural inclination to think along the same lines. However, when it seems important to distinguish "who's talking now," we will employ this usage: I [Joe], or I [Brian].

The case examples. We have used anecdotes based on experiences with clients in our counseling and medical practices. The names are not real and, in most cases, the personalities are fictional composites of people we have known or worked with.

A note about the Relationship Survey. See Appendix A for an evaluation exercise entitled "Survey Your Own Relationship Patterns." You may wish to start this survey immediately as a way of applying the principles of this book; add to it as you move through the chapters. Or you might want to wait awhile, and read a few chapters of the book before starting this personal analysis of your relationship patterns. In any case, realize that the survey is not meant to be done in one sitting. It should be an ongoing personal investigation over a period of time.

Love: The Persistent Invitation

Fathers and teachers, I ponder: "What is hell?"
I maintain that it is the suffering of being unable to love.

          —Dostoevsky, *The Brothers Karamozov*

We were created for love.

And when we are unable to love—to give and receive—we suffer.

Love is the reason for our existence. Therefore a life without love leads to disaster, even though the evidence of such spiritual bankruptcy may remain well-concealed behind success and acceptability . . . and even a certain degree of congeniality. I think of Professor Borg in Ingmar Bergman's classic film, *Wild Strawberries*, the story of a life lived mostly outside the bounds of love. Through the eyes of an old man the question of life's meaning presents itself. Dr. Borg's life is normal, and beyond that, successful. But it is, in his own estimation, a special kind of hell. "My daily life has been fully occupied by hard work," he says proudly. Yet when he asks his daughter-in-law what she thinks of him, she risks being frankly honest:

> You're completely selfish, Father Isak. You're completely inconsiderate. . . . And you never listened to anyone but yourself. . . . But you hide it well, with an old man's civility, and friendly charm.
>
> You're as hard as nails, even though the magazines call you the great friend of humanity. We, who have seen you at close quarters, know how you are.

What do our close-quarter observers know of us? In the case of Borg, he has been selfish but never realized it. His children do not like him, but he has always believed he had their respect and understanding. So now Professor Isak Eberhard Borg, seventy-six years old, a seemingly kind and gentle old man, is ready to review the significance of his life. He envisions a hearse carrying a coffin. As its wheels crash into a lamp post the coffin tumbles to the street, opens, and reveals the occupant: Borg himself. He must face his own mortality.

> The last few months I've had the oddest dreams . . . it's really absurd. It's as if I was trying to tell myself something that I didn't want to hear when awake.
> *What, for example?*
> That I'm dead . . . though I live.

What better description of hell: a living death! All of this is a call to the old man, a call to consider whether any embers of sensitivity or affection in his being might yet be fanned into the flames of compassion.

We speak of this call in the chapters to come. It comprises a decision facing us each moment of our days: whether to believe that—and live as though—love is the grand pervading principle of the universe, the motivation that started it all ("For God so loved"), and that it is, at the same time, available in the most intimate way.

For you. Now.

The story of your life is the story of your response to this persistent invitation. We will begin by sharing our stories, a bit about our own response so far. We ask you to think through your own story along the way. Our experience is neither earth-shattering nor unique, simply illustrating that the most imposing of life's requirements—that we learn to live in love—can come packaged in the most mundane circumstances of our daily lives . . . and be ignored for years.

The sad part is that some of us leave the investigation of love to the end of our lives, like Dr. Borg, or never consciously enter the search at all. Yet the invitation—felt as a deep and abiding longing—is there all the time, working its subtle effects in all of our attitudes and choices and relationships. We need not relegate this pursuit to the end of life, though, to uncover the places in our histories where love could have, and should have, been. It is better to start early, right now, this day, on the journey to love. For we can refuse the invitation though we cannot rid ourselves of the longing. We can only let it speak to us and move us toward its divine source. That is what has happened to us.

Is This All There Is?

I [Joe] grew up in New York, the second of four children. Ours was a typical Italian family with a lot of cousins, aunts, uncles—and confusion—at holidays.

With so much going on all the time, it was hard for me to feel special.

I have always endeavored to *do* enough, or to *be* enough, to attain a worthiness for any droplets of love that might flow my way. I have always been goal-oriented and very accomplishment-oriented, trying to work my way to love. The more work I did, the more work I had to do. I felt as though I always needed to be accomplishing and doing to be worthy of approval, much less love. The problem is I could never do enough to earn the gift. I felt I was in a never-ending race.

I'd never *experienced* love. From early on I knew something was missing—but what?—so I just *did more.* Intuitively kids know that if they produce what a teacher wants, then they will be accepted. I felt that way all through school, and I think that's why I was a successful student. I carried this over into my life with friends and family: If I could just be what they wanted me to be, then I would be acceptable. I never realized how far my dry and parched inner landscape was from the oasis of unconditional love.

A person who has an approval-approach to life as I did looks at everything good that comes into his life as some form of reward for something produced. So if someone did genuinely love me (which was the case with my wife, for instance), I would feel as though she loved me only for what I produced: going to medical school, becoming a doctor, being successful. Because my perspective was warped, I saw everything that way. I needed to put on a new set of glasses, to look at things in a different light. Much of the time, people were loving me, but I just couldn't receive it as love. I decided relatively early that I was going to become a doctor, and I can see that even that decision was a striving to do and to be *more worthy* ("Won't they finally be proud of me?").

I had gone through medical school, and then to internship, and then to residency. I had worked hard, and I remember that, as a second and last year resident, my new wife and I didn't have any money at all. I was on call every third or fourth night, which meant thirty-six hours straight. I didn't sleep and I didn't come home. On my "off" nights I would moonlight at a clinic to make some extra money. When I came to the end of that long, exhausting period of my training and finally went into medical practice, I had great expectations: *I've finally reached the goal; I've come through; I can relax and enjoy the good life.*

Instead, I was overwhelmed with a dark, heavy feeling of letdown, of yawing emptiness. I remember talking with my brother-in-law, who is an Episcopal priest, and saying: "This is it? This is what I've worked for all these years?" Somehow it wasn't enough. Doing things just didn't fill me with the right stuff. But what was missing?

It took me several years after that to realize where I was in life, that I had always been striving, and that the incredible workload in itself had been filling a good part of the emptiness in me. Now I was in practice, successful and accomplished, and this void began to gape at me and demand my attention. Work wasn't filling that dark spiritual chasm, patients weren't filling it, my home life wasn't filling it. I think of that car commercial on TV: "I have a good career, nice house, great wife. So now it's time for . . ." what?

In the commercial the answer is: a luxury sedan.

But that's not the real answer, is it?

> I pray that out of His glorious riches He may strengthen you with power through His Spirit in your inner being, so that Christ may dwell in your hearts through faith. And I pray that you, being rooted and established in love, may have power, together with all the saints, to grasp how wide and long and high and deep is the love of Christ, and to know this love that surpasses knowledge—that you may be filled to the measure of all the fullness of God.[1]

I suppose I chose this passage because, as I talk about my story, I realize that it has been one long quest to experience love in its fullness. I don't think any of us experience the fullness of God until we die, but I do believe we are allowed to taste of it during our lifetimes. And that fact is what brought this book into being—the aim of opening up our spiritual taste buds a bit (we call them "love receptors"), to taste and see that God, and what He has created, is good and filled with love.

Being a "Great Guy" Isn't Easy

I [Brian] grew up in the South, in a large family, the fourth child of five siblings. My father was self-employed, a hard worker. My mother was a stay-at-home mom who worked hard too, taking care of us all.

I suppose one of the things I learned early on from watching my family, and from watching my two older brothers, was how to avoid problems, how to avoid getting in trouble (although I certainly had my share of getting into trouble). Just watching what those guys did and how they dealt with things when they got into trouble, I learned how to stay out of the same predicaments. As a result, I learned to "schmooze" people, to manipulate people for my good.

Not that I was doing anything harmful toward them. No, I was a very friendly guy, a helpful guy. That's how I got people liking me, and I discovered quite early on that my role in the family was to be the helpful one. I did spend a lot of time helping to keep the house clean, helping with the laundry, with shopping, even as a young kid. I found a lot of my approval coming through my performance. Dad would come home and be proud that the basement would be clean or see that I had helped with the housework. He'd give me a nice pat on the back.

As I grew into my high school years, my "servant attitude" personality jelled even more. I enjoyed it. But part of the reason I enjoyed it was not due to the sincere joy of serving, but because of the positive feedback and acceptance I got from people. It was meeting a deep need in me. It felt like love.

I remember in high school reading the book *How to Win Friends and Influence People* by Dale Carnegie. One of the major ideas that stuck with me was this: you can win more friends, in a relatively short period of time by showing genuine interest in others than you can win in a very long period of time, by trying to get others interested in you. So that became my life theme. In every conversation I had, I was inquisitive. I encouraged people to talk about themselves. I showed a lot of genuine interest in them. Of course, they left thinking, "Gee, Brian's a great guy."

But I was controlling the love I received through my good deeds and my helpful attitude. In a sense, I was getting false love. I wasn't getting true love because I wasn't putting much of my true self on display. The things that were negative about me, things that people might not like, remained locked away. If I didn't like something, I wouldn't say, "No, I don't like that." I would just suck it up and go on and put on a happy face.

That is how I learned to cope with life, how I learned to fill myself with what appeared to be love. Not that most people didn't genuinely care about me, but they weren't loving the real me. They were just loving the me that they saw, the me that I allowed them to see.

Several things changed in my life when I entered seminary and got involved in a counseling training program. I had to take a look at my life and some of the self-destructive strategies that I was using in order to attract people and keep them interested in me. I began recognizing how I'd manipulate others to be involved with me. I was dating (and eventually married) Debi at that time. She was also going through this counseling program, and she made a statement that continues to have profound impact on me:

> You know, Brian, what I really long for? I long to have someone truly know me. Not just be attracted to me because I may have some physical beauty, because I am a sweet person, or because I am a kind person. I long for people to know the ugliest inside of me—the side of me that I rarely allow anyone to see—and yet not be scared off by it. And they would continue to love me in spite of those things.

What a different outlook compared to my well-worn love-getting methods! I was keeping the "ugliest inside of me" locked up inside . . . in hopes of achieving the very same goal for which Debi had been willing to be self-revealing: genuine love and acceptance. Surely, two opposite approaches couldn't produce the same desired effect! Debi's words helped me squarely face some of the ways I avoided dealing with the real issues, how I avoided conflict, for instance, because I didn't want anyone upset with me.

I had to work through those things, and it wasn't easy. And now a lot of what I do in my counseling practice is help people recognize the futility and sadness of the love-getting strategies they live with, how are they covering up who they really are, or manipulating and showing only a part of themselves to keep people happy with them.

It seems worth all the hard labor to work on myself, and work with others, in opening up to love. Because it's certainly not easy being a "great guy" with no love; it's no fun being half a person. In fact, the hurt runs pretty deep.

Why a Book about Love?

One patient came to us, complaining of burnout, of utter exhaustion. He said:

> I think I've come to a point in my life where my personal needs and desires are strangers to me. I'm beginning to see that my goals and plans have always come from the outside, from the others I sought to please. But now, no one seems to be telling me what to do with my life. I'm goalless, depressed—like I'm extremely busy with living, but not engaged with life.

We came to an interesting conclusion: *Burnout is the opposite of being too busy.* It is the loss of meaning in life. In the midst of busyness, we discover that we have nothing very important to be busy *about.* At those times, we may need to explore where we are headed, and why. We've become like a ship without a port of call. We keep bumping off various relational islands, shouting: *Tell me, everybody—Is this it? Or this? What do I really want?*

We want love—we long for it—first and last. Not even the luxury sedan will do. Yet I [Joe] realized that I had never really felt anybody's love before. There was always a block there, this love-block. And although my wife, who is a very kind and loving person, loved me about as unconditionally as someone can love, I never really *experienced* that love.

I came to a point, desperate for love, of trying to do things that would help me experience it. I began experimenting with ways to connect, what I call connecting with other people, letting this love-block down so I could feel their love and experience their love. I found out it worked. The answer was not a matter of accomplishment, but *relationship.* And then, in a similar fashion, I began connecting with God and feeling His love, instead of living as an isolated person.

That's what led to this book. We began building on this initial experience of longing for, and finally beginning to receive, the love around us. We began to talk to people about all of this and found that they struggle with receiving love too. We became aware of a gigantic problem—a huge void—in our medical and counseling practices, seeing how many patients had love-blocks that made them miserable. They struggled with numerous complaints, often related to stress and overproduction of adrenalin, or with psychosomatic illnesses. Others experienced mild to severe depressions, still others retreated back into abusive and destructive relationships with little hope of change. But most important, we began to see that each of these responses to inner pain was an unconscious cry: "Please, please love me!"

> By common estimation most people realize only about ten percent of their life-potential. They see only ten percent of the world's beauty and hear only ten percent of the music and poetry of the universe. They are alive to only ten percent of the deep and rich feelings possible to human beings. They stumble along the path of an unreflective life in an unexamined world. They survive with only a shriveled capacity for giving and receiving love.[2]

And so this book is unashamedly about love, because it is the thing we all need the most. It is about learning to accept the love that is around each of us every day and being able to process it into ourselves. It is about learning how to love ourselves as we are commanded by God to do. As we do this, we will begin to trust, and in our growing faith that love will be there for us, we will break the bonds of isolation and loneliness. We'll begin to connect with other people and with God. In the healing process we'll begin to feel that we are deserving of love and, therefore, we'll be open to receiving it. Only then will we be able to give love to others.

How Is It with You?

So many of us are working out of depleted love reserves. Instead of realizing and embracing our need to receive love from God and others, we often close ourselves up and accept "counterfeit fulfillments" at crucial moments in our relationships. And we may be tragically sidetracked into other questionable self-improvement endeavors revolving mainly around this key question: *How can I change myself in order to make people love me?* But if that is our approach to life, then the changes will never be enough. For the true problem is not that love is unavailable until we deserve it. Love is available, now, when we are ready to receive it.

Where does all of this intersect with your own experience? We invite you to see that you have been right in the middle of this discussion, to recognize it with just a moment's reflection. We have been describing the love-block, and you can feel it in yourself by just recalling some of the things that happen regularly in your life. For example:

❏ You have a brief, minor argument with a friend. It's over, and there is a moment of silence in which the relationship can go either way . . . if only someone would say: *"Hey, I guess I was wrong about . . ."*

❏ You've just been turned down for sex by a tired spouse. You turn to the other side of the bed, close down the conversation, and think: *But wouldn't it be better if I turned back around and said something kind before we go to sleep?*

❏ You face a rebellious teenage son who once again smarts off with a wisecrack. You lay into him with a few cracks of your own (instead of trying to uncover the real problem). Later, he comes up to apologize, and you'd like to hug him, *but your arms feel stiff and don't move.*

In each of those situations—that is, in the similar, but unique ones in your own life—just ask yourself: *What was the thing that held me back? What was it that kept me from reaching out?*

Whatever that "it" was, however you label it, that was the love-block in action. The question that ought to follow your reflection on such experiences is: *Why haven't I received enough love to be able to give a little bit of it away when my friend, spouse, or child needs it?*

Open New Routes . . . and Rest

Perhaps Dostoevsky was right in telling us that the inability to love is a hellish kind of suffering. In this regard I think of Corrie ten Boom, the World War II concentration-camp survivor. In her book *The Hiding Place* she tells about being young and deeply in love with a man, engaged to be married. The man broke off the engagement, though, and married Corrie's best friend. Of course, Corrie was devastated and became quite isolated and lonely. Until her father told her:

> Corrie, do you know what hurts so very much? It's love. Love is the strongest force in the world, and when it is blocked that means pain.
>
> There are two things we can do when that happens. We can kill the love so that it stops hurting. But then of course part of us dies, too. Or, Corrie, we can ask God to open up another route for that love to travel.[3]

Wise words from a kind father, words that released torrents of love throughout Corrie's life, even in the midst of a Nazi hell. The Scripture says: "Love is kind." We hope you will find this a book full of kind and helpful words. If we occasionally slip in a "should" or an "ought," please forgive us. For we do not presume to offer you the answer to life. We can't cure all the hurts of your past or guarantee a painless future. We hope only to invite you to investigate further the power of love to transform us all. We speak primarily of what has happened to us and to others we know. We seek to encourage you, but not by marshaling the evidence to convince you of a principle or philosophy. For what would that do? You already know the ache in your heart for love, just as we know it.

But we do believe that ache can be embraced . . . and much of it eased. Though some of it will always remain, in itself a loving reminder of our earthly incompleteness and our eventual fulfillment in the One who said:

Take My yoke upon you and learn from Me,
    for I am gentle and humble in heart,
        and you will find rest for your souls.[4]

PART ONE
The Need for Healing

1

The Love-Blocked Personality

Not only is it the most difficult thing to know one's self, but the most inconvenient.

—Josh Billings

Let's look into the lives of some people you may know—

❏ David Norton, vice-president of finance, wheeled his silver Mercedes into the driveway, stepped out, and gave the door a shove with his elbow. *It's always something,* he thought, kicking a stone across the asphalt. The hassles at work, the squabbles with his wife Betty, or just the upkeep on everything he'd been able to accumulate over his thirty years of business success.

He trudged up to the front door and saw Betty move away from a bedroom window. He could look forward to . . . what? Another night of TV? A few drinks to help him numb-out for the evening? David supposed he needed friends. Yet despite being around countless people during the day, he couldn't conjure up the face of a single person he would call a close companion. *Isn't that what a wife is supposed to be?*

He wandered into the living room and flicked on the evening news. *Big-time successful exec! But is this really all there is to my life? All there's gonna be?*

❑ "We have your son down here, and we need you to come get him. He's being charged with shoplifting; you'll receive a court date in the mail." Lisa Jensen, many years' divorced, mother of three, wasn't really surprised by the call, though she was definitely upset. Fifteen-year-old Michael had been wild and unmanageable for years now.

If only I could find "Mr. Right." It was a bitter thought, for the merry-go-round of relationships over the years had been anything but right for her. *Just a little help with all this, that's all; it's too much for one person.*

She knew it wasn't right that the kids woke up to a new "daddy" pouring coffee in the kitchen every few months. She knew Michael's acts of public defiance were thinly camouflaged missiles of bitterness launched at her. And she knew it couldn't go on like this without a dam-burst of serious trouble soon to come.

Lisa paused at the mirror and looked into her eyes for a moment before heading to the police station. She decided there were too many crinkles of flesh at the corners of those once-perfect brown eyes—too many for a thirty-four-year-old young lady who should be having a good time in life.

❑ John Rios didn't inhale all that much, but it was enough, he knew, to start the buzz. *And I'll have to keep doing it too the way things are working out for me.* Sitting in a circle of friends like this, though, gave him some peace. He had thought he'd be through with college by now, but after six years—two spent "just seeing the world" (mostly on the southwest side of Chicago), he still hadn't hammered out an economics degree. His mother, of course, was definitely ticked.

John shifted his weight and let the haze wash over him. "Yesterday, all my troubles seemed so far away. . . ." *Old song, but that's what this stuff'll do to you; put all your troubles way behind you, yeah.* A psychologist had once told him that the only way to deal with his anxiety attacks would be to face the pain of his past. That cauldron of hurt had been threatening to bubble over ever since the day his dad had checked out of the family with a truly prize-winning coronary. *But why bother?*

John could hardly hear the music now, or even tell if anyone was near him. *Nobody's there for me, stoned or sober. What's the point?*

❑   ❑   ❑

Do you recognize these people? No doubt you've seen them, worked with them, lived with them as neighbors and family members. You may even see a bit of yourself in these folks. After all, they're simply doing their best to cope with life as it comes to them. Yet though each of them is a unique human being, each is tied together by a thin thread of dysfunction, a special kind of failure in living called the love-block.

The love-block is a chronic pattern of relating that closes off the wellsprings of our joy. It hampers our ability to reach out, deadens our potential to be fully alive in each moment. Love-block is a state of heart and mind that makes us too fearful to trust another human being. As we develop a shell that closes off the pain in our lives, we deflect the available affection too. Thus, the love-block runs interference with all our relationships in mysterious and baffling ways. And it has many personalities.

Persons Who Fail to Receive Love

"I guess I just don't deserve to be loved."

"I can't seem to accept love, even when it's offered to me."

The soul-deep feeling of unworthiness to receive love shows up in an array of inauthentic relational arrangements. We might call them interpersonal disguises, or masks. Sadly, they hide the fear that we won't receive love under an ironic approach to the thing most needed: "See, I don't *need* your love!"

Someone has said that "we mold our faces to fit our masks." The personalities developed by the love-blocked individual are there for self-protection. To acknowledge the fear that we might be unworthy of receiving love would be too painful. So we mold our lives to fit our fears.

Consider these eleven common personality types developed to protect from love-block pain. It is not an exhaustive list, and no one is strictly one or the other in full-blown manifestation. Most love-blocked people blend two or more of these qualities in their approach to relationships.[1]

Wounded Child

One way we can be sure to have Mom's attention as a child is simply to be physically sick. Who could blame us when we're so needy? The wounded child grows up in other ways, but holds onto his unfortunate and immature method of milking love from his relationships. He clings to a childlike inner logic: "Since I'm desperate, I'm *allowed* to be loved."

The twisted beauty of this approach is that it works. Forty-year-old Keith still hasn't settled on a life vocation, but people at church reach out to him with odd jobs; Maria constantly mismanages her money, so her father bails her out periodically with "loans" that never get repaid; Allen keeps having accidents at work, and the pastor comes to the hospital every day for a visit. Some chronically wounded people cling to the meager comfort they find in knowing "something is always wrong with me." They are in and out of doctors' offices with a wide variety of symptoms and complaints. As long as relatives and friends offer sympathy, the woundedness is working.

Wounded-child Savior

Here the love-blocked person seeks out the wounded child in order to feel the worthiness that comes from "saving" another's life. In the face of doubts about the availability of genuine love, the savior clings to the hurting and needy in order to tell himself: "Look, I am obviously needed here."

A friend of ours told us about the minister in a small town near his home. He has watched this elderly pastor take numerous women under his wings, young ladies who admired him and went to him with their significant problems. He convinced some of them to seek the ministry. He'd make them interns, teach them about preaching and counseling, even enroll some of them in seminary and help pay the tuition. The young women absolutely adored their spiritual mentor, and some truly blossomed. But many developed inappropriate romantic attachments to him. Sadly, once these women began to heal their wounds and become competent on their own—no longer clinging to the minister as their savior—he dropped them. And the search for a new, needy protégé would begin once again.

Insatiable Feeder

This person cries out, "I *must* have your love—more, and more, and more of it." Here is an unquenchable thirst for affection and nurture, a constant demand that significant others demonstrate commitment without boundaries. This love-seeker is hunting for what he needs, virtually on the prowl. When he finds it, though, it will not be enough.

Low-level Tolerator

Here the love-blocked person seeks out a relationship that will remain one-sided . . . and not in her favor. The unspoken rule is this: only one person will be the receiver of any potential affection. The other chooses to tolerate the meager love-morsels that might occasionally fall from the table. "I simply don't deserve more," reads the inner script. Though perhaps secretly acknowledging that something profound is missing, the tolerator can at least rest in a familiar security. The arrangement validates the "rightness" of the way things were growing up.

All-out Assailant

This pattern could be called the "Rambo Reaction." In this particular style of love-block, the individual can only cope with love's loss by turning the need for others upside down. The best defense against the pain of neediness is an all-out storming of the ramparts. Who of us hasn't felt the harshness of a modern-day Rambo at the workplace—or on the church board—someone who lashes out with constant criticism, hurling verbal grenades, simply to keep his own fears and needs at bay?

Consecutive Conqueror

The Don Juan of the love-block seeks one romantic relationship after another. The whirlwind of sexual encounters offers at least a tolerable illusion of genuine intimacy. As we write this, the local paper reports:

> Kato Kaelin, fast-fading O.J. sideshow, is stretching his 15 minutes of fame with a daily talk show that started Tuesday on L.A.'s KLSX-FM between 2 P.M. and 4 P.M. The houseboy said he won't answer trial questions. What will he talk about? "Girls are more like it," he said. "Since all this happened, I'm getting so many girls I had to put airbags on the headboard of my bed."[2]

Is this a person experiencing the joy and fulfillment of love?

Yet there are payoffs in this type of love-block. For one thing, the conqueror can control intimacy to meet his own need, without worrying about having to give. And, of course, this one who so ingeniously hides his fear of rejection always does the rejecting *first*, before he can be given the "heave-ho" himself.

Counterfeit Connector

Some of us become desperate enough even to attempt buying the love of others. One husband lavishes his wife with diamonds and new cars in hopes of feeling loved by her. Of course, he has to work long hours to keep the prizes flowing. Yet he's inevitably defeated, wooing a wife who feels abandoned by his workaholic absences and offended by his apparent belief that he can pay for her love.

Isolated Loner

Fear has an amazing paradoxical power; it can cause us to run directly toward the object of dread in utter, mindless panic. The isolated loner most fears being left alone. Yet out of this fear, she may consciously or unconsciously seek out an island oasis of loneliness. A place that is at least safe. Withdrawing from others keeps her from having to engage in the healthy risk-taking required of intimate relationships. Such chronic isolation assumes many different disguises and hides under various rationalizations, including:

❏ "I'll *never* find the right person to settle down with." (The middle-aged matron who keeps trashing her relationships as soon as the "M" word comes up.)

❑ "Don't tell me I'm lonely; I *am* married, you know." (The spouse who puts up sexual or emotional walls, avoiding vulnerability.)

❑ "If I'm going to be good at it, I've got to give it my all." (The career person who invests most of her time in work or some other solitary, life-consuming endeavor.)

❑ "It's just that I'm never able to be home." (The executive who is away on business trips for months at a time, guaranteeing isolation from his family.)

❑ "It just happens to be where the main office is located." (The young person who accepts geographic isolation in the name of career advancement.)

❑ "I just don't like or need people that much." (The older single adult who stays locked indoors unnecessarily.)

Dependency Maker

Some people attempt to resolve their fear of "not deserving" love by attaching to another in an apparently warm and close relationship. But the apparent closeness, when viewed up close, reveals itself as essentially parasitic. The underlying premise: "You would never genuinely want or need me; therefore, I will set things up so that *you* are forced to depend on *me*."

A friend of ours, a love-blocked parent, emotionally buffers every life trauma for her adolescent son. "Don't you see that he can learn some things about life through experiencing a few hard knocks?" we asked.

"Oh, but I'm only trying to protect him! Isn't that what parents are for?"

Inappropriate parental insulation can hide itself under the laudable claim of protective love. In reality, this parent is engineering emotional neediness in her child. Apparently it eases her insecurity about whether anyone "really needs me, or wants me." A parasitic parent/child relationship may culminate in an adult-child who is never able to leave home emotionally. He's the nice young man who remains unattached, who invests his deepest loyalty back into the parasitic relationship rather than fully investing his love in a marriage and children of his own.

Submissive Power-giver

People who relate in authentic love know how to maintain the balance between controlling and submitting. It is a give-and-take relationship in which one or the other relinquishes the power at certain times, depending on each unique situation and what is called for to move through it. But the love-blocked person confuses love with control. And the submissive power-giver enters relationships with a secret pact of self-surrender: "I will give up all my needs and desires in order to make sure you'll love me." She gives away legitimate power, virtually asking for inappropriate domination.

Most of the time, Edith Bunker was like that with her husband Archie (in the seventies TV sitcom, "All in the Family"). Whatever Archie wanted, whatever he demanded, whatever abuse he dished out, Edith would submit. She loved him! What else was there to do? Of course, she'd occasionally stand her ground in a decidedly less-than-conventional way. We laughed then, but we also cheered the occasional genuineness when it erupted in a mostly superficial relationship.

Managing Director

This is the opposite of the submissive approach to relationships. It's the distorted internal premise that says: "I can't be sure I'll ever receive genuine love from you; so I'll just control every move you make." It may not be love, but it is a relationship. Though a sad one, indeed.

❏   ❏   ❏

Time Out

Before moving on in this chapter, take a moment to think:

❏ *Which of these personality qualities seem to show themselves in my life?*

Possible examples:

_____

_____

❏ *Which of these patterns of living and relating keep me from being fully alive every day?*

Some ways this has worked recently:

_____

_____

❏   ❏   ❏

Do I Have the Love-Block?

The experience of the love-block may be overt and conspicuous. For example, we may feel painfully awkward about receiving gifts and compliments. Or we may know someone who, on theological grounds, openly chastises himself for being "selfish" and constantly searches for new avenues of vindication through sacrificial service. On the other hand, the experience of love-block may be quite subtle and even unconscious, as it was with Rhonda.

When Rhonda was growing up, her parents had long ago decided to "stick it out together" and delay a divorce until the kids were grown and married. The pair lived in the same house together, but treated each other as virtual strangers. In fact, one side of the house came to be identified as "Dad's side." The other side was Mom's. No one ever actually said this was the case; the pattern of living just developed that way and was accepted. "Sometimes I was secretly relieved when the two of 'em would have a good, barn-burner of a scrap," Rhonda said. "It scared me at the time, of course. But part of me took pleasure in it. I mean, at least they were doing *something* together."

Rhonda and her needs were drowned in this swirl of avoidance and aggression. And a woman like Rhonda, who failed to receive childhood nurture under two parents barely tolerating one another, will move into adulthood "on guard" toward all relationships. On the surface she may tell herself, "I don't really need people." Beneath this veneer of toughness, however, the unconscious message will be, "I feel completely unworthy to receive love from anyone."

Addressing the love-block can help people like Rhonda, or any of us who desire deeper levels of whole-person wellness. But where do we start? A good first step would call for carving out little swatches of time for quiet self-examination. You might begin by asking the most general questions:

"Do I know how to accept love?"

"Am I able to love someone else?"

"How do I know?"

Then gradually become more specific. Consider blocking out an extended period of time—covering perhaps weeks or months—to build "recollection sessions" into your daily life. You would spend quiet time recalling experiences in your family of origin and doing a personal inventory of times of emotional deprivation. You might take a friend or counselor along with you on this journey. It would be "time travel" for you, going back to *who you were* as a child, and gaining insight into how you came to be *who you are* today. But first, here's a self-test that can help you see where you stand on the love-block scale right now.

❑   ❑   ❑

Where Do You Stand? (A Self-Test)

Most love-blocked people rarely take time to think candidly about what happened to them in their family of origin. Many will say they "had a happy childhood" and leave it at that. But what was really going on during those critical, formative years at home?

Here are nine questions you can use to assess how well you have learned to receive and give love. For each question, first mark the scale from 1 to 5, and then jot a response to the sentence-completion.

You may prefer just to think through your responses during a moment of quiet, perhaps focusing on a question or two each day. Better still, plan to jot longer responses and recollections in a separate notebook or a personal journal. You'll no doubt benefit from referring back to these questions often, augmenting your responses and adding insights as you move toward healing.

❑ In your family of origin, was it easier for you to do things for others than to allow others to do things for you?

1_____2_____3_____4_____5
Doing for others   Accepting from others

One thing I always did for others in my family was . . .

❑ Do you feel that you were loved for "just being you," rather than for what you could accomplish?

1_____2_____3_____4_____5
Always   Never

A time when my parent(s) expressed warm affection for me, unrelated to my performance, was when . . .

❑ To what extent were you held, listened to, and taken seriously by your parents?

1_____2_____3_____4_____5
Always   Never

An example of a time when my parent(s) held and comforted me was when . . .

❑ How important were your personal needs in your family?

1_____2_____3_____4_____5
Very Important   No Importance

A personal need of mine that usually remained uncared for was . . .

❏ Did it seem that your happiness was more important than your parents' need for you to be "successful"?

1_____2_____3_____4_____5
Always   Never

One time when my needs came before everything else was when . . .

❏ Did your parents model a loving, spontaneous relationship, rather than a superficial and rigid one? Did they openly express their love for one another?

1_____2_____3_____4_____5
Always   Never

One way I could tell that my parents were/were not deeply in love was . . .

❏ Were you required to play the role of the parent, sacrificing what you needed in order to satisfy their needs? That is, were you your parents' parent?

1_____2_____3_____4_____5
Never   Always

I had to play a parental role when . . .

❏ Was your uniqueness cultivated, even when you did not "fit" into the family patterns?

1_____2_____3_____4_____5
Always   Never

I remember being able to be "uniquely me" when . . .

❏ Are your public and private selves one and the same most of the time?

1_____2_____3_____4_____5
Exactly the same   Very different

One way I had/have to cover up "the real me" was/is . . .

A higher score (in which most of your scale markings fall along the right-hand side) indicates a higher degree of love-block in your life. Also, if you had trouble coming up with childhood examples of love, acceptance, affirmation, holding, and other forms of nurture, you may have a problem accepting love as an adult. Because of this, you may be unable to give love freely as well.

❑   ❑   ❑

Why Is It So Difficult to Give and Receive Love?

Just the mention of the word "love" fills our minds with romance and inspires poets to lofty imagery . . .

> Love! the surviving gift of Heaven,
> The choicest sweet of Paradise,
> in life's else bitter cup distilled.[3]

"We are all born for love," said Benjamin Disraeli. "It is the principle of existence, and its only end." Yet it remains elusive to most people.

In the beautiful film *A River Runs Through It,* Norman McLean, as the elderly narrator, reminisces about his youth among the rivers and mountains of Montana, highlighting his relationship to his minister father and younger brother Paul. The film portrays the very different ways the two boys respond to their father's love and example.

In the McLean family, fly-fishing at the river was virtually a form of worship. To the Reverend McLean, "all good things—trout, as well as eternal salvation—come by grace." Norman and Paul grow up in their father's grace, his kind love and guidance, learning the lessons of life and religion largely through training in the "art" of fly-fishing. The father admires his boys in all their adolescent strength and zest for life. But Paul, even as a young child, seems to have trouble accepting that admiration. Perhaps he wants too much from his father—and suffers the despair of never receiving it—for he does everything in a manner tinged with self-destructiveness.

As the film unfolds, we begin to wonder: Will Paul ever be able to receive the love his father has to offer? Or will he just keep searching for what is clearly at hand? In a most significant line in the film, Norman's future wife asks about Paul: "Why is it that the people who need the most help won't take it?" Later, Paul himself unwittingly speaks to his own condition when he says of someone else: "Maybe what he likes is someone *trying* to help him."

It becomes clear to his family that Paul is on a path to self-destruction. He starts drinking early in the morning. He stays out late at night, gambling his money away in a dingy part of town. He gets into trouble with mean-spirited creditors. So when Paul is violently murdered, the family is stunned, but not without a sense that it was somehow inevitable. For all along Paul just couldn't drink in the love that his brother had gratefully imbibed from his parents. Paul couldn't let down and stop competing long enough just to be . . . *needful.*

Wanting to be loved; not knowing how to be loved.

If we were to ask most people if they desire more love in their lives they would almost without exception answer yes. However, many would be immobilized by such an enormous undertaking, not knowing where to begin. Like Paul in the movie, they know they lack love—both the ability to receive it and the energy to give it—but it is easier to salve the longing with things such as power, alcohol, and even fishing. Easier than following the longing to its Source. For all our deepest desires are a call for us to come Home.

So we continue to ask: Why is love so elusive? I think the main reason there is so little love in the world today, and so little love shared in relationships, is that *we do not know how to accept this love and incorporate it into ourselves.* Love surrounds us each and every day of our lives. But the challenge is to learn how to open up to it and internalize it.

There Is Hope

God created each of us with an enduring need for love. Is it any wonder, then, that our lives become so disordered and even disastrous as we encounter a hardened shell within us that keeps love at bay? David Norton is bored with success and can't seem to connect with his wife. Lisa Jensen searches for a lover to bring her lasting fulfillment. John Rios just wants to escape his yearning for a father. Three faces in the crowd. Ordinary people infected with a soul-pathology that masquerades under multiple disguises. Is there hope for them and us?

> Across the gateway of my heart
> I wrote "No Thoroughfare,"
> But love came laughing by, and cried:
> "I enter everywhere."[4]

> Many waters cannot quench love;
> rivers cannot wash it away.[5]

The poets and the prophets all proclaim: Yes! There is more than enough hope, for love can hardly be thwarted. But, whether you approach this quest as a means of "self-help" or in hopes of becoming a more effective helper of others, it will not be an easy adventure. It will take courage, particularly if you are on the outside looking in, hoping that a spouse, a friend, or a loved one will open her arms and finally rest in your love.

In the closing scene of *A River*, the Reverend McLean preaches a sermon, years after Paul has been killed because of his gambling debts:

Each one of us here today will, at one time in our lives, look upon a loved one who is in need and ask the same question: "We are willing to help, Lord, but what, if anything, is needed?" For it is true we can seldom help those closest to us. Either we don't know what part of ourselves to give, or more often than not, the part we have to give . . . is not wanted. And so it is those we live with, and should know, who elude us. But we can still love them. We can love completely, without complete understanding.

Yes, there is hope for those we love. And there is hope for those of us who wish to receive love more readily and fully. For it may be your own arms that need to stretch and reach out to the love all around you. Once you learn how to accept and internalize love you can begin to feel and enjoy the love others have for you. You may not be able to understand it all as it is happening, for love can never be completely explained. But as the soul's floodgates are opened, and love flows in, your life will blossom with new meaning and deepened relationships.

How will you do it? The steps for healing that we lay out in this book suggest a step-by-step process of opening our "love receptors." In the following chapters you'll see that, just as our physical brain cells have chemical receptors, so we have, by analogy, receptor sites in our emotional and spiritual makeups. We do have the potential to receive unconditional love from God and others as we progress toward wholeness. The steps in this healing process include:

1. Renewing of the mind, through replacing false thoughts with truth (chap. 5)

2. Dealing with depression, through a renewed perspective on loss (chap. 6)

3. Opening up love receptors, through transformed interactions with people (chap. 7):

    ❑ Risking vulnerability

    ❑ Choosing forgiveness

    ❑ Cultivating awareness

4. Opening up love receptors, through deepening the relationship with God (chap. 8):

    ❑ Discovering the true God

    ❑ Practicing the presence

    ❑ Offering praise

5. *Committing to self-nurture as the basic approach to daily living (chap. 9).*

As you can see, there certainly are ways to unblock our love receptors, and we'll learn about them in the chapters to come. But first, let's take a closer look at what happens when the love offered to us has strings attached—when conditional acceptance works its special brand of failure.

2

The Failure of Conditional Love

Love is a decision to move into others' lives
pursuing their good,
steadfastly hoping, but not demanding,
that the ones being loved will respond
by developing a life of love.

—Deborah R. Newman

For the garden is the only place there is,
but you will not find it
until you have looked for it everywhere
and found nowhere that is not a desert.

—W.H. Auden

In the 1995 movie *A Walk in the Clouds* a young woman of the wealthy Arragon family in California discovers the failure of conditional love. The family's wealth comes from its sprawling grape vineyards, which cover the rolling hills with green leaves for as far as the eye can see. Her father, Don Arragon, has given his life to those vineyards, loving and nurturing the grapes year after year, building his wealth as his way of loving his family. Out

41

of his riches he can lavish his wife and daughter with all the good things of life. He is a good man, though stern and fiercely concerned with family honor, loving the only way he knows: through his unrelenting hard work.

The girl is on her way home from college to tell her father that she is pregnant out of wedlock. "I know my father will kill me," she tells a soldier on the bus. But the young man decides to go home with her and pretend to be her husband (for one day), in order to save her honor.

Toward the end of the film, Don Arragon discovers the truth and disowns his "failure-of-a-daughter." And in a fit of rage, he throws a lantern at the young stand-in husband. The flames lick up the vineyard, one vine at a time, until the hillside becomes an inferno of smoky destruction. The next morning the proud father has nothing . . . except the possibility of love from his family. He takes his sinner-daughter in his arms and cries: "It was the only way I knew how to love. Teach me to love. Please, teach me to love like you love."

Most of our own parents, like Don Arragon, did not learn how to be loved—or to love us without great demands. And that is such a joyless thing. As Spanish philosopher Miguel de Unamuno said:

> It is sad not to be loved,
> > but it is much sadder not to be able to love.

This, then, is the condition many of us grew up in: the condition of conditional love. How does this fact continue to affect us as adults? Let us survey some of the ways.

The Painful Effects of Conditional Love

Most children growing up, at best, receive conditional love from their parents. Conditional love is a level of acceptance that must be earned by doing something or behaving in a certain way. Children will try to obtain any semblance of this acceptance from their parents by any means they can. They will do and become things that they were not meant to do or become just to receive this counterfeit love. (You might wish to silently observe it happening every day in your own world: adults doing things they really don't want to do—even very successful people. Take a look at the unhappiness in the workplace, for instance.)

So children feel they must perform to get love. In this type of environment, as children do not feel loved for who and what they really are, two things happen. First, at some point they will stop looking for and trying to receive love. Second, they will develop a mistrust of the world and a deep, ongoing dissatisfaction with life; they become love-blocked. Psychologist Arthur Janov described the phenomenon in terms of neurosis. Though he holds a decidedly non-Christian worldview, his words here hold true for our purposes:

The hallmark of normality is the ability to be satisfied. The neurotic is often dissatisfied with almost everything. He is missing something, something crucial, so there is never enough money, security, love, sex, power, prestige, or fame. Just feeling satisfied with one's life is an enormous achievement. For the neurotic, no matter what the gift, no matter what the achievement, it won't make an unloved person feel loved. Being completely loved as a child is what makes someone feel satisfied. It is the most relaxing thing on earth.[1]

If we were to catalog the *least* relaxing aspects of conditional love, we might name three of its most painful effects: losing choice, creating a public self, and fixing the original family.

Perceiving a Loss of Choice

Perhaps most abuse finds its way into our lives quite passively, in the guise of emotional abandonment and conditional love. Some have called what happens to a person who grows up in such an environment "codependency." Though the word has been overworked of late, it is still a valuable term. It can provide insight into what we are describing in this chapter as the effects of conditional love. Here is a helpful, extended definition from Charles Whitfield's exhaustive study *Co-dependence: Healing the Human Condition:*

> Co-dependence is a disease of lost selfhood. . . . We become co-dependent when we turn our responsibility for our life and happiness over to our ego (our false self) and to other people. Co-dependents become so preoccupied with others that they neglect their true self—who they really are.
>
> [It is] any suffering or dysfunction that is associated with, or results from, focusing on the needs and behavior of others. When we focus so much outside of ourselves we lose touch with what is inside of us: our beliefs, thoughts, feelings, decisions, choices, experiences, wants, needs, sensations, intuitions, unconscious experiences, and even indicators of our physical functioning, such as heart rate and respiratory rate. . . .
>
> Co-dependence is the most common of all addictions: the addiction to looking elsewhere. . . . The "elsewhere" may be people, places, things, behaviors or experiences. Whatever it is, we may neglect our own selves for it.[2]

In light of this description, we could say that codependency is primarily about an actual loss of choice. I give my life away to others. Thus I come to believe that I am powerless to choose my own way. Life becomes a series of virtually automatic *reactions* rather than adventures in freedom. For I don't even know what I truly want.

This sad process tells us why control is such a big issue with codependent people. As they feel their lives are getting more and more out of control they "tighten up" and seek to regain more control. They become inflexible and intolerant.

Because such folks react instead of choose, most make very few genuine decisions in their lives. They are unaware of this and often have the illusion that they are, indeed, directing things. However, usually they are merely reacting to the circumstances with habitual responses. It's as if they turn off the thermostat in their own house and rely on the neighbor's thermostat to regulate their inner environment. The feelings and desires of others determine the course of their lives. They do not realize there are alternative ways to live.

> Most of us are taught from an early age to pay far more attention to signals coming from other people than from within. We are encouraged to ignore our own needs and wants and to concentrate on living up to others' expectations.[3]

The codependent—or the conditionally loved—operate on false beliefs about themselves and their families, and this further limits their perceived alternatives. For example, rules in the family, spoken or unspoken, can dominate all decisions and rob of personal freedom. This is the root of love-block.

❑   ❑   ❑

Typical "Dysfunctional Family Rules"

Here are some of the things parents "tell" their children. These rules come through, whether in spoken words or in the general atmosphere and ordering of family interactions:

❑ You must make me happy.
❑ Don't get excited (or angry, sad, fearful, etc.). Such emotions threaten to unblock my own tightly controlled feelings.
❑ Your job is to take care of me.
❑ You will be loved if you perform up to the standards.
❑ Walk on eggshells.
❑ Keep things orderly and calm around here.
❑ Live in denial.
❑ Don't speak the truth if it will make any of us feel bad.
❑ We must not openly grieve our dead loved ones; it's too painful for us.
❑ We must not touch one another. It could lead to problems.
❑ If you need something, I'll give it to you. I know your needs better than you do.

❏   ❏   ❏

In a dysfunctional family of origin you were taught that such rules had to be obeyed at all costs. Because "the good of the family" (or, more specifically, the good of the parents) was all-important, the right to make personal choices was rarely cultivated. As a result, in the adult, particularly in stressful circumstances, the subconscious mind takes over and tries to protect. You respond as you did when you were a child.

Take Bill for example. At forty-eight years of age, he had worked numerous jobs. "I just can't find an employer who will treat me right," he says. "I go into a job thinking everything is great. Then, a few months or a year down the road, and wham! The guy becomes a jerk. Starts making all kinds of unreasonable demands. That's happened to me so many times I can't begin to count them all. Why do I have to have such rotten luck?"

"Tell me a little bit about your father, Bill," I say. And then the broader picture emerges: I learn that Bill's father was "standoffish" and quite critical of Bill's performance in school. Bill began to see this. He became more aware of his past—not just the facts, but how much *he was hurt by his father's coldness.* He was able to make the connection that whenever one of his bosses would be a little critical of his work, or ask him for just a little bit more, he would feel just as he had felt when he was six years old, when his own father would criticize his performance for, let's say, an average report card. Those old stored-up feelings would make Bill extremely uncomfortable and angry. He handled this by putting his bosses in the wrong and eventually quitting another job. Reacting, not choosing.

As Bill became aware of his loss of choice (his virtually "programmed" overreactions), he was able to take this first step toward change: he determined that whenever he first felt those old feelings surging he would simply become more aware of them and name them for what they were—old business. Next, he would make a conscious decision not to react, but to remove himself from the conflict and think about the situation for a few minutes. After doing this he was able to make decisions appropriate for his age, instead of reacting as a child would. He could begin to see that most of the time, when someone criticized something he did, that it was not an attack on his personal worth.

The past can powerfully control the present if we let it. Thus, many of us aren't even aware that we do not make true choices in our lives; our reactions happen so quickly and so automatically. It doesn't take long for a child to learn that if he does what is approved of he will gain acceptance, and if he does what he wants to most of the time he will be rejected. This behavior becomes so ingrained that we go through our lives merely reacting and making very few genuine choices. We will often do a thing because we secretly believe it will gain us our longed-for acceptance, instead of considering our options and making the best choice.

We have more freedom than that. And we must take the responsibility for our God-given freedom, as scary as that may be. As someone has said:

Take your life in your hands and what happens?
A terrible thing: no one to blame.

Yes, it is a fearful thing to acknowledge that I do indeed have choices, to finally admit that not even my parents are to blame for the way I am right now.

We should all acknowledge that we are fully responsible for our beliefs, attitudes and behaviors. Being loveless, for example, is not a mean trick that life has played upon us. More likely, it is a conscious decision on our part to close love out. It's often easier to think of ourselves as victims of a cruel fate than to accept our part in the problem. But it's neither accurate nor conducive to bringing love back into our lives to ignore that we were at least partly responsible.[4]

Acknowledging painful parental failures gives us impetus and direction for change. Yet this must never become a Mom-and-Dad Blaming Game. It is simply part of the process of seeing who we really are—and why—and then taking personal responsibility for change.

Creating a "Public Self"

As we've seen, most of us in our families of origin experienced conditional acceptance at best. We were loved not for who we were, but for what we did. As children, when we did the behavior that was applauded by our culture or by our parents, we were rewarded. When we acted as individuals and chose different paths, we were almost always punished or rejected. For example, whenever one little girl got angry, she was punished. Now she never gets angry as an adult—at least *never feels it as anger,* only as nervousness and shame. She successfully split off authentic parts of her self.

Conditional acceptance leads a child to doubt her own feelings and decisions. Eventually, she feels flawed deep inside. Becoming a "people pleaser" she will try to do anything to please parents and others—even if it means giving up a part of herself. She thus creates a public self and a private self.

The public self is the part of us we show the world, but the private self is our true self, our true identity. It is where our unique thoughts and genuine desires reside. It is our individuality.

I [Brian] think about a time when Debi and I had been married for probably ten months. We had just left Indiana where I had graduated a few months earlier with my master's degree in counseling. We had moved to

Dallas to begin working for the Minirth-Meier Clinic. I was also going to start a doctoral program, working on my doctorate in counseling. I chose not to start in the fall of that year, but to start in January the next year, for two reasons. First, I didn't have all the money together. Second, I wanted to give myself every opportunity to be available for counseling appointments in order to establish a client load. I wrote and told my dad about my decisions.

I remember receiving a letter back in the mail from him expressing his disappointment in my decision to delay my doctoral studies. Before I really had a chance to think about it, I decided to call him. And my hands were shaking as I picked up the phone.

For me, this was the first time, as an adult, I had directly addressed my father with the issue of my own right and power to make life decisions that I thought were best for me—apart from considering his approval. "I'm sorry, Dad. I know you don't agree with it, but I am having to look out for the best interests of my new family," I said.

Coming out of that child role with him, and putting myself on a level with him to the point that we could agree to disagree was one of the toughest things I've had to do in growing up. But I suddenly felt I could approach my dad as the adult that I had become.

Sadly, this is something some adults have never done. They are so plagued by love-block that they continue playing a part with their parents and others. It does not take long for a child to learn that he must be what somebody else wants him to be in order to be accepted and loved. This conditional acceptance breeds anger and resentment in the child, and he quickly gives up his own reality, or private self.

When conditional acceptance is applied to our personality (instead of our behavior only) it becomes an even more damaging tool. This conditional acceptance of "acceptable" character traits molds us into a constantly changing caricature of ourselves. We become what the world wants us to be instead of the person who is uniquely us, who God created us to be. Therefore, our true self goes into hiding. When we must hide the true self, we feel damaged and take on a deep sense of shame. And the more of this shaming there is, the deeper the true self must hide, thus creating more shame. Internal confusion results.

"Who are *you?*" said the Caterpillar.

This was not an encouraging opening for a conversation. Alice replied, rather shyly, "I—I hardly know, sir, just at present—at least I know who I *was* when I got up this morning but I think I must have been changed several times since then."

"What do you mean by that?" said the Caterpillar sternly. "Explain yourself!"

"I can't explain *myself*, I'm afraid, sir," said Alice, "because I'm not myself, you see."

"I don't see," said the Caterpillar.

"I'm afraid I can't put it more clearly," Alice replied very politely, "for I can't understand it myself to begin with; and being so many different sizes in a day is very confusing."[5]

How terribly confusing—and sad—not to *be* who one *is!* I [Joe] remember being in that discovery period of who I was. I was needing some space from my folks, and though I had always talked to them often and shared, I kind of stepped back from that. I wouldn't call them as much and I wasn't sharing as much about my life. They felt bad about it.

We talked about all of this and I acknowledged that their feelings were hurt. I essentially told them I wasn't able to visit as much for a while. I needed time for me, and I was working on certain issues of personal growth. I had a sense that I was taking a step back to go forward again. The more space they gave me, the more I could grow . . . the very thing that happens when we repot a root-bound plant.

We all need that space in order to provide room for our truer selves to blossom. Otherwise, we become stuck in the old, stereotypical roles. We whither on the vine.

❑   ❑   ❑

Time Out

What Role Did You Play in the "Family Drama"?

One of the first steps in learning to receive love is coming to understand who the real you is and accepting yourself as you really are. Sometimes that requires pulling away from those who have shaped us over the years into their own desired image of us. That is not easy, for coming from conditional-love families, we became "type cast" in the roles our families gave us. As eventually happened with Yul Brynner (as the King of Siam), the role we played became inseparable from the person playing it. Here are some typical examples:

The Star Performer
She courageously keeps the family going, "keeps things together," and fixes the problems that arise. She heroically leads the way through adversity in the family. She keeps being the straight-A student in everything that she does.

Blamer
Always the first to say: "No fair; it's your fault!" He avoids personal responsibility or taking on tasks to help the family.

Scapegoat
The one who gets dumped on for everything that goes wrong. Playing the role of the "bad boy" he or she is the sacrificial lamb when anyone needs to take the blame. A black sheep among the others, his or her failings and shortcomings become the explanation for the family's dysfunction. "If only brother Bobby wasn't a compulsive gambler (or convicted felon, or incorrigible womanizer) this family would be all right." His actions, in a sense, define the family's purpose.

Saintly Sufferer
The one who constantly goes the extra mile for the family's sake. No cost is too great to ensure the family is cared for. Sometimes the care is "forced" upon others in smother-love fashion. A martyr at heart, she maintains an identity through being a victim. She never rocks the boat by saying, "But this is what *I* need!"

Enabler
With a sense of helping, he actually keeps dysfunction strong. For example, a key role is keeping the addicted family member from being found out, or from getting into trouble that would spark change. He smooths over the problems in order to keep some semblance of peace.

Merrymaker
She plays the role of family clown, approaching all problems with a wink and a joke. Operating at the height of denial, she tries to laugh away the pain. Her theme song is: Laughing on the outside, crying on the inside. She wears the mask of the happy clown.

Placater
The one who tries to make peace at all costs. Usually this means he'll be the one to do the work, or suffer in some way to keep things calm. Always attempting to bring people together, he is constantly frustrated. Needed by the family, they wait on him to at least try to bring some intimacy to the relationship.

Rescuer
He's always ready to bail out the family member in trouble. He keeps addictions going strong by "saving" the addicted one from the consequences of his actions.

❏   ❏   ❏

Even in Scripture we see family role playing. Think through the following biblical passages and consider which roles the characters are playing:

> But the Lord God called to the man, "Where are you?" He answered, "I heard You in the garden, and I was afraid because I was naked; so I hid." And He said, "Who told you that you were naked? Have you eaten from the tree that I commanded you not to eat from?" The man said, "The woman You put here with me—she gave me some fruit from the tree, and I ate it." —Genesis 3:9-12

What role does Adam play in relation to Eve?

> Judah said to his brothers, "What will we gain if we kill our brother and cover up his blood? Come, let's sell him to the Ishmaelites and not lay our hands on him; after all, he is our brother, our own flesh and blood." His brothers agreed. So when the Midianite merchants came by, his brothers pulled Joseph up out of the cistern and sold him for twenty shekels of silver to the Ishmaelites, who took him to Egypt. When Reuben returned to the cistern and saw that Joseph was not there, he tore his clothes. He went back to his brothers and said, "The boy isn't there! Where can I turn now?" —Genesis 37:26-30

What role did Judah play with his brothers?

> So Joseph settled his father and his brothers in Egypt and gave them property in the best part of the land, the district of Rameses, as Pharaoh directed. Joseph also provided his father and his brothers and all his father's household with food, according to the number of their children. —Genesis 47:11-12

What role does Joseph play for his family?

> As Jesus and His disciples were on their way, He came to a village where a woman named Martha opened her home to Him. She had a sister called Mary, who sat at the Lord's feet listening to what He said. But Martha was distracted by all the preparations that had to be made. She came to Him and asked, "Lord, don't You care that my sister has left me to do the work by myself? Tell her to help me!" —Luke 10:38-40

What role does Martha play in relation to her sister?

❏   ❏   ❏

Time Out

❏ *What role (or several roles) do you think you played in your family of origin? (You may add your own role; it may be a variation of the ones given, but name it or describe it in your own words.) Jot an example—your memory of an event or conversation—that shows you acting this part:*

_____

_____

_____

❏ *Do you still play this role? In what ways have you seen this "role playing" come through in your adult interactions?*

_____

_____

_____

❏ *As a child, did you ever play the role of "parent" because of a death or divorce in your family? How did you fill that void? How do you continue to fill it?*

_____

_____

_____

❏   ❏   ❏

At some point early on in life, most of us developed masks, or a false persona, almost as though we were acting a part for a play. We wanted to appear more acceptable to others, seeking always to please. These acceptable behaviors were not necessarily what we wished to express at the outset; however, we were discouraged from having our own true feelings and desires. We thus became confused as to who we really were and even confused as to what our basic needs are. We became addicted to people's approval and sought it at any cost, the cost of our true self. It is primarily this loss of our self that causes an inability to love ourselves. After all, if the "genuine me" has to be hidden, I must be unlovable.

We must experience a rediscovery of ourselves. This happens when we go back and do an inventory of our lives. We can enter this process with a friend, spouse, or professional counselor, depending on the level of abuse experienced in childhood. In this rediscovery we come to better understand the persona we took on over the years. We slowly strip these layers away, as if peeling an onion, until we get to the core of our personality: usually a hurt, fearful, and sad child.

If this process is carried out in a loving, accepting atmosphere we begin to learn that we are acceptable and no longer need to hide the truth of our lives. This is the beginning place of intimacy for us: becoming less and less afraid for people to see us as we really are. For intimacy is all about self-discovery leading to self-disclosure.

❑ ❑ ❑

Time Out

Self-Discovery through "Picturing" the Past

Gather one or more photos of yourself that were taken when you were a child. Study them for a while. Recall what it was like to be there, in the pictured scene or activity. Ask yourself:

❑ What sense of happiness comes through in these photos?
❑ What is sad about these photos?
❑ What kind of face did I display when I was with my family? What did that face say to the world at the time? What does it say to me now?
❑ What secrets was I keeping?
❑ What fears resided below the surface?
❑ Who was aware of these things—aware of my inner life—at the time? How did these persons respond?
❑ Who was comforting me during this period of my life?
❑ If I had the opportunity, what would I like to say to the child in this photo? What forms of comfort or encouragement might I offer this child?

The last question, about what you want to say, can launch you into a very powerful exercise. Over the next few weeks, consider filling in some of the blanks below. Think about the thoughts that filled your mind as a child. Then consider what you would say as an adult to your child. This process can help you grieve the hurts of your childhood, and should be done over and over for an extended period. As you begin to counteract what you were saying to yourself as a child you will stop falling into shaming thought patterns as an adult.

❑ The Child's thought: (Example: I wish Mommy and Daddy would stop yelling at each other.)

Possible Adult words to the child: (Example: You look sad; you must be feeling afraid. But Mom and Dad's behavior is not your fault.)

❑ The Child's thought:

_____

_____

Possible Adult words to the child:

_____

_____

❑ The Child's thought:

_____

_____

Possible Adult words to the child:

_____

_____

❑ The Child's thought:

_____

_____

Possible Adult words to the child:

_____

_____

❑   ❑   ❑

"Emotional health" is when the public self and private self become one and the same. In confronting our public self and the roles we played, we can begin to leave behind a conditional-love, dysfunctional upbringing, and lifestyle. Only by doing this can we learn about genuine love and learn to accept and give love freely. Certainly, it is painful and yes, it requires a lot of work and courage. But the alternative, remaining stuck in old roles, leads to a dead end.

Fixing the Original Family . . . Again and Again

In healthy families, the parents are there to meet the child's needs. In conditional-love families, the behavior that is desired and approved of is usually an expression of the parent's needs rather than the child's needs. The child's true needs are superseded by the parent's insatiable "neediness."

The child gets the message, "You are here for me and you need to take care of me." The child sees himself as having no choice in the matter and becomes a parent to the parents. Sadly, in highly dysfunctional families, some children spend their whole lives taking care of their parents, ignoring their own needs and desires.

Imagine a thermometer scale that tracks the level of conditional-love dysfunction. It is a matter of degrees; no family is either completely healthy or completely unhealthy. Yet someone who comes from a conditional-love family that would measure 80 degrees or greater on the thermometer scale will often marry someone with a similar reading on their own thermometer.

Struggle is the symbolic way the neurotic goes about getting fulfilled. The neurotic rarely goes straight for love. On the contrary, the pattern is first to find a neurotic like your parent then *struggle* to get love. You find a cold woman and try to make her warm. You find a critical, unsatisfied man and try to make him accepting. The struggle for love is what is ingrained, not the getting of it. Getting apparent love often makes the neurotic feel worse because the underlying feeling is of being unloved.[6]

People will often subconsciously pick out someone who is at least as dysfunctional as they are. This only causes the problems to continue into the next generation. As they begin to form families of their own, they will almost always try to re-create a family similar to the family of origin. There are at least two reasons for this, both of which operate subconsciously. First is the general principle that we will end up parenting the way we ourselves have been parented. The way we were raised is what we consider to be normal.

The second reason we attempt to re-create the family of origin is to give the conditionally loved person a chance to finally "fix" the family, to solve the problems originally experienced in the family of origin. The child once felt powerless in the face of family problems and lack of intimacy. Now the adult, by re-creating similar dynamics in her own family, thereby creates an opportunity to set things right. But reliving the past will never fix the present.

This is illustrated by Mary, whose father was a raging alcoholic. She swore she would never have anything to do with a "drinking man." Yet she is now married to her third raging alcoholic husband. Mary is still trying to "fix" her father in each new relationship with an abusive man.

Deep down, if you come from a conditional-love family, although you may have been desperately unhappy, you felt the situation to be normal. The body uses a host of subconscious activities, including denial and repression, to keep us from dealing with the serious problems of the past. This serves to protect us as children; however, it makes matters worse as we grow into adulthood by continuing the cycle of dysfunction in our own new families. So, although denial helped us survive the "crazy-making" parental behavior, this same denial eats away at our ability to experience love as an adult. It is as though "ghosts from the past" continue to haunt us.

A First Step Toward Healing

Exactly how shall we confront the ghosts of the past, these painful effects of conditional love? Leo Buscaglia, the hugging professor, suggests a starting place:

> If we are going to be lovers, we must be as open to the wretchedness as we are to the bliss it can bring, for both are a part of the reality of loving. Earthly love is imperfect. . . . Perhaps we would feel less frustrated if we could accept the fact that on this earth there is no perfect love, only human love. Then we could expend our energies appreciating and enhancing the love we have.[7]

Acceptance of human love's imperfection. Buscaglia fails to mention the divine love that is available to us—a perfect love—even as we live on this earth. But his point remains: purely human love is always imperfect. How, then, shall we heal the wounds it delivers? It certainly does have to do with acceptance.

Accept Acceptance

We have been speaking of the ravages of conditional approval, but let us once again point to the incredible healing power of perfect, unconditional acceptance, and its only source: the Creator and Lover of this world. The Apostle Paul penned his great ode to the Great Lover's unconditional love in Romans 8:

> Who shall separate us from the love of Christ? Shall trouble or hardship or persecution or famine or nakedness or danger or sword? As it is written: "For your sake we face death all day long; we are considered as sheep to be slaughtered."
> No, in all these things we are more than conquerors through Him who loved us.[8]

In the thrilling movie *Braveheart*, Scottish freedom fighter William Wallace is crushed by the knowledge that he has unwittingly caused the death of his new bride. He stands at the grave with the girl's parents and watches as the beautiful young woman is lowered into the ground. He wishes to speak to the parents but, of course, words have little power at such a time. He can only kneel silently before the grief-sick father and hope . . . for forgiveness, for pity, for his aching heart's absolution. Everything depends on whether he will feel the gentle touch of the father's hand upon his head.

And we watch as the father slowly, painfully unfolds his fist. . . .

The deepest truth of our lives, when we finally come to the end of our fighting against the things that threaten our sense of control, is that nothing can be said; nothing can be done. Only a bowing and a kneeling remains, a hope that the hand will reach out and heal.

> For I am convinced that neither death nor life, neither angels nor demons, neither the present nor the future, nor any powers, neither height nor depth, nor anything else in all creation, will be able to separate us from the love of God that is in Christ Jesus our Lord.[9]

Every aspect of our existence, our every breath, hinges on the grace of our already being touched by Him. Either that, or life itself is a sad exercise in the most profound emptiness. How could it be otherwise? For to *demand* acceptance is to presume that its attainment is in our own power.

But to *accept* acceptance . . . that is our blessed opportunity. The alternative, as we shall see, is sickness.

3

The Physical Fallouts
of Lost Love

*People will do anything, no matter how absurd,
in order to avoid facing their own soul.*

—C.G. Jung

Sure, I'm OK. Everything's fine.

Lilian honestly couldn't think of anything that was going wrong in her life. In fact, she had the comforting thought that things were finally getting under control: career goals taking shape, a marriage becoming more stable, even a weight-loss program yielding pleasing results. One problem, though: her stomach hurt her almost every day.

The thing that made Lilian begin to question whether perhaps all was *not* well with her (she was working on an ulcer, after all) was what she called "my flashback times." Memories of her father had bubbled to the surface. They seemed to shoot out of the blue and cause a lump in her throat and a pain in her abdomen.

Lilian's father had left her at age six, but she had never felt the pain of it, not like this, until *forty*-six.

Why this? she wondered. *And why now?*

❑   ❑   ❑

Most of us know the physical sensations that accompany grief. Clearly there is a connection between the powerful emotions entwined with love and the physical sensations of love's loss. As the old popular song laments: "Can't live without you. . . ." Some people do waste away for love.

In this chapter we'll focus on something a bit more subtle, but no less real: The unexpected physical fallouts when the loss of love is less obvious than the temporary heartache of a romantic jilting. The songwriters don't tell us this: Most of the time *we have no idea* that we feel ill because we feel ill-treated. We fail to make that crucial connection.

The Mind-Body-Spirit Connection

Love is such an important human need that without it life can become disastrous. The psychological and spiritual wounds of the lack of love may seem "acceptable" to us. But it is much more difficult to recognize and accept that our immediate symptoms of physical illness have anything to do with a profound inability to receive love. Yet I've observed that the lack of that ability, either directly or indirectly, leads to many physical illnesses. Not that this inability is always the sole cause; however, it usually is a major factor.

In my practice of internal medicine, not a day goes by in which I do not see several people who have legitimate physical illnesses that have been caused by their inability to experience and accept love. Someone might immediately say: "Well, then, it's all in their head, right?"

No, the physical illnesses I see are not imagined but indeed real. The cause, however, is unresolved psychological and spiritual conflict. To me this is all the more tragic because people will readily blame a physical illness for all of their problems—taking pills and even having surgery—and will only grudgingly admit that they might be avoiding an underlying psychological or spiritual cause.

After all, who wants to have psychological problems? It is easier to deal with an infection or backache than a profound sense of boredom or meaninglessness in life, for instance. It is much more palatable to deal with a hole in the stomach lining than with a hole in the soul. And to believe that such physical manifestations are completely separate from our deepest spiritual longings provides us a kind of high-priced security. Yet, we cannot ignore the intimate connection between mind and body, spirit and biology.

> The pathways along which the human mind makes its registrations on physiology are being probed more deeply than ever before. A biology of the emotions is coming into view. For example, discoveries have been made that both the neuroendocrine and immune systems can produce identical substances (peptide hormones, or neuropeptides). . . . The two systems also share the

same array of receptors with which these substances can interact and transmit their messages. Such evidence has led Dr. Blalock to believe that the central nervous system and immune system convey similar information to each other through such hormone signals. These facts fit in with the last article written by the late Franz Ingelfinger as editor of the *New England Journal of Medicine,* in which physicians were reminded that 85 percent of human illnesses are within the reach of the body's own healing system.[1]

Of course we are *not* healing ourselves of 85 percent of our illnesses. But we may well wonder whether that fact is largely due to our refusal to recognize and accept their true causes, our denial of the extent to which we ourselves cause sicknesses by our sickened approach to living. The cost to the health care system in treating psychosomatic illnesses has been estimated—way back in 1983—as $20 billion per year.[2] Imagine what it is now. Yet many of our physicians do not help us in this matter. Just as it is easier for patients to deal with physical problems only, so it is with doctors.

Doctors Prefer Treating the Physical

Doctors' offices are filled with people who have physical problems stemming from psychological and spiritual pain. The tragedy is that most doctors today address the physical problems, but rarely attempt to investigate the deeper, fuller picture presented by the emotional and spiritual lives of their patients. Why? First, *they are unaware of the connection.* Most doctors receive little training in the art of treating the person as a whole, so that the mind-body-spirit aspects are all taken into account.

The ancient Greeks recognized the importance of this approach. Socrates said, "As it is not proper to cure the eyes without the head, nor the head without the body, so neither is it proper to cure the body without the soul." Similarly, Hippocrates said, "In order to cure the human body it is necessary to have a knowledge of the whole of things." To treat only the body without acknowledging the interplay of mind and soul puts the doctor at a great disadvantage. And the curative process will be hampered.

The second reason most doctors do not address the whole person is that *they prefer cases to be clear-cut.* That's how M.D.s are taught to think and react. Throwing in the psychological and spiritual profiles of the patient muddies the diagnostic waters. Certainly it is easier for a doctor to prescribe a medicine than to delve into what could prove to be deep-seated, "sticky" problems. As one doctor put it: "I have just enough energy to take on the physical problems of my patients and carry them around with me—along with my own personal and family concerns. If I tried to shoulder the load of all their self-torturing hangups too, I'd be a basket case in no time."

There is a third reason: *Patients get angry.* Most people become angry if you tell them that psychological or spiritual issues may be playing a role in their physical illnesses. So why alienate a patient when you can play the expected role of beneficent healer by dispensing a pill or ordering a blood test? Of course, patients themselves compound the problem by demanding the quick fix. They will medicate themselves, and even accept surgery, rather than address their spiritual and psychological woundedness.

As an example, consider Munchausen's syndrome, a condition in which people arrive at hospitals with a variety of symptoms trying to gain admission. Many do gain admission and have multiple surgical procedures done to them, such as having their appendix or gall bladder taken out for no good reason. Some people have five or six operations done on them that are completely unnecessary.

One older man was convinced he had cancer of his lung. After I did chest X rays to reassure him, he immediately developed symptoms that made him think he had cancer of his prostate. After being tested "OK" for these things, he later came in with symptom reports that sounded like cancer of the stomach. When I tried to reassure him, he ended up going to a specialist to get endoscoped (a procedure in which a tube is put down into the stomach). We were able to view the lining of his stomach to convince him that he did not have cancer. This man was married to an alcoholic whom he cared for like a child. When I placed him on antidepressant medication, his symptoms of worrying about having cancer went away. But I wondered whether he would continue on with counseling, whether he would have the courage to explore the true nature of his problems.

Peace does not come in capsules! This is regrettable because medical science recognizes that emotions such as fear, sorrow, envy, resentment and hatred are responsible for the majority of our sicknesses.[3]

Why Such Fear?

Why would people be so afraid to face the pain in their souls along with the pains of a physical illness? I believe there are several reasons for this. One is the simple fact that most people are not knowledgeable about the mind-body-spirit connection. Medical publications for lay people burst with articles about strengthening your heart, lowering cholesterol levels, and healing peptic ulcers. But rarely do we see an article dealing with, say, strengthening one's personal faith as a means of contributing to overall well-being. So, ignorance plays a great role.

Also the mechanism of denial is so powerful in most of us that it causes a type of spiritual and psychological blindness. We fail to see our internal scars, which remain deeply hidden in the subconscious. It hurts so much to bring them into consciousness that we do not let them surface. And it is impossible to deal with something when we won't even acknowledge its existence. The words of James Thurber strike a chord here:

> All people should strive to learn before they die:
>   what they are running from, and to, and why.

But we do continue to run, without substantial knowledge of ourselves. For to address previous spiritual and psychological woundedness gives us pain. And who wants that? Most of us would rather give up our fullest potential for growth, and the freedom that comes with that growth, than deal with all the pain (that's why drugs and alcohol are so prevalent in our society). Yet what appears to be the solution, the short-term avoidance of facing past hurts, is not only damaging in the long run, it is crippling. Consider Cathy, one of my patients. She had consulted me several times in the course of a year, experiencing asthma attacks and requiring several admissions to the hospital for chest pains. She also suffered high blood pressure and was taking two medications to regulate it. To top it off, she had battled obesity for most of her adult life. She now sat before me with all the signs and symptoms of a peptic ulcer.

"Tell me, Cathy," I began. "What's stressing you out these days?"

Without skipping a beat, she replied: "Nothing that I know of."

"Perhaps *knowing* would help," I said. "You do have an ulcer, and the pain is clearly severe. But there are *reasons* for the excess production of acid. Suppose we take some time to explore possible causes a little further?"

As I dug deeper, I discovered that Cathy's husband had emotionally abandoned her, calling her "an ice-cold fish." Although they still lived together, they barely spoke. She had also only recently become aware that he had had several affairs during the course of their marriage. On a subsequent visit to my office the inner wounds became more apparent as she tearfully recounted the story of her childhood, which included a workaholic father whom she rarely saw and a mean-spirited, punitive mother.

Cathy had no sense of being loved as a child. "I can't even remember a single time when my mother looked at me with kindness in her eyes. She had these huge, green eyes, and they always looked like they were saying: 'What are *you* doing here, anyway?' "

This horrifying deprivation was so painful to Cathy that she could neither address nor accept it. To do so would require coming to a conscious, soul-wrenching conclusion: "So this is the truth of who I was—a sad, lonely, hurting little kid, with nobody to help me." Who wouldn't be overcome with grief at the prospect of accepting such a life sentence? Instead, Cathy translated the terror of being unloved into multiple physical problems. She overate, causing her cholesterol and blood pressure levels to rise higher and higher. Her false internal message was: *I am not lovable.* And under the crushing, anxiety-producing spell of being unloved by her parents, she ended up marrying a man who also did not love her. In effect, it was the type of relationship she had been groomed for since her earliest days.

How Feeling Unloved Makes Us Sick

Let's look more closely at how the emotional stress of feeling unloved leads to physical illness. I stated earlier that giving and receiving love is a basic, God-given *need*, not just an "extra" that would be nice to experience. When this need goes unmet we get into trouble. People who are unable to accept love are constantly frustrated and angry because of the loneliness and isolation it fosters. Loneliness, isolation, and anger are all great stressors to the human body.

Simply stated, the body was designed to deal with stress immediately. Yet people who don't know how to receive love experience a chronic state of ongoing stress. They are unable to get close (or feel close) to others, making them feel alone and empty. Under the surface this profound disease rumbles like an ever-present earth tremor beneath a seemingly solid skyscraper. The unstable core rattles the windows and pounds away at the foundation, compromising the integrity of the entire superstructure. Until one day . . . the inevitable collapse.

The ANS and Chronic Stress

The part of the body responsible for handling stressors is called the autonomic nervous system (ANS). Here's how it works: You back out of your driveway in the family sportster without looking to the right, and suddenly a trumpet-blast of a horn rips into your eardrums and you look up to see the local garbage truck preparing to demolish you. Your pupils dilate, your heart races, and your entire body becomes poised for action in what is called the "fight or flight" reaction. Quick! your foot pounces on the break pedal. That's your ANS at work; it can save your life. Ideally, the stress passes and the lifesaving adrenalin surge quickly dissipates.

Unfortunately, there is no system set up for managing *chronic* stress. We just weren't meant to be under pressure all the time. Adrenalin is constantly being secreted in large amounts during chronic stress and its effects are not only devastating to our psychological health but also to our physical bodies. Simply put, this constant secretion of adrenalin is bad medicine for any organ system in the body. It's too much of a good thing.

Take, for example, hypertension. The constant secretion of adrenalin in a love-blocked person, through a variety of mechanisms, makes blood pressure go up and stay up. Chronically elevated blood pressure is bad enough, but that's only the beginning. High blood pressure is a known risk-factor for heart disease, leading to early heart attacks and heart failure. It is also one of the primary causes of strokes and atherosclerosis (commonly called hardening of the arteries). Hypertension can also damage the kidneys and lead to kidney failure. Do you see the domino effect, how the lack of love can even cause kidney failure?

Is there any hope, then, for the chronically stressed—which includes just about all of us? Yes, if we develop the ability to distinguish between external stress *factors* and inner stress *reactions*. It is not how many external, stressful circumstances or situations bombarding us that causes us to become ill. Rather, it is how we react to those circumstances that makes all the difference.

There are great differences in the ways people react to stress agents such as experiencing an automobile accident, speaking in public, disciplining a child, deciding the brand of refrigerator to buy, chasing the neighbor's dog out of the flower bed, or being awakened at 2 A.M by a philandering cat. Physicians are kept busy treating people who react poorly to these and other stressful situations. Some patients develop sieges of abdominal distress that last three or four weeks and require a great deal of medication. Others suffer the agonies of severe migraine headaches . . . a few succumb to coronary heart attacks. On the other hand, some people who are subjected to the identical stress factors adapt so well that they experience no ill effects at all.[4]

In other words, you might begin asking yourself as you confront each stressful event in your daily routine: *How much* inner stress *am I allowing this* outer stress *to generate inside me?*

Some Killer Maladies

It's obvious why we must learn to deal with chronic stress. The topic of this book is not a benign, take it or leave it thing. The physical fallouts of love-block can be deadly. When I was struggling so hard to become a success, unleashing torrents of adrenalin to course through my system, I was silently killing myself. I could never truly relax. Of course, I was not alone. Consider some of the more common examples I see in my practice all the time.

The Obesity Complex. Take a stroll down the aisles of your local supermarket and secretly tabulate the number of overweight people loading their carts with Cool Whip, Twinkies, and Triple Chocolate Delight Butter-Crunch Munchies. You don't have to look very far today before you notice people who are overweight . . . and getting heavier.

I call obesity a complex because it is so often bound together with at least three other health problems and their damaging effects: anxiety/-depression, hypertension, and heart disease. Studies clearly show that as body weight increases so does blood pressure. We've just seen all the problems high blood pressure can cause. As if that's not bad enough, obese people also have higher cholesterol and triglyceride levels and almost always have lower HDL (good cholesterol) levels. High blood pressure and high cholesterol levels all lead to increased incidence of heart disease, such as heart attacks and congestive heart failure.

(Just a note on cholesterol: It is a fat-like substance that we get from many of the foods we eat, and there are two main components to it: the low density lipoprotein [LDL], which is the so-called "bad" cholesterol, and a high density lipoprotein [HDL], the "good" cholesterol. LDL is associated with the plaque or the blockages in the arteries. The higher it is the more at risk you are for heart disease. On the other hand, the good cholesterol, HDL, actually clears the LDL out of the arteries. It's like a transport, picking up the bad cholesterol and bringing it to the liver to be destroyed. Therefore, the higher your HDL, the less your risk of heart disease. Also, triglycerides are another kind of "bad" fat, which are usually at higher blood levels in the obese.)

What a cavalcade of physical problems obesity causes! Yet these people are trying to satisfy a need in themselves that goes far deeper than the physical. Obesity is almost always caused by an addiction to food. People who are obese eat compulsively rather than because their body needs the extra calories, and these extra calories lodge themselves as fat. A food addiction is a ravenous search for self-acceptance and love, an engorging with food to quell the anxiety that facing the love void naturally releases. Counselors at the Minirth-Meier clinic report:

> Many people in our eating disorder unit at the hospital suffer from anxiety. Now we aren't talking here about a specific fear—worry about the final exam next week, worry about the pay raises you're going to ask for tomorrow and may not get. We're talking about a persistent, vague anxiety: fear of the unknown. Anxiety is fear of finding out the truth about one's own hidden thoughts, feelings, or motives.[5]

Obviously, dieting alone is not the answer when you are dealing with food addiction. A doctor must go further and deeper and deal with many of the psychological and spiritual issues, particularly the issue of the hunger for love. When a person learns how to receive love and gets the need for love met, he or she will no longer try to fill up with food in hopes of somehow filling the emptiness that is deep inside where love should be.

So the obesity complex comes packaged with anxiety and depression. People who do not experience love, who eat to fill the love void, have higher anxiety levels and this anxiety can lead to high levels of acid production in the stomach. Over a period of time the increased acid production damages the wall of the stomach and causes an ulcer.

High anxiety levels can also lead to high blood pressure and heart disease. Remember that many times there is a connection between several of these illnesses in people who have love hunger. Obesity, hypertension, and heart disease are often all connected in one single patient.

Infections. Although it has never been proven definitely, I believe that many infections stem from people's psychological and spiritual maladjustment, particularly their inability to receive love. Such people probably have more viral as well as bacterial infections. I know that in my practice the patients who don't appear to have the fulfillment of love come in with infections much more frequently than those who do. They just get sick more often.

Some researchers believe that the constant stress of living without love, and its resulting high adrenalin production, causes the white blood cells that fight infection to work less effectively. Of course, this would lead to more frequent infections.

If one asks, What are the primary influences on the immune system? the answer is, Practically everything. The immune system can be affected by biochemical changes in the body, by an invasion of microorganisms, by toxicity, by hormonal forces, by emotions, by behavior, by diet, or by a combination of all these factors in varying degrees.

The immune system is a mirror to life, responding to its joy and anguish, its exuberance and boredom, its laughter and tears, its excitement and depression, its problems and prospects. Scarcely anything that enters the mind doesn't find its way into the workings of the body. Indeed, the connection between what we think and how we feel is perhaps the most dramatic documentation of the fact that mind and body are not separate entities but part of a fully integrated system.[6]

If the immune system is indeed as susceptible to our emotions as many medical researchers now believe, is it any wonder that love-blocked souls suffer greater incidence of infection?

Headaches. Here is one of the most common illnesses associated with stress and the inability to receive love (and also one of the most common reasons to see an M.D.). That is not to say that all headaches spring from the lack of love; however, I'm convinced that a great many of them do. Not a day goes by that I don't see at least two or three people in my office with this very common complaint.

Consider the case of Sam, a forty-five-year-old accountant who came to see me for frequent headaches. He was a recovering alcoholic with twenty years of sobriety to his credit. He complained of almost daily headaches so intense that he felt his head was "being pumped full of concrete that just keeps expanding inside my skull."

"How are you managing to cope with that kind of pain?" I asked.

"With about thirty Tylenols a day—and anything else I can get my hands on through the pharmacist. I've got to find a cure for this thing. Or I don't know how I can keep my job. And without that, I'm sunk."

The desperation oozed from Sam, in his voice, in his eyes, in his contorted facial expressions as he spoke. Yet a thorough physical exam and laboratory tests failed to reveal any physical reasons for his headaches.

On Sam's return appointment when I related that all his lab tests had come back normal and that there might be some other reasons for his headaches, he grudgingly consented to talk, beginning with a painful topic: his father.

"I hate to say it this way, but Dad was nothing but a drunk. No other way to put it. And when he was really fried—which was most of the time—he was one heck of a mean cuss around the house. At one time or another, I was hit with just about every piece of furniture that old guy could manage to pick up and toss in my direction."

"You had to put up with that kind of thing, day in and day out?" I asked.

"Not really. Actually, he was gone most of the time. We never knew where. So it was like: I wished I had a father around, but then—No, it's better if he stays away. You know?"

Sam admitted to being depressed, having difficulty sleeping, often being at odds with his wife and children. When I asked him if he had ever been able to receive love, even God's love, he blurted: "What in the world kind of question is that?"

I explained to Sam that he was taking Tylenol in such dangerously large amounts that it could damage his kidneys and liver. But then we got to the heart of the matter: we discussed the fact that though he had stopped drinking alcohol, he had never really worked through the rage he felt for his father, nor had he ever learned to connect with other people or God. I believe this all combined to cause his splitting headaches.

With this initial insight encouraging him, Sam began seeing a psychologist. When I saw him a few months later, he had an intriguing report: "When I first came here, I thought it would be just one more series of needle pricks and little paper sample cups. You know, one more crummy disappointment. I never really considered that *my head was hurting because my heart hurt so bad.*" He said it with tears in his eyes.

Certainly, there are many causes of headaches. But I believe the majority of them are related to depression and anxiety, which both, in many cases, spring from an inability to receive and process love. The gripping stress and pain of depression and loneliness leads to headache.

Cancer. One of the more nebulous illnesses that I think can also be psychologically and spiritually related is cancer. This is addressed marvelously by Dr. Bernie Siegel. This cancer surgeon tells us that cancer—its cause and often its healing—may be strongly connected to the psychological and spiritual well-being of the patient. He invites us to consider, for example, that our white blood cells, the cells that fight infection, are also the cells that travel throughout the body removing any precancerous or early cancer cells, thus preventing the cancer from developing.

The critical point here is that white blood cells do not function well in people who do not know how to receive love. Therefore it makes sense that cancer may also be more common in these folks.

What we get back to again and again is that, although there's no question that environment and genes play a significant role in our vulnerability to cancer and other diseases, the emotional environment we create within our bodies can activate mechanisms of destruction or repair.[7]

Depression and Hypochondria. A discussion of physical illnesses stemming from psychological and spiritual distress would not be complete without talking about depression and hypochondria. (I will discuss depression in greater detail in the next chapter.)

By hypochondria I am referring to people who display the symptoms of a certain physical illness—without actually having medical evidence of that physical illness. Because of the havoc stress wreaks upon the body, almost any of the symptoms of any physical illness can be felt by a patient. Every doctor has had patients who bore symptoms of paralysis, with no nerve damage; choking without obstruction; even pregnancy without a baby. In fact, there are cases of men being "pregnant" (their abdomens bloat with gas) due to their intense identification with their wives who will actually bear the child.

Suffice to say that hypochondria is very common in many doctors' offices. Most of these people are highly anxious and somewhat depressed and often are completely unable to experience love. Many are addicted to being "sick" just as an alcoholic would be addicted to drink.

Consider forty-eight-year-old Ann, who came to my office with a history of asthma. She constantly suffered shortness of breath and wheezing and had been seen by other doctors several times with similar complaints. Medical tests, however, including pulmonary function studies, chest X-rays, and blood oxygen tests, revealed no asthma—even when she was short of breath.

Ann had also been treated for angina in the past and was on three different heart medicines when I first saw her. She was having prolonged chest pains, which appeared very much like angina. I hospitalized her at that time and performed numerous tests on her. Eventually she underwent cardiac catheterization and was found to have normal coronary blood flow. None of her heart arteries showed any blockage.

"Good news, Ann. Your test results are all normal," I told her.

She looked at me with wide eyes as the color drained from her face.

When I went on to tell her that I would have to take her off all heart medications, she began twisting the wooden arms on her chair. "But, but. . . ."

I wanted to find out more about Ann, about her life, past and present, as it became apparent to me that she was depressed. She did admit to having trouble falling asleep and then waking up almost every night at about 2 A.M. without a return to sleep. She also admitted to feeling "down in the dumps" most of the time.

As I discussed with her the possible need for seeing a psychologist and perhaps taking antidepressant medicine, I thought she would actually rip off the chair arms she was gripping so tightly. She eventually left me to see another physician.

I believe Ann had a need to be sick, a need that substituted for an even deeper longing to be loved.

Alcohol and Drug Addictions. If you are addicted—to anything—you suffer a self-image that is shame based. Addicted people are all searching for love, but because of the shame are never able to receive it. Shame is the fuel for addictions. (We all have shame, because all sin is dysfunctional and leads us into it. For example, after "the Fall" Adam felt shame. This is humanity's plight. See Gen. 3:8-10.)

Let's focus just on alcohol for a moment, and its connection to physical illness. Alcohol, when used to excess, damages almost every organ system of the body. Probably the most well-known alcohol-related illness is cirrhosis. Cirrhosis itself has multiple effects on many organ systems and ultimately results in death.

As I write this, baseball legend Mickey Mantle has just died, wasted away with liver disease and lung cancer. A couple years earlier he had admitted himself to the Betty Ford alcoholic rehabilitation center and talked about his life in a *Sports Illustrated* article.

> Whenever I tried to talk about my family, I got all choked up. My four sons drank too much because of me. When they were growing up, I was too busy to play catch in the back yard. But when they were old enough to drink, we became drinking buddies. My kids have never blamed me. They don't have to. I blame myself. . . . I'm going to spend more time with all of them now—show them and tell them I love them.[8]

It's interesting to me that Mantle spoke not only in terms of the physical side of addiction. He was also willing to pour out the emotional anguish—the guilt and shame—that flooded his soul.

Cirrhosis is just one of many physical problems associated with alcoholism. For example, since alcoholics get most of their calories from alcohol, they frequently suffer malnutrition. They commonly suffer from multiple vitamin deficiencies. And that, coupled with the malnutrition, suppresses the immune system, leading to more frequent infections.

Another devastating effect of alcoholism is dementia. Alcohol is toxic to brain cells and as these cells are killed off over a period of time they do not regenerate, leading to the gradual loss of the ability to think and reason, clinically called dementia. Some of the other effects of alcohol on the body include pancreatitis, gastrointestinal bleeding, subdural hematomas (bleeding around the brain), strokes, and frequent cuts and lacerations from falls. The effects of alcohol are devastating to the body.

Other Addictions. Everybody has heard it said kind of smugly that you could probably be addicted to almost anything, and it's probably true. For any time we are *driven* to do something there are hidden reasons behind that drivenness. Alcoholism and drug abuse are so common that we may gloss over the devastating effects of the many less obvious addictions that hound us.

How do you know if you're addicted? Consider this extended description of addiction that comes from a counselor friend of ours:

> An addiction is any unhealthy relationship, which has life-damaging consequences, with: (a) a mood altering substance; (b) an experience, or series of activities that comprise an experience; or (c) a person or persons. The addiction is:
> ❑ what you rely on for nurturing
> ❑ what you trust (because it always delivers)

❑ what you rely on for stability, escape, and reassurance (and eventually, isolation and alienation)

❑ what allows you to ignore the need to cultivate other interests and interest in others

❑ what allows you to organize your life to prevent knowing and feeling a deeper anguish, a deeper unresolved hunger

❑ what structures your life

❑ what allows you to ignore unresolved childhood conflicts

❑ what gives you the illusion of perfection or perfect control

❑ what you lie about or hide

❑ what you do to relieve the tension of resentments[9]

Do you see yourself here?

Someone has said: "To live is to be addicted." In light of the list above, wouldn't you agree? Just consider two of the more "acceptable" addictions you've no doubt encountered: workaholism and perfectionism. These traits are applauded in our society today. The more you have the more you are worth; the more you accomplish the better you are.

If you step back and look at your own childhood you'll likely see that you were applauded for accomplishments and rejected when you were not accomplishing. This is carried over into our adult lives as we attempt to squeeze our sense of meaning and worth out of what we produce. As one local TV commercial drones: "A man *is* what a man *does.*" Such a false message produces an addiction to doing more and more, to winning, to being successful, to rushing and worrying.

Simply stated, *people are getting ahead of you.* All the time.

While you're at your desk, people working out at the gym are getting ahead of you.

While you're at the gym, your coworkers are getting ahead of you.

If a friend gets a promotion at work, she has gotten ahead of you.

If a colleague reads a book you haven't read, he has gotten ahead. The entire U.S. swim team has gotten ahead of you.

While you're reading this book *everyone* is getting ahead of you. . . . Always judge any situation in relation to how much the people involved have gotten ahead of you, and in what ways.[10]

So work becomes addictive; we've got to stay ahead of the pack. Yet it is not the particular "object" of the compulsion that is so important but the reasons behind the compulsion, the driving forces behind it. A person unable to receive love thinks accolades will fill the crater left. It is the need for love and acceptance, then, that drives the cycle.

The point is that addiction has physical symptoms and effects and we try to "medicate" ourselves by using even more alcohol, drugs, or sex, or spending, or prestige. Sadly, we only succeed in stoking a cycle that has its own perverse irony: it is fueled by our attempts to stop.

Your History of Hurt

Just from this brief survey of killer maladies, we can see that physical illness stemming from psychological and spiritual pain is extremely common. Some researchers estimate that between 75 and 85 percent of all patients in doctors' offices with real or imagined physical complaints have those problems because of psychological and spiritual issues that are unresolved. The chronic stress generated can cause almost any physical illness. Some of the ones I have not talked about are: skin rashes, vascular headaches, irritable bowel syndrome, colitis, congestive heart failure, hypoglycemia, amenorrhea and infertility, as well as accident proneness.

What about you? Most people have been touched by one or more of these illnesses. They are so very common. Suppose you were to look a little closer at your health history to discover how love—or the lack of it—has affected your physical well-being?

❑   ❑   ❑

My Health-History Time Line (and the Meaning of My Illnesses)

Suggestion: On a separate sheet of paper, draw a horizontal line representing the years of your life so far. On the line, mark the dates of physical illnesses you recall.

Here's a brief example:

1961	1973	1978	1988	1994
• Pneumonia	• began to have asthma	• broken arm	• heart attack	• shingles

After you've jotted significant times of illness, go back to one of those times and analyze it (you might do so with each illness during the next few weeks):

❑ Describe some of the life events that occurred within the year before you got sick (or addicted). Do any "defining moments" stand out to you now?

_____

_____

_____

❑ Jot some descriptions of your state of mind at the time. How did you feel? Who was there with you? Who helped you?

_____

_____

_____

❑ Did your illness give you anything that you couldn't get without being sick? Name some of those things:

_____

_____

_____

❑ Now focus on a current affliction or addiction. If you had to assign a "meaning" to your illness, what would you say it means to you? What would you gain, and what would you lose, if this suffering were miraculously taken away?

_____

_____

_____

❑   ❑   ❑

Why write a chapter detailing the physical destruction that comes packaged with the love-block? "You're trying to scare me into changing, right?"

This could indeed be a scary and disheartening chapter, but that's not my goal. I have seen in myself, and in so many others, a *need* to be sick because physical symptoms protect us from our deeper need to be accepted without condition, without having to change ourselves. So the physical symptoms themselves are simply a plea for love. And we become addicted even to them.

But let's go back to the "addictions list" and fill in the last item on our friend's descriptions. I've saved it until now because of its profoundly encouraging truth:

> An addiction is "a spiritual *emergency* that is waiting to be transformed into a spiritual *emergence*."

What emerges when we come to a place of acceptance? A self that is being transformed: spiritually, emotionally, physically. Over three decades ago, medical doctor S.I. McMillen, in his brilliant little book, *None of These*

Diseases, summarized a wonderful—though radical—approach to life based on Romans 8:36-37:

> As it is written: "For Your sake we face death all day long; we are considered as sheep to be slaughtered." No, in all these things we are more than conquerors through Him who loved us.

McMillen recommended that we play off this passage to put on a "victorious adaptation to life's insults." His suggestion was this: to awaken each morning with the expectation of a sheep that is on its way to the slaughter. "If you take that attitude of mind," he says, "then nothing that comes up should frustrate or disturb you."

> A man awaiting death is not disturbed by many stress factors that upset people. He is not upset because his neighbor's chickens are scratching up his flower bed; his arthritis is not worsened because the taxes on his house have been raised; his blood pressure is not raised because his employer discharged him; he doesn't get a migraine headache because his wife burned his toast; and his ulcerative colitis doesn't flare up because the stock market goes down ten points. The crucified soul is not frustrated. The man who willingly, cheerfully and daily presents himself as a "living sacrifice" can excellently adapt to the severest situations and, with Paul, be "more than conqueror."[11]

Paul learned the bittersweet art of submitting to God, a pleasure alloyed with pain. He said: "I die every day."[12]

The idea of acceptance, then, has two distinct and powerful applications to encourage us: (1) God has perfectly *accepted* us with a love that cannot be overcome, and we can therefore (2) *accept* the daily stress factors as natural, expected components of our prior surrender (i.e., our "death") to His beneficent will. This call to acceptance also has great influence on how well we will be able to handle the inevitable depression in our lives.

4

The Despair of
Unfelt Love
(Depression: Part 1)

*All night long I flood my bed with weeping
and drench my couch with tears.
I am bowed down and brought very low;
all day long I go about mourning. . . .
I am feeble and utterly crushed;
I groan in anguish of heart. . . .
My heart pounds, my strength fails me;
even the light has gone from my eyes.*

—David, King of Israel[1]

King David showed us centuries ago how depression feels. Things haven't changed much . . .

The mornings themselves were becoming bad now as I wandered about lethargic, following my synthetic sleep, but afternoons were still the worst, beginning at about three o'clock, when I'd feel the horror, like some poisonous fogbank, roll in upon my mind, forcing me into bed. There I would lie for as long as six hours, stuporous

75

and virtually paralyzed, gazing at the ceiling and waiting for that moment of evening when, mysteriously, the crucifixion would ease up just enough to allow me to force down some food and then, like an automaton, seek an hour or two of sleep again.[2]

This is how depression felt to William Styron, the Pulitzer Prize-winning author who journaled his experience in *Darkness Visible*. His sufferings resonated with his readers because most human beings, at some time or another, have fallen prey to some level of depression—from a simple case of "the blues" to the full-fledged severe variety. It's a universal experience, transcending time and culture.

Recently we sat down to talk about the cases of depression we see today, the depressed people who walk into our offices. We wanted to compare notes about how a medical doctor and a counselor respond. We found that, typically, people come to us with multiple physical complaints—back pain, stomach pain, nervousness, tiredness—it can be anything. One person came with a sheet of paper, filled out on both sides, with lists of things that were hurting her. Usually that is a red flag and we'll ask: "Do you think you may be depressed?"

About 50 percent will say, "Yeah, I'm depressed," and heave a sigh of relief that it's finally been named. The other 50 percent will say, "No, I don't think so. I'm not depressed." But then I [Joe] will ask them how they're sleeping, and they usually have sleep-disturbance patterns. I'll ask them if they are interested in doing things that used to be fun, and they'll say no. Often they will give all the standard responses showing they are depressed. I'll put them on antidepressant medication, and three weeks later I'll see them again, and almost 80 to 90 percent of them will be better.

Other people come to our offices in different ways. Some come in and sit down and they're fairly cheerful, fairly expressive. But pretty quickly we'll get past that and begin asking them about the typical symptoms of depression:

"How are you sleeping at night?"

"Well, I'm not sleeping at all," or "I want to sleep all the time."

"How's your energy level?"

"Well, it's down."

"How's your concentration level?"

"I just can't remember things as well."

"How's your motivation level?"

"I don't enjoy doing the things I used to do. I have to force myself to go places."

"How's your appetite?"

"I either want to eat all the time or I don't feel like eating at all."

"How's your anxiety? Have you had increased anxiety?"

"Yes. I don't like this feeling."

"Have you had suicidal thoughts?"

"Well, you know, I wish Jesus would come back," or "I know I would never hurt myself, but I wish God would kill me in an accident."

So we see people who look fine, but once we probe under the surface a bit, and get them talking, they show depression.

Or there's the other way people come in. In John's case, I [Brian] went out and met him in the waiting room and as soon as I looked at him, I could see in his eyes that he was depressed. There was a sadness, an affect of utter despair. Once we came back to my office and we talked, he shared how he had tried praying about his moods and had talked to his pastor about it. He had done all these things and nothing seemed to work. I said, "Have you ever considered the possibility that there could be a medical, physiological component to your depression?"

"No, I never thought about that," was his listless response.

When we make a diagnosis of clinical depression we'll talk to a patient about what's going on in their lives before suggesting they go on medication for a while. Most people nowadays have heard of Zoloft, Paxil, or Prozac and they're willing to try it. So those people we'll put on the medicine. When they come back, we don't necessarily discuss future counseling the first time, if they've been in a major depression. We just tell them there's hope and that there is no question that they can feel better. When they come back, we talk about their part in this, their need for counseling.

Many times a person can be so depressed initially that counseling is premature. It would do no good until we get the chemicals in his brain right. When he comes back in three weeks and says, "Boy, I didn't realize how bad I felt," at that point, we start to lay the groundwork for a healing process that often includes counseling. This type of depression—depression as a physical disease—is out there and should be understood.

Depression as Physical Disease

Since some forms of depression are clearly tied to organic malfunctions of our bodies, it will do little good to try to "talk someone out of" this type of illness. Helping such a person with suggestions about opening up to more love, getting more exercise, or eating better can't hurt, and may well spark some improvement. But by and large, the "cure" will initially call for an adjustment of the chemical balances in the brain through medication.

The Biochemical Side of Depression

At the base of most depression is a disruption of the physical, emotional, and spiritual elements of a person. We have spoken of the love-block as both the cause and result of such a disruption deep within the fabric of our beings.

Depression is part of that disruptive cycle: We become isolated and develop a psychic "shell" that simultaneously holds in our pain and blocks out the possibility of love. This thoroughly unnatural way of being, which causes our whole system to break down, is invariably manifested as chronic stress. Chronic stress eventually leads to a depletion in certain brain chemicals. And this depletion causes the state of physical depression, which, in turn, usually leads to more isolation. The cycle feeds on itself.

Other biochemical factors can lead to certain forms of depression too. Take, for instance, the malfunction of the thyroid gland. A young woman called my secretary and said, "I feel like I'm going to die. Will Dr. Biuso see me right away?" This lady was a nurse at the hospital and liked the way I always said hello to her. So she came in to see me specifically for depression. She had been to another doctor who told her, "It's all just part of your age." Several weeks later she felt as if she were going to die.

I suspected when I looked at her, even before ordering the blood test, that she had a thyroid problem. And the tests later confirmed that her thyroid just wasn't working. Her TSH level was 122. Normal is up to 6. And that showed her thyroid just wasn't working. Of course, she did not need antidepressants, but she did need medication—thyroid medication. I started her on medicine immediately, and within two days she came in and said she was feeling so much better. After six weeks, she said, "I didn't realize how bad I felt. I think I would have died."

Actually, she could have died. A lot of times people with depression do not realize how much of a sinking disease this can be. I use the expression, "the old frog in the kettle." You stick a frog in a pot of water and slowly turn the heat up. That frog will continue adjusting its body temperature to the temperature of the water until the point at which he is boiling and can't jump out.

What happens in working with people is that medication does not give them an instantaneous high but it slowly reduces the heat in their body, so to speak, and as the depression comes down and they start feeling better, then they say, "I did not realize how bad I was feeling now that I know what feeling good is. I didn't realize how deep a hole I was in or how bad I felt." Because the descent happens so slowly, even with a medical cause of depression.

Most people don't go into depression quickly. It's a slow process. And they gradually adjust to it. The human body and brain makes an allowance. Like the thermostat, the frog resetting its thermostat. People get used to more and more pain, and they learn to live with it. "I guess this is how I'm supposed to feel," they say.

So there clearly are medical reasons for depression. In other words, not every case of depression is caused—directly—from a lack of love. Prescription drugs can cause depression. Low thyroid function can cause it. Also, people who have tumors of the adrenal gland can sometimes produce too much adrenalin, which leads to depression. But in any case the main factor in organic depression is the depletion of brain chemicals.

The Brain Chemical Connection

As we saw in the previous chapter, the "fight or flight" reaction gives us the spurt of energy we need to avoid an immediate, threatening catastrophe. Once the danger has passed, our heightened adrenaline level is supposed to go back to normal.

But some people suffer chronic stress, constantly maintaining high levels of adrenaline in their bodies. The stress may stem from the external circumstances in their lives, past or present, or may be the result of internal conflicts they have buried in their subconscious. At any rate, because of the constant stimulation to the nervous system, the brain becomes depleted of certain neurotransmitter chemicals it needs to function properly: serotonin, epinephrine, and norepinephrine. These are used up quickly in the "revved up" nervous system of the high-stressed, high-adrenaline person. Eventually the brain can't keep up with the demand for them.

It is this depletion process, from a purely physical standpoint, that causes depression. Specifically, here's how it works: at the synapse, the area between two cells in the brain, a chemical is released from one cell. It goes into the space between them (the intracellular space) and then goes to the other cell, causing a reaction. Once the reaction is over, the chemical (serotonin, for instance) is metabolized in that space. In other words, it is digested. Certain medicines prevent that "reuptake" of the chemical (i.e., the digestion, or metabolism of it) and increase the serotonin levels in the brain. In cases of depression—when levels of serotonin and epinephrine are low—we give drugs that prevent the reuptake of these chemicals, and the depression abates. Drugs such as Prozac, Zoloft, and Paxil are SSRIs (selective serotonin reuptake inhibitors). They prevent the digestion of serotonin (a neurotransmitter linked to feelings of well-being) at the nerve endings.

❏   ❏   ❏

Brain-Chemical Depletion . . . And How Antidepressant Medications Work

As we said, chronic stress leads to chronically high adrenaline levels, causing not only depression but anxiety. That is why the two are often experienced together. High adrenaline levels can be treated medically with drugs called beta-blockers. Picture adrenaline working on the cell surface. The cell has

The Mechanism of Action of Antidepressant Agents

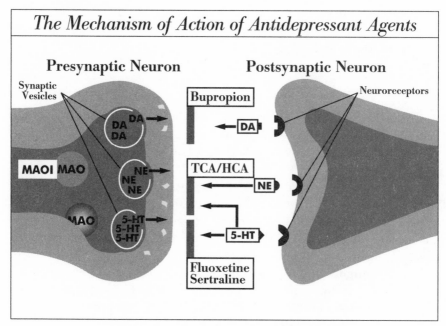

DA, dopamine; NE, norepinephrine; 5-HT, serotonin

what might be called keyholes in it (like a lock on a door), but the keyholes are shaped differently for different chemical "keys." Adrenaline affects two keyholes—the alpha-receptors and the beta-receptors. Like the key to your garage door and the key to your front door, they are two separate keys and they produce different effects in the cell. When adrenaline goes into the beta-receptor site on the cell it causes an increase in heart rate and causes the bronchial tubes in your lungs to dilate so you breathe better. The alpha-receptors cause an increase in your blood pressure by constricting the blood vessels, contributing to a heightened sense of awareness.

Certain drugs block these receptors. A beta-blocker "key" fits into the beta-receptor site, but it does not open the door. It doesn't unlock the lock. So it fools the cell. It blocks that receptor so adrenaline can't get there but it doesn't produce the effect of high heart rate or high blood pressure.

So if we prescribe a beta-blocker medicine, like Inderal, Corgard, or Tenormin, which we do for people who have high blood pressure or high anxiety levels, this medicine goes and fits into the receptor but blocks it from creating the fast heart rate and the high blood pressure. We fool the cell by giving it a drug to take up those receptor sites so now no other key can fit in those receptor sites, even though the correct key is there. In other words, the adrenaline is there to act but it can't act because the receptor site is already taken up.

Neurotransmission Within the Synapse*

Synapse

Presynaptic Neuron

Neurotransmitter (Serotonin)

Postsynaptic Neuron

SYNAPTIC CLEFT

Axon Terminal

Dendrite

Receptor

Direction of Nerve Impulse

Presynaptic Neuron

Postsynaptic Neuron

Receptor

Neurotransmitter

*Adapted from: Bristol-Myers Squibb Co. (Princeton, New Jersey).

Impulse Transmission in Brain Cells*

Presynapse   **Synaptic Cleft**   **Postsynapse**

Steps

A Nerve impulse goes to end of presynaptic cell

B Stimulated vesicles release neurotransmitter (e.g., serotonin) (Ⓝ)

C Neurotransmitter (Ⓝ)diffuses across synaptic cleft

D Neurotransmitter binds to postsynaptic receptor

E Impulse transmission in the postsynaptic cell creates desired effect (with serotonin that would be a sense of well-being)

*Adapted from: Bristol-Myers Squibb Co. (Princeton, New Jersey).

Some people naturally have higher levels of adrenaline in their bodies than others, so they are generally more nervous, or "higher strung," than others. Also, because they are more prone to secrete adrenaline, they deplete their serotonin levels more often, or quicker, and are more prone to depression. People are definitely wired differently.

❑   ❑   ❑

Time Out

Do I Need Medication for My Depression?
(Ask the Experts)

Scenario: You have been feeling uncommonly anxious lately. You wake up early in the morning, unable to return to sleep. You swallow and sigh a lot. You sometimes stare into space or feel like crying for "no reason." Life seems to hold no purpose; you can hardly get up in the mornings for work.

You believe you are depressed, and you have heard that there are some marvelous drugs on the market to help people in your condition. Suppose you could ask a medical doctor and a counselor about it. What would you ask?

Here are some common questions our patients raise, along with our answers.

1. Suppose I want to be checked out for possible "organic" causes of my depression. What should I do? What procedures or tests might be done?

Initially, you would want to see your family doctor and have a thorough physical exam. Typically I will order two key tests to check out possible organic causes of depression: (a) CBC test (for blood count), in order to make sure you are not anemic; (b) a thyroid test that includes a TSH (thyroid-stimulating hormone) level measurement. TSH levels will be high if your thyroid is not working.

If these tests do not reveal a problem, you may be advised to see a psychiatrist or counselor, along with being given a prescription for antidepressant medication. It is important to distinguish pure organic *causes* from organic *indications* of depression. No matter what the cause, there is always evidence of depression in the fact that brain chemicals will be depleted. Purely organic causes—without any life-situation and/or emotional problems involved—are very rare.

2. What prescriptions might I receive for medication? What about side effects?

Antidepressant medications prescribed today include: Prozac, Paxil, Well-butrin, Imipramine, Serezone, Elavil, and a host of others. Every prescription drug has some side effects, and these are no exception. Some of the more common complaints are: insomnia, weight gain, blurry vision, drowsiness, dry mouth, diarrhea or constipation, and sexual dysfunction (the failure to reach orgasm during sex, for instance). Prozac has been known, in rare cases, to cause suicidal tendencies. Other antidepressants can even *increase* anxiety in certain dosages.

3. *What are some of the benefits and limits of taking medication for depression?*

Around 70 percent of patients report feeling better after a few weeks of taking an antidepressant or beta-blocker prescription. They have increased energy, begin sleeping through the night, and display a greater enthusiasm for living. However, merely taking a prescription does nothing to treat the underlying causes of the depression. That is why counseling is normally recommended alongside drug therapy. Also, most physicians expect to take their patients off a medication within a year or two. It may not be a permanent solution.

4. *I've been told that medication only delays true healing. Is that true?*

No. Actually, medication aids in the counseling process. It frees a person to focus less on symptoms and more intently on emotional pain—past and present. In effect, the medications help free up more energy for focusing on this part of the healing process.

5. *Some of my Christian friends believe all emotional problems can be solved through prayer and faith in God. What do you think?*

Of course, faithfulness and prayer are essential ingredients of Christian discipleship. But they do not rule out taking prudent action on our behalf when common sense tells us to do so. God expects this, for He has given us intelligence and wisdom to do what is good and right.

God has given doctors and medicine to humankind as part of His providence in the world. So, in a way, it's true that only God solves our emotional problems. But the means He uses are broad and varied. We should not ignore a gift He places before us to use, just as a Christian diabetics would not refuse to take their insulin. Wisdom is the key, for God often uses our pain as His means of transforming us. No pill can take the place of that gracious work.

❑   ❑   ❑

Depression as "Emotion Stuffing"

The debate over whether depression can be treated solely through the use of medications is a topic too broad to cover in depth here. Suffice to say, however, that whether we seek healing at the physical level or the emotional/spiritual level, we must always treat the three parts of the person as solidly interconnected. "Purely organic" depressions are still linked to chronic stress, since depletion of brain chemicals stems from overactive adrenaline production. And stress, as we have seen, has a connection to the love-block.

Clearly, in every case of depression, something is wrong in the whole-person balance. If we move our focus from the depressed person's brain down to his heart, we'll very likely find "stuffed" emotions. Depression in this sense is a loss of awareness, an out-of-touchness with emotions. Contrary to popular belief, a depressed person is not someone who has little feeling (though he may appear that way on the surface); he is actually overloaded with feeling that has been pushed down, suppressed, or repressed. Those stuffed emotions are doing their destructive work, wreaking havoc as muscle tension, adrenaline production, and anxiety—all resulting in depression.

Goethe once said: "Few people have the imagination for reality." We might rework his epigram and make it more relevant to depression by saying: Few people have the *courage* for reality—the reality of their emotions, the courage to experience them head-on. Especially anger.

The Anger-Isolation Connection

Anger can be a fearful thing. "Suppose I get totally bent out of shape? What if I lose control?" Even when such fears are not expressed directly, they do linger just below the surface for most of us. We fear what might happen should we give free reign to our raging frustration.

And, of course, most of us have been taught that it is always better to "be nice." Anger has been made the enemy of our healthy social develop-ment. A friend of ours who consulted us remembers one of his father's favorite sayings. He says: "Whenever I was experiencing any kind of powerful emotion, especially when I was on the brink of getting really angry, he'd always chime in with: 'Oh, Jay! Don't *feel* that way!'

"The trouble is," says Jay, "I *did* feel that way. What was I supposed to do?"

Jay spent decades learning to stuff his real feelings. And he spent years in counseling dealing with depression.

Loneliness and isolation are trademarks of depression, but we may fail to see their connection to anger. As we become more lonely and isolated we are less able to process and receive love, simply because we feel so unworthy of any gift offered to us. This, in turn, makes us more angry.

Without intervention this cycle remains intact and becomes very powerful in our lives. We soon become separated, not only from the people around us, but alienated from our true selves. Our relationships become more meaningless to us and lacking in intimacy. The need for love is so powerful that if it is left unmet it creates a huge void leading to more intense anger and depression. This void has to be filled, and so people use a variety of substances or activities to try and fill it. Unfortunately, this always ends up in failure.

❏   ❏   ❏

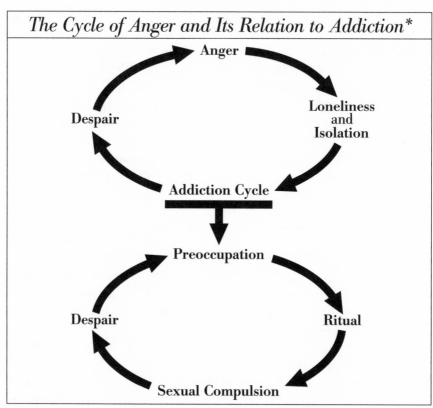

The Cycle of Anger and Its Relation to Addiction*

Anger

Despair

Loneliness and Isolation

Addiction Cycle

Preoccupation

Despair

Ritual

Sexual Compulsion

*Adapted from: *Out of the Shadows, Understanding Sexual Addiction* by Patrick Carnes (Minneapolis: CompCare Publications, 1983).

Anger, then, is about our unmet emotional needs telling us when our needs are not being met. It should not be ignored. The most important of these needs was to be loved and nurtured as a child for just the one we were. This would have been the exact opposite of being isolated and lonely.

Probably one of the most common complaints in any doctor's office, be it a psychiatrist, psychologist, or family doctor, is that of loneliness. Almost everyone who seeks psychological or psychiatric help complains of it. It is the awareness of being separated and isolated, of feeling disconnected from other people. That was Marcy's story.

Marcy was a thirty-four-year-old ICU nurse who came to my office complaining of being depressed. Indeed, she had all the symptoms that go along with depression, including: lack of appetite, difficulty falling asleep, irritability with her husband and children, and lack of interest in life in general. She was not suicidal, although she did say that the thought had crossed her mind. Marcy's main complaints were that she was very lonely and becoming more and more isolated from those around her. She felt angry, defeated, separated from those closest to her, even her family.

Marcy's complaints are common. Her feeling of separateness and isolation were a source of anxiety for her. The more anxiety and anger she felt, the more she continued to isolate herself. The anxiety and guilt grew. And though constantly surrounded by people, her loneliness deepened.

> Loneliness is not the same as aloneness. I know that, because loneliness seizes me most acutely when I am in a crowd. There, surrounded by laughing, self-assured people, I feel awkward and clumsy. I am afraid that anything I say will be ignored, or worse, I will be interrupted by someone with a more fascinating, winsome personality. So I retreat inside and head toward the corners of the room.[3]

So it is that a person can be around others all day long, be part of a "happy" family, be an active member of a friendly church . . . and yet feel isolated and lonely. Even working in a busy ICU, like Marcy.

❏　　❏　　❏

Time Out

How's Your IQ (Isolation Quotient)?

❏ How often do you involve yourself with people or activities outside of work? How often do you have people over for socializing at your home?
Example:

_____

_____

❏ How often do you feel deeply connected to people, perhaps sharing an intimate detail or feeling with a friend or spouse? Or do you feel disconnected most of the time?
Example:

_____

_____

❏ How often do you go out to other people's homes or involve yourself in going out with other people?
Example:

_____

_____

❏ How often do you do things that you find pleasurable, just for yourself?
Example:

_____

_____

❏ How often would you say that you feel lonely?
Example:

_____

_____

❏ Do you tend to avoid other people, even when you are not under stress?
Example:

_____

_____

❏ Do you have three other people you could say know you well, meaning they know you emotionally?
Example:

_____

_____

❏ If you were to die today, do you have people in your life who would really care? How many people would be concerned?
Example:

_____

_____

❏ Do you feel like you are watching things from the outside looking in and not really "involved"?
Example:

_____

_____

Without assigning a number as an Isolation Quotient, you should still be able to tell from your responses and examples how isolated you tend to be. If you see room for improvement, try reaching out to a friend or neighbor today.

❑   ❑   ❑

The Love Connection

As shame is the fuel for addiction, so love is the fuel for relationship. We've seen that depression, even when organically caused, is usually linked with escalating loneliness and isolation. It's essential, then, for the "disconnected" person to reconnect in relationships. And love is our connection to other people and to God. There are no exceptions.

Even sexual intercourse, outside of love, provides only a fleeting connection, which ends abruptly after orgasm, leaving one feeling more isolated and lonely than ever. In Josephine Hart's haunting novel, *Damage*, Roger, a successful doctor, Member of Parliament, and respected family man, seems to have engineered a perfect life for himself. He reflects back over half a decade:

> All my ambitions were fulfilled. All had been my own choice. It was a blessed life. It was a good life.
> But whose life?[4]

> Later, Roger meets Anna . . .

> A stillness descended upon me. I sighed a deep sigh, as if I had slipped suddenly out of a skin. I felt old, and content. The shock of recognition had passed through my body like a powerful current. Just for a moment I had met my sort, another of my species. . . . I had been home. For a moment, but longer than most people. It was enough, enough for my lifetime.[5]

He succumbs to an affair with this woman, the same woman that his own son was planning to marry. The physical aspect of this relationship seems to meet all his needs, giving him an absolute, perfect fulfillment of his soul—for he has found his soulmate, the perfect match.

Yet the scandal, when it finally comes to light, ends up destroying Roger's family, actually killing his son, and condemning Roger to perpetual exile far from his home. All of the devastation started with a simple kernel of isolation, a sense of emptiness, which Roger recognized in himself: "But *whose* life?" Within himself alone—surrounded by family and fame, but still alone, he could not find peace. He tried to connect through sex—not love—and that was his downfall.

There is an emptiness inside that, no matter what we do, we cannot fill outside of intimate connection in love. This void can make us feel that all we do is meaningless. This isolation and loneliness, coupled with the unrealistic expectation that we should come to a point of perfect fulfillment in this life (that I can "have it all," or that I will meet "my sort" of person, someone who can heal my soul), leads to anger, bitterness, anxiety, guilt, and eventually depression. In some people it becomes so intense that suicide seems the only way out—

> A still small voice spake unto me,
> "Thou art so full of misery,
> Were it not better not to be?"[6]

Many of our greatest artists and writers, in spite of brilliant minds brimming with creative talent, have ended up killing themselves. They became isolated, angry, and depressed. And never found the unconditional love they so desperately sought.

PART TWO

The Healing Process

Living in the Truth

The mind is its own place,
and in itself
can make a heaven of Hell,
a hell of Heaven.

—John Milton

Almost all our misfortunes in life come from the wrong notions
we have about the things that happen to us.

—Marie Stendahl

It is very obvious that we are influenced not by "facts"
but by our interpretation of facts.

—Alfred Adler

We have spent four chapters surveying the many aspects of our need for love's healing. We have explored the ways we long for love—and the ways we consciously or unconsciously block it off. We want love, we seek love, and we become physically, spiritually, and emotionally sick for its lack. When we do find an occasional relationship-oasis, a trickling source of affection, it so often comes packaged with a price tag attached, conditional upon our ability to reciprocate or our determination to keep on pleasing the giver. We need healing.

93

The first broad step in the healing process is to renew our minds. We do this through replacing distorted thinking with truth. This task is intimately related to our growth journey as Christians. Becoming a Christian and coming to know God is only the beginning of a lifelong process of learning to recognize and receive God's grace and love, which is a sanctifying transformation that leads us to be Christlike. And in this new life, we are to do two basic things: (1) "put on the new self" and (2) "renew our minds."

Putting Off and Putting On

Putting off the old self and putting on the new self is obviously a two-step process. Here is how the Apostle Paul described it:

> You were taught, with regard to your former way of life, to put off your old self, which is being corrupted by its deceitful desires; to be made new in the attitude of your minds; and to put on the new self, created to be like God in true righteousness and holiness.[1]

The process involves total life transformation in the sense that we exchange our old lifestyle habits for new ones, motivated by God's Spirit within us. For our purposes, in our context of learning to receive love, we start with the most foundational aspect of this transforming process: dealing with our thoughts and attitudes. The first step here, then, is to begin recognizing what kinds of thoughts and beliefs swirl in our minds, telling us that we are unworthy of love. We call this phenomenon "self-talk" and it is happening all the time, whether on a conscious level or just below the surface.

Recognizing the Lies

Many of the things we believe about ourselves are simply untrue—virtual lies—but we live by their precepts nevertheless. What are the sources of these lies? Let's consider three possibilities.

Satan. Talking about the devil is tricky business today. Even sincere and devout Christians disagree about who, or what, Satan is. And surely in society at large it is not considered an "enlightened" view of reality to speak of a real devil these days. Yet consider Jesus' words about Satan's identity:

> He was a murderer from the beginning, not holding to the truth, for there is no truth in him. When he lies, he speaks his native language, for he is a liar and the father of lies.[2]

At the very least, there is something important here to consider when we're faced with the task of ferreting out the sources of the lies we tell ourselves. Surely it can do no harm to check out the influence of the "father of lies."

Scott Peck, noted psychiatrist and author, was skeptical about the reality of the devil, and of evil in general. In *People of the Lie* he relates his struggle with this very question:

> Is there such a thing as evil spirit? Namely, the devil? I thought not. In common with 99 percent of psychiatrists and the majority of clergy, I did not think the devil existed. Still priding myself on being an open-minded scientist, I felt I had to examine the evidence that might challenge my inclination in the matter. It occurred to me that if I could see one good old-fashioned case of possession I might change my mind.[3]

A good portion of Dr. Peck's book deals with his experience of witnessing satanic possessions and exorcisms. He saw evil literally speak, saw it try to kill those who fell into its clutches. In one case, a patient regressed to severe, life-threatening illness. As a result of his observations, Peck concluded: "I now know Satan is real. I have met it."

Obviously, possession is extremely rare and not well understood by anyone. And, in any case, it is too broad a topic for us to do justice to it in this book. The point is, however, that in these unusual cases, the reality of one source of lies becomes crystal clear. Satan, or "the spiritual forces of evil" (Eph. 6:12), do influence our minds. This became clear even to one who approached the whole subject as an academic inquiry, purely as a scientist. Listen again to Peck:

> The list of lies it spoke was endless—sometimes almost a boring litany. The major ones I remember were: humans must defend themselves in order to survive and cannot rely on anything other than themselves in their defense; everything is explainable in terms of negative and positive energy (which balance out to be zero), and there is no mystery in the world; love is a thought and has no objective reality; science is whatever one chooses to call science; death is the absolute end to life—there is no more; all humans are motivated primarily by money, and if this appears not to be the case, it is only because they are hypocrites; to compete for money, therefore, is the only intelligent way to live. . . . The best definition I have for Satan is that it is a *real spirit of unreality*.[4]

Though Peck speaks of an "it," while the Bible attributes personhood to the devil, we must, in any case, take him seriously. As Frederick Buechner said in his book *Wishful Thinking*, "To take the Devil seriously is to take seriously the fact that the total evil in the world is greater than the sum of all its parts. Likewise the total evil in yourself."[5]

Why is it so crucial to recognize the role of the devil? Our self-esteem is significantly affected by the lies we tell ourselves. These lies, when repeated daily over the course of a lifetime, shape us to no small degree. When we repeat the lies often enough, we live the lie and become the lie. "I am unlovable" becomes the premise on which we base our actions and interactions with the world and, yes, even God. This kind of thinking leads us into a downward spiral that blocks us from being able to praise God or effectively witness for Him. It also prevents true joy in our lives. Satan apparently has his part in this. If we relegate him to the realm of mere myth then we are allowing a pernicious, ongoing destruction in our lives to remain unnamed and unaccounted for. We fail to confront the enemy, assuming he doesn't exist.

Childhood Interpretations. Everything that happens to a child is interpreted and misinterpreted with childlike logic. We have seen a pattern develop at an early age in many of the people who come for counseling. Consider the effect of living for years with an overly critical parent, for instance. We had a man report that his father repeatedly told him that he "wasn't worth the gunpowder it would take to blow your brains out." Repeatedly hearing that message in his mind, he began believing in his total unworthiness. "I'm not worth the gunpowder that it would take to blow my brains out" was the deep, ingrained message in his soul, whether he consciously thought about it much or not. I think Satan can use the cruelty of humanity to set these lies in motion and to dig a ditch of negative thoughts in our brain.

Of course, children interpret the *unspoken* things that a critical parent can do as well. It may be Dad coming home and doing nothing but sitting in the chair and reading the paper, watching TV, and never paying attention to you. Or Mom is a cleanaholic. All she does is clean her house and worry that you are getting the table dirty when you're eating . . . spilling milk and obsessing over that. It may be just the fact that your parents rarely spent quality time with you that conveys the negative message, "I'm no good, I'm not worthy of someone spending time with me." Interestingly, a lot of time those people go on to marry a spouse who won't spend time with them, just to continue to fulfill that prophecy.

This is not an exercise in parental "piling on." No parent is perfect, and every parent sends messages that hurt his or her children as they grow up. The point we're making is that the severity of the influence is largely determined by *the interpretation or misinterpretation* the child makes and how that child translates those messages into life-shaping self-talk tapes of unworthiness. Sometimes, in fact, a parent is minimally at fault, as in the case of Suzanne.

When Suzanne was eleven years old, her mother told her to take her little sister Carrie with her to the grocery store down the block. They would have to cross a rather heavily traveled intersection, but the girl knew how to read the lights and was instructed in severe tones: "You be sure to hold onto your sister's hand, no matter what."

So the girls walked along the sidewalk and came to the light just as the "Walk" sign was beginning to flash. Suzanne decided to run across the street, calling for her little sister to follow. But Carrie had been lagging behind a bit. Suzanne got across the street, and when she turned to look back, she was horrified to see her little sister still on the other side. The light had changed, but Carrie looked as though she were going to cross anyway. Seeing this, Suzanne began to wave her arms frantically. Carrie looked up, saw her sister waving to her, and smiling brightly, she jumped into the street.

Carrie was killed instantly by a heavy truck barreling down the street.

Suzanne went into a catatonic state for many months, speaking to no one, simply laying on a bed in fetal position, a mask of terror on her face. It took years of psychiatric care before Suzanne could begin to deal with the searing guilt she harbored inside, before she could even speak the horrible interpretation that had shaped her life for those years: *Carrie thought I was waving her across; I killed her.* She did eventually come to grips with her false interpretation, speak it, and grieve out its pain in a group under the auspices of Compassionate Friends (a self-help group for parents and siblings of killed or murdered children).

Distorted, Irrational Thinking. There isn't a person alive who hasn't experienced the falsehoods we're talking about, even on the most mundane level—certain things we believe about ourselves that aren't true, or things we *don't* believe about ourselves that *are* true.

> Many lie tapes play in your mind without your even knowing it. They play unconsciously when life presses the play button. Unconscious or not, these tapes dramatically affect your feelings and actions each day. Ignorance is not bliss when it comes to these tapes. Unless they are made conscious, you are at their mercy.[6]

With distorted and irrational thinking, it's possible to self-talk ourselves into a continual state of depression and low self-esteem, hardly even recognizing what we are doing. We become so confused by our love malnutrition that we unknowingly begin to shut down our love receptors.

Recall the standard cartoon-image of a man crawling in the desert when he finally sees a mirage offering him a pool of fresh, cool water, just what his body is longing for. But the moment he reaches the place where he saw the pool of water, it instantly disappears. Wouldn't it be dreadful if, just a few feet from the place where the man left the path to chase his mirages, a real spring of water had awaited him?

Similarly, we are each lost in a desert, desperate for love to quench our thirst. Too often we chase mirages promising love but delivering nothing that will quench what a soul needs. Let's begin to recognize our mirages— especially the ones that come in the form of our automatic thoughts.

❑   ❑   ❑

Time Out

What Are Your "Automatic" Thoughts?

Think back to the last "tense situation" you faced. Maybe it was a confrontation at work, or a fight with a neighbor, or a criticism from your boss. Imagine being back in that situation, and recall some of the thoughts that ran through your mind.

1. On a piece of paper or in your journal, jot the thoughts that automatically flashed through your mind.

Examples: Oh, no! I couldn't stand it if he thought I was incompetent. I must not appear to be nervous about this. Making mistakes is unacceptable. I should never hurt anyone. I always do stupid things. People are looking at me. Everybody sees how afraid I am.

2. Look back over those thoughts, and reflect:

❑ *Which of these thoughts do I often have in similar situations?*
❑ *Which of these thoughts are true? Which are NOT true?*
❑ *For each of these thoughts, what alternative interpretation would be possible?*

Example:
<u>Automatic Thought</u>: I must *not* appear to be nervous about this.
<u>Alternative Interpretation</u>: Actually, most people would be nervous in this situation; it's only natural.

3. Plan to jot automatic thoughts as soon as possible after your next "tense situation." Then spend time reflecting and finding alternatives, as in step 2 above. Eventually, you will "automatically" begin to think more rationally in such situations.

❑   ❑   ❑

What are the practical, daily implications of all this? We can quote hundreds of cases of people who are helped simply by changing their thinking. We see women who are being emotionally, verbally, physically abused by their husbands. One woman said to me: "Actually, deep down, I think I deserve this. Part of me is saying that I haven't been a good enough wife, that I have provoked this. He has reason to do this to me."

When a person begins looking at why she has that lie in her mind, change can begin. In this case, the woman had grown up in a home where her father abused her mother. She bought into the lie that "I'm no good and this is the kind of treatment I deserve." So she goes out and attracts that kind of person to marry.

When she finally confronted the lie, and began working to build truth into her life—that she was worthy of being loved, that she was created in the image of God—then a first step for her was to begin saying, "I'm not going to allow you to abuse me. I'm going to leave home. I'm going to call the police. I'm going to get to a safe area in order to protect myself."

That's a tremendous step. Even the simplest step of saying, "When you talk to me that way, I'm going to walk away and go to another room" can make all the difference. If someone just kind of talks harsh to her now, she can say, "When you can talk to me in a nice tone of voice and you can talk about this rationally, then we will discuss it." What gave her the strength to change so dramatically? She discovered that just because her father and her husband didn't love her, it didn't mean that she was unlovable. Once catching sight of this she not only learned how to receive love, but also how to love others better.

Her willingness to be victimized and abused by others did nothing to help them grow toward love. When she became unwilling to be the target of her husband's and other's lack of love, she actually became an agent of love in their lives—by not being there to reinforce their wrong belief that she was the reason for their problems.

❏   ❏   ❏

Time Out

Psychologist Albert Ellis developed a system of Rational Emotive Therapy which he called the ABC system. This stands for:

Activating event: something happens

Belief system: the event or experience is *interpreted* by a person's beliefs

Consequent emotions: the interpretations create resulting feelings

According to this theory, the events themselves do not cause our feelings. It is our *interpretations* of the events which make us afraid, sad, anxious, or angry. For (a silly) example:

Event: John sees Mary walk up to him with a knife in her hand.
Belief: *A knife is always a weapon.*
Emotion: John feels panicky and anxious.

The *event* did not cause John's feelings. This was proven when Mary said: "Would you be able to take this knife out to the garage and sharpen it for me, John?" John's task would be to attempt to replace his belief in such a situation, not to change the situation or try to change his emotions. Events cannot cause our emotions because A does not leap immediately over to C. But events do start up our internal self-talk (B). It is then our task to identify the self-talk (which is usually some form of irrational thinking) and counter it with rational thinking. This brings to bear the next two steps in Ellis' method:

Dispute irrational beliefs: replace the distorted or false beliefs with the truth.
Eliminate the misconception: feel the appropriate emotion.

Think: How could you apply this approach in the future to an event or experience that keeps "making you feel bad"? *(For example: a coworker criticizes your idea for a fund-raising campaign. Possible distorted belief: "Criticism is always a sign of malicious attack.")*

❏   ❏   ❏

Replacing the Lies

The bad news is that our thoughts can have a profound, deleterious affect on our emotions and the quality of our "love life." The good news is that we can learn to monitor our thinking rather than just continuing to let our false beliefs damage us. If the first step in the putting off/putting on process is recognizing our distorted, "lying" thoughts, then the second step is replacing those false beliefs with God's truths. It does no good just to create a vacuum in our minds, trying to wipe out the negative with nothing to replace it.

We are working at two levels here: the psychological and the spiritual. So we speak both of distorted thinking and of Satan's lies. No matter what the source, these false beliefs need to be uncovered, recognized, shared with others, and countered with the truth. Some of the countering can be done on a purely psychological level, replacing the irrational with the more rational. On a spiritual level the process calls us to the task of replacing lies about our true nature and situation in the world with biblical truths about who we are in God's love. And that is a daily process. Even though we may not feel it at first, we can begin living as if the truths are true. Feelings eventually follow reality, the reality of who God says we are.

Many Christians are stuck, knowing all these things: God loves me, God cares about me, God would send Jesus if I were the only person on earth. Yet, we don't live that way, and we don't feel that way; we don't believe it deep down in our bones. Feeling comes from learning to believe it, and learning to believe it comes from having it in our minds over and over until it is part of us. Our emotional reactions spring from the way we view ourselves and our world, for in a significant way, our interpretations *are* our world.

> Man is disturbed not by things
> but by the view he takes of them—Epictetus

What, specifically, can we do to begin replacing lies with truth? It has to do primarily with our relationship to the Scriptures.

Focusing on the Promises. We can't go into every verse of Scripture that helps us counter the falsehoods we have believed, but a few examples may help get you started in your own explorations of just the right Scriptures to help you counter your particular false beliefs or distorted thought patterns.

For example, many people tell themselves that they are unworthy of love. They believe that they are so unworthy of love that they are not able to accept even God's love for them. Some people even go so far as telling themselves that they are bad. However, the Scripture tells us differently. Jesus tells us in John 1:12-13:

> Yet to all who received Him, to those who believed in His name, He gave the right to become children of God—children born not of natural descent, nor of human decision or a husband's will, but born of God.

He goes on to say in John 15:9, 11:

> As the Father has loved Me, so have I loved you. Now remain in My love. . . . I have told you this so that My joy may be in you and that your joy may be complete.

I think that it is clear from such Scriptures that God wants us to have a joyful, love-filled life. He wants us to be able to experience His love and joy in its fullness. After all, if the God of the universe loves us, it really makes no difference how anybody else feels about us.

We are sons and daughters of the King. He chose us, not because we were nice or good, but because we were "dead."

> But because of His great love for us, God, who is rich in mercy, made us alive with Christ even when we were dead in transgressions—it is by grace you have been saved. —Ephesians 2:4-5

This is the greatest miracle of love: God's free and unearned grace. Just as we didn't choose to be born, so we don't choose to be born again.

> For He chose us in Him before the creation of the world to be holy and blameless in His sight. In love He predestined us to be adopted as His sons through Jesus Christ, in accordance with His pleasure and will—to the praise of His glorious grace, which He has freely given us in the One He loves. —Ephesians 1:4-6

What love! All we have to do is receive it. As believers, we also have available to us the promise of God's power, as Paul tells us in Philippians 4:13:

> I can do everything through Him who gives me strength.

These are some of the awesome promises that are given to us by God in His Word. Learning to receive love and focusing daily on such promises is not easy. However, it can be done. Especially through Christ who strengthens us. His Spirit can and will give the strength to identify the lies and replace them, if we ask and then receive.

The problem for many of us is not that the power and the love are not available to us. It is that we do not feel worthy enough to accept God's promises. We are not able to receive God's full blessing upon us because we don't approach Him with outstretched arms and open hands ready to accept all that He has for us. Instead, we approach as damaged goods.

Drinking in the Truth. The task involves something much deeper than mere intellectual assent. We can know the truth, but if it is to set us free, it must become a part of our being.

> Oh, it is not that you will think about what you have read, but you will *feed* upon what you have read. Out of a love for the Lord you exert your will to hold your mind quiet before him. When you have come to this state, you must allow your mind to rest. In this very peaceful state, *swallow* what you have tasted. . . . Have you not, at times, enjoyed the flavor of a very tasty food? But unless you were willing to swallow the food, you received no nourishment.[7]

Once we understand what the truth is, then we can begin saturating our minds with that truth throughout the day. I've heard it described in terms of a tennis player or bowler who has an extremely strong arm as a result of using that one arm all the time. What happens is that with our negative thoughts we build up that one arm. What we need to do is take that weaker arm and start using it and building that up with the truths of God. Build up the truth muscle and let the lie muscle deteriorate.

In his book, *Please Let Me Know You, God* Larry Stephens[8] has compiled a massive list of truths about the believer that can be utilized in positive self-talk. The list in Scripture of things about us that are true—and blessed—is astonishing. Here are just a few of the examples Stephens lifts up for us:

❏ I am the apple of my Father's eye (Ps. 17:8)
❏ I am the salt of the earth and the light of the world (Matt. 5:13-14)
❏ I am set free (John 8:31-32)
❏ I am dead to sin (Rom. 6:7)
❏ I am free of shame and condemnation (Rom. 8:1)
❏ I am being changed and conformed to the image of Christ (Rom. 8:28-29; Phil. 1:6)
❏ I am the temple of the Holy Spirit (1 Cor. 6:19)
❏ I am a new creation (2 Cor. 5:17)
❏ I am holy and without blame before God (Eph. 1:4)
❏ I am forgiven; all my sins are washed away (Eph. 1:7)
❏ I am alive with Christ (Eph. 2:5)
❏ I am God's workmanship (Eph. 2:10)
❏ I am strong in the Lord (Eph. 6:10)
❏ I have the peace of God, which surpasses understanding (Phil. 4:7)
❏ I can do all things through Christ (Phil. 4:13)
❏ I am complete in Christ (Col. 2:10)
❏ I am seated in the heavenlies—right now (Col. 3:1-4)
❏ I am God's forever-child (1 Peter 1:23)
❏ I have overcome the world (1 John 5:4)

Personalizing the Word. What we are speaking of requires a lot of hard work and meditation on Scripture. Make it a personal quest by beginning with verses that are particularly meaningful to you and to your specific situation. God's Word is full of promises telling us who we are and what we have in Him. One of the most powerful verses of the Bible is in Ephesians 2, where Paul says,

Immense in mercy and with an incredible love, He embraced us. He took our sin-dead lives and made us alive in Christ. He did all this on His own, with no help from us! Then He picked us up and set us down in highest heaven in company with Jesus, our Messiah. Now

God has us where He wants us, with all the time in this world and the next to shower grace and kindness upon us in Christ Jesus.[9]

So, as believers we not only have eternal life to look forward to after this life, but we have been raised up with our Lord at the right hand of the Father *at this very moment.* Just think about that. At this very moment you are seated at the right hand of the Father. We are also told that not only are we in Christ, He also lives within us. He is with us in everything that we do and present in every circumstance of our lives. Ephesians 2:19 tells us that we are fellow citizens and actually considered a part of God's household. And Paul tells us that the Lord cares so much for us that, in some inscrutable way that involves our own assent in the decision, He picked us, not that we picked Him.

For those God foreknew He also predestined to be conformed to the likeness of His Son, that He might be the firstborn among many brothers. And those He predestined, He also called; those He called, He also justified; those He justified, He also glorified.[10]

So, we are living with Christ in His glory, and He indwells us with His Holy Spirit each moment of every day. And it is all present tense, not something that is going to happen to us, but is happening at this very moment. Surely Christ wants us to make those kinds of promises precious to us. After all, this is what growth and recovery is—taking the intellectual knowledge and making it personal.

❑   ❑   ❑

Examples of Scriptures for Daily Meditation

It's important to fill our minds with promises and encouragements from God. This truth-immersion-process is how we "put on" our new person in Christ. Try these Scriptures for starters. You may wish to focus on just one per day (or week).

❑   ❑   ❑

The Lord is my light and my salvation—
whom shall I fear?
The Lord is the stronghold of my life—of
whom shall I be afraid?
—Psalm 27:1

I have told you these things, so that in Me
you may have peace.
In this world you will have trouble. But take
heart! I have overcome the world.
—John 16:33

Wait for the Lord; be strong and take heart
and wait for the Lord. —Psalm 27:14

Set your minds on things above, not on
earthly things. —Colossians 3:2

Delight yourself in the Lord and He will give you the desires of your heart.
—Psalm 37:4

Be still before the Lord and wait patiently for Him; do not fret when men succeed in their ways, when they carry out their wicked schemes. —Psalm 37:7

Why are you downcast, O my soul?
Why so disturbed within me?
Put your hope in God, for I will yet praise Him, my Savior and my God. —Psalm 42:11

I lift up my eyes to the hills—where does my help come from?
My help comes from the Lord, the Maker of heaven and earth.
He will not let your foot slip—He who watches over you will not slumber.
—Psalm 121:1-3

You will keep in perfect peace him whose mind is steadfast, because he trusts in You.
—Isaiah 26:3

So do not fear, for I am with you; do not be dismayed, for I am your God. I will strengthen you and help you;
I will uphold you with My righteous right hand. —Isaiah 41:10

Therefore do not worry about tomorrow, for tomorrow will worry about itself.
Each day has enough trouble of its own.
—Matthew 6:34

Therefore, since we have been justified through faith, we have peace with God through our Lord Jesus Christ.
—Romans 5:1

Therefore, there is now no condemnation for those who are in Christ Jesus.
—Romans 8:1

"My grace is sufficient for you, for My power is made perfect in weakness."
Therefore I will boast all the more gladly about my weaknesses, so that Christ's power may rest on me. That is why, for Christ's sake, I delight in weaknesses, in insults, in hardships, in persecutions, in difficulties. For when I am weak, then I am strong.
—2 Corinthians 12:9-10

Do not be anxious about anything, but in everything, by prayer and petition, with thanksgiving, present your requests to God. And the peace of God, which transcends all understanding, will guard your hearts and your minds in Christ Jesus.
—Philippians 4:6-7

Praise be to the God and Father of our Lord Jesus Christ! In His great mercy He has given us new birth into a living hope through the resurrection of Jesus Christ from the dead.
—1 Peter 1:3

Cast all your anxiety on Him because He cares for you.—1 Peter 5:7

Renewing the Mind

We have been speaking specifically about changing our thought patterns as a "putting off and putting on" process. But perhaps we are now ready to back up and take a broader, more general view of the challenge before us—to see it all in context. Exchanging false beliefs for the truth is part of a wider and deeper calling that God has given us. The specifics of putting on a new attitude and lifestyle are the result of *having our entire mind renewed in a total transformation of outlook.*

Do not conform any longer to the pattern of this world, but be transformed by the renewing of your mind. Then you will be able to test and approve what God's will is—His good, pleasing and perfect will.[11]

Renewing our minds is the second of the twin callings we mentioned at the very beginning of this chapter. In biblical terms, ever since Adam and Eve came upon the scene, the human race has become quite vulnerable to distortions about the true nature of life. This vision of reality fails to grasp the loving Lord at the center of everything. How shall we transform this vision? Here are three suggestions.

Change Your Perception of Reality

True and lasting change demands a change in our personal perception of reality, what author John Powell calls our "personal vision"—the foundational beliefs we hold about the overall nature and purposes of life. They are unique and different for each of us, but invariably shaped to a great degree by the "pattern of this world," the culture and values that surround us. Consider some examples of various personal visions we may hold:

-Life is exciting; it is a real adventure.
-Life isn't easy; it is everyone for himself.
-Life is to have things: your own home, enough money for an emergency, security for old age.
-Life is to get ahead, to prove yourself, to make people respect you.
-Success in life is judged by how popular you are—by how many people love you.
-You are worth only what you are worth in God's eyes.
-Success in life is spelled M-O-N-E-Y.
-Be sure you own your own business. Don't ever work for anyone else.
-You only go around once, so grab all you can while you can.
-Life is for having good times.
-It isn't whether you win or lose; it's how you play the game.
-Get your own plot of land and build high fences around it.
-If you've got your health, you'll be all right.
-Education is what is important. They can take everything away from you except your mind.[12]

Even those of us who profess to hold Christian values are influenced at some level by these kinds of ingrained visions. They work below the surface, influencing the choices we make in our careers, determining our methods of working with others, affecting the kind of guidance we give our children. And so we need to work with our vision and open ourselves to having that vision transformed by kingdom values. As we become more aware of what basic perceptions are influencing our lives, we can hold that vision of reality up to the light of the Scriptures and let its distortions reveal themselves. It is not an easy task, for most of us have spent decades forming our personal vision. To dismantle and transform it is a step-by-step, tedious process of deconstruction and rebuilding, accompanied by growing pains. How many of us will take up that challenge?

Choose Your Attitude

The failure to take on responsibility is the cause of most, if not all, problems in life. And one of the most basic, God-given responsibilities we have as human beings is simply to choose our attitude within each circumstance of our lives. For it is not so much what happens to us that makes the difference in what we are becoming, it is the attitude we bring to those events, especially the painful ones, that will determine our satisfaction in life. How well we take up this responsibility determines, in the long run, how much progress we make in our growth toward Christlikeness.

The point is, I can always choose my attitude, no matter what circumstances intrude into my life. This was powerfully illustrated by the experience of Victor Frankl in the Nazi concentration camps of World War II. Frankl was a psychiatrist in Vienna who ended up spending most of the war in various German camps, suffering extremes of deprivation and brutality, narrowly escaping the gas chambers on numerous occasions. His father, mother, brother, and wife all died in the camps, leaving only himself and a sister as survivors. Literally everything was taken from him.

> While we were waiting for the shower, our nakedness was brought home to us: we really had nothing now except our bare bodies—even minus hair; all we possessed, literally, was our naked existence.[13]

Throughout his book, *Man's Search for Meaning*, Frankl gives countless examples supporting his thesis that when we are reduced to our most basic essence, our pure existence, the thing that remains, which cannot be taken away, is our ability to decide how we will respond.

> The experiences of camp life show that man does have a choice of action. There were enough examples, often of a heroic nature. . . . We who lived in concentration camps can remember the men who walked through the huts comforting others, giving away their last piece of bread. They may have been few in number, but they offer sufficient proof that everything can be taken from a man but one thing: the last of the human freedoms—to choose one's attitude in any given set of circumstances, to choose one's own way.[14]

When all external distractions have been removed, the critical importance of attitude shines through. The renewal of our minds, then, requires a foundational conviction that we have a part to play in the process. God has given us a freedom that cannot be taken from us under any circumstances, the ability to respond to Him and the choices before us.

> Two men looked out from
> prison bars.
> One saw mud,
> one saw stars.

For, as we have been saying, your mind is the most potent power at your disposal each day. With it you alone are determining the value of your work, the meaning of your relationships, even the worthiness of your whole life to this point in time. Some people believe it has been the invincible, inevitable circumstances that have landed them in an unhappy place. But what situation or event could possibly overpower our ability to interpret our lives in a manner that gently leads us out of self-recrimination and into a hopeful future?

So how might you use your mind in this moment of reflection as you read this chapter? Suggestion: As an opportunity to reflect on the power of interpretation. What guilt-brimmed event of the past might blessedly evaporate from significance under the blazing light of final self-forgiveness? And what fearful situation in the present might shrivel down to size as you reframe it in the lens of objectivity? Or what dreaded step into the future might you now recognize as a benevolent call to walk onto the bright fields of perfect acceptance? May we more and more learn to make full use of our power to see everything that happens in the light of God's loving plans for us.

Accept the Chaos

But this is not easy. It means a transformation of our whole orientation to life. The reason it is not easy is that it requires the courage to "be in process" for a while, to accept a certain amount of chaos as normal. Like Tarzan swinging through the jungle on one vine to the next, the process is a letting go of one form of security to reach for another. And it's never easy to let go of the familiar—even if it is something that is hurting us.

> To live is to be separated from what we were
> in order to approach what we are going to be
> in the mysterious future.[15]

We can't hold on to our own distorted visions of reality while expecting to grasp in full-orbed completion the kingdom vision God offers us. We must experience the fear of falling along the way, the limbo of the in-between at each bend in the road that calls for risky faith.

So we come full circle, back to where we began in this chapter: the call to put off and put on. We might say it is, in essence, the challenge to give up the old self for something new, a self that is in a much better position to receive the love offered by our great Lover. For all of life's blessings come as a result of giving in and giving up. Grace allows for no other way.

> Until you have given up your self to Him you will not have a real self. . . . The principle runs through all life from top to bottom. Give up yourself, and you will find your real self. Lose your life and you will save it. Submit to death, death of your ambitions and favorite wishes every day and death of your whole body in the end: submit with every fibre of your being, and you will find eternal life. Keep back nothing. Nothing that you have not given away will ever be really yours. Nothing in you that has not died will ever be raised from the dead.[16]

What is the first step for you in this journey of giving up? For some it is acceptance of the truth that life does not always work out as we wish. There is always a lot to lose. And we'll see in the next chapter that this too demands a particular kind of response from us, the kind that will not close us off to love.

6

Embracing the "Hope" of Loss (Depression: Part 2)

Blessed are those who mourn, for they will be comforted. . . .
Unless a kernel of wheat falls to the ground and dies,
it remains only a single seed.

　　　　　　　　　　　　　—Jesus

Not only creativeness and enjoyment are meaningful.
If there is a meaning in life at all,
then there must be a meaning in suffering.
Suffering is an ineradicable part of life, even as fate and death.
Without suffering and death, human life cannot be complete.

　　　　　　　　　　　　　—Victor Frankl

The moon in the water;
　　Broken and broken again.
　　　　Still it is there.

　　　　　　　　　　　　　—Chosu, Haiku poet

He was just a rookie cop. As he begins telling me what happened, his story comes tumbling out: He's racing to the scene in his cruiser, squealing around curves, blue lights flashing, going real fast. The call was "fighting in the street . . . with weapons . . . officer in danger." So he's got the adrenaline pumping, pounding the steering wheel. A few seconds either way can mean the life or death of his fellow officer.

He comes to a red light and protocol says he's got to stop, make sure the intersection is clear, then proceed. But he figures, just this once—since he's got his lights and siren at full blast, and a buddy is in trouble—he can run through and make some time.

But the young lady in the little Ford Escort didn't hear him. Or see the lights. . . .

So this young man comes in to see me [Joe] a couple weeks later and says: "What's wrong with me? I am so down, about as down as anybody could be. I can hardly get up in the morning. What's wrong?"

"Maybe what's wrong with you is what *should* be wrong with you."

"What do you mean? I should be depressed?"

"If you weren't, then *I'd* begin to wonder what was wrong."

❏   ❏   ❏

Depression as "Normal": The Awareness of Loss

There is an approach to living that is thoroughly dishonest. Whole groups of believers live by its crushing assumptions. At its heart is this fundamental doctrine: With God, life is happy; without God life is sad. So choose!

With this type of theological underpinning, all sorts of conclusions spring to life. For instance, if you are depressed then you must be sinning. If you aren't happy, then you must have "backslidden." If things are going wrong in your life, you've moved away from the Lord. In the Bible, Job's so-called comforters applied this point of view with cold, precise logic to their suffering friend:

> Consider now: Who, being innocent,
>   has ever perished?
> Where were the upright ever destroyed?
> As I have observed,
>   those who plow evil
>   and those who sow trouble
>   reap it.[1]

There is too much pain in the world—God's world—for anyone to sell us the line that grief and sadness have no place in our spiritual journey. And most of the time we can't even point to any redeeming qualities of that pain, as much as we would like to. Yet so many ordinary people have testified to discovering the love of God in the midst of their suffering. Some have even been grasped by the joy of God and have taken the energy that flows from it and put it to work in coming alongside others who suffer.

More often, this work of being with our own and another's pain can bring us to the depths of human sorrow. Who could blame a rookie police officer for suffering over a pointless fatal accident? In other words, we may well become depressed. Legitimately.

A Legitimate Depression?

No one need remind us of the things in this world that ought to make us sad: war, poverty, racism, crime. Not to mention our own sins and serious blunders that cause loss to others that can't ever be fixed. To be aware of this life *as it is,* is simply to have a lucid awareness of loss.

In "Depression: Part I" of this book, we spoke of a disruption of normal physiology, the kind of clinical depression that is abnormal because it is a disease of the brain, which in turn affects the heart and soul. But here we approach depression from another angle by raising the possibility that some of it is normal and to be expected. We cannot cure it because, as someone has said: "You cannot cure life."

But perhaps we can allow our depression to become part of our healing. For in the recognition that we are incomplete, that we are only finite, that we are unable to heal everything in perfection, resides the hope that a source of help infinitely greater than ourselves stands ready to come to our rescue. This is the secret wish of depression: Might it offer a divine opportunity that could come to us in no other way?

> God brings into our lives the loss of what we have been holding onto, what identifies us, what is "saving" our ego. We are forced to let it go and given the opportunity to just be in His love.[2]

Some may not call what we are speaking of here, in the strict sense, "depression." All of us suffer losses regularly: the death of our loved one, the end of our job, the divorce of our children, the deterioration of health and youthfulness. We grieve, and grief reactions are not necessarily clinical depressions. However, whether we choose to label our reactions as grief or depression, the point is that we do enter states of being in which life seems barely worth living. We survey the wreckage after we have been laid off or have buried a child. And we become listless, empty-feeling, silent observers of night following day in grim, gray procession.

In the midst of such deprivation of energy, joy, and hope, should we add guilt to our predicament? Is it helpful to be told: "Cheer up! You are a

Christian, after all." If not, then what, indeed, will help us?

The Paradox of Health and Illness

What is happening to us in depression has its aspect of normality. Simply recognizing this may be the first step in coming to terms with it. There may even be strictly biological reasons for the human being to experience illness in general as "normal," as suggested by Larry Dossey in *Meaning and Medicine:*

> The paradox, glimpsed occasionally by saints and mystics, psychologists and scientists, is that health and illness "go together," and even illness has its place. . . . For a certain period following birth, we are protected from infections by the antibodies that originated in the body of our mother. But this "passive immunity" soon dwindles and we begin to develop our own resistance. This can be done only through repeated exposures to pathogens of various sorts—viruses, bacteria, fungi—that create temporary "mini-illnesses," which spur us to develop the appropriate immune responses. If this process does not take place, life is cut short by overwhelming infections. The paradox, carved into our biology: life and health depend on illness and cannot exist without it.[3]

Again, we cannot cure life. We seek a greater openness to its possibilities, the possibilities existing because of the One who authored it, who chooses to convey grace in the midst of all of its circumstances. We, if given the power, would be tempted to eliminate the bad parts. We would prefer a colorless, painless existence to one that held the potential for both ecstasy and agony.

Believable Fiction

Certain false suppositions and unrealistic expectations contribute to our normal depressions and threaten to carry them over the brink into the abnormal. The culprit is denial. In our skewed thinking we attempt to deny the role that pain, suffering, and loss will always play in our lives. Such denial leads inevitably to a needless prolongation of normal depression. Let's look at just three of the incorrect beliefs, or believable fictions, that can cloud our thinking about what is "normal":

I Should Always Be Happy. Remember the cute little song you sang in Sunday School?

> I'm inright, outright, upright, downright
>   happy all the time.

Since Jesus Christ came in
    and cleansed my life from sin,
I'm inright, outright, upright, downright
    happy all the time.

Cute, yes. But is it a fair description of the normal life, even if our lives have been "cleansed from sin"? One psychologist, Lesley Hazleton, made a case for *The Right to Feel Bad*. She says: "The insistence on happiness can place sometimes intolerable strains on ordinary people. Constantly set up as the desired norm, it becomes oppressive." She speaks of a young health worker, one of her clients, who linked his depressions directly to the demand that he be happy. The young man told her:

I remember how in sixth grade, I was a good student, and my parents said to me: "We don't mind what you want to be, a road cleaner or a scientist, an artist or a businessman. We just want you to know that we'll love you whatever you do, so long as you're happy."
And the implied message seemed obvious—if I wasn't happy, then they wouldn't love me anymore. And *that* made me unhappy! Since then, whenever I get depressed, it seems to be at a time when I haven't been happy when I *should* have been.[4]

Pursuing happiness *as a goal* can create havoc in our lives. How hard it is for us to accept that happiness comes after the fact, always. Usually it is the result of striving for a goal that focuses attention away from our own selves, away from our own preoccupations with our state of mind or circumstances.

To become totally involved in pursuing our passions, rather than our happiness, brings us to the point, later, in which we realize that we have reached a state of peace and contentment. A wall poster shows a beautiful butterfly about to land on a dazzling yellow flower. As a caption, the poster has words uttered long ago by Nathaniel Hawthorne:

Happiness is like a butterfly;
    The more you pursue it,
        The more it eludes you.
But when you turn your attention to other things,
    It comes,
        And sits gently on your shoulder.

As we go about our days, we can let happiness land where it will, in its own time and place. For when could we ever control it?
Which brings us to the second major believable fiction.

I Must Always Be in Control. Naturally, I feel that my life is my own to direct as I see fit. That if I face problems, it is up to me to generate solutions; if I have success, it is myself who should be congratulated; if I am going to have happiness and love in my life, then it is I who must produce it.

In the Academy Award-winning movie *Babette's Feast*, set in nineteenth-century Denmark, a young army officer believes he must choose between his ambition to become a great military leader or give his heart to a devout and beautiful young lady in a remote fishing village. He makes his decision, choosing the army. He leaves the tiny village, saying to the young woman he loves: "I will never see you again."

Decades later, when the man has risen to the top of his profession (now a general), and has accomplished his goal of "public renown and prestige," he is invited to return to the village for a dinner with a small group of believers. There he meets his young love again (though now an old woman), the one with whom he could have lived a life of love and good works in the small town. As he sits down to dinner, he glances at the woman and feels deep sadness as their eyes meet. *How good life could have been for us over these many long years!*

However, the miracle of grace breaks through in the most unexpected way during the dinner. For though the old general had expected to sit down to a simple meal of fish and rough beer-bread, he is instead served course after course of the finest French cuisine in the world. He is overwhelmed and feels that his youthful, impulsive decision—which had seemed so wrong to him before the dinner—has somehow been redeemed, simply through the gift of the heavenly meal. He stands and makes a speech to the rest of the gathered group:

> Man, in his weakness and shortsightedness, believes he must make choices in this life. He trembles at the risks he takes. We do know fear.
>
> But, no! Our choice is of no importance.
>
> There comes a time when our eyes are opened. And we come to realize that mercy is infinite. We need only await it in confidence and receive it in gratitude. Mercy imposes no conditions.
>
> And, lo! Everything we have chosen has been granted to us. And everything we rejected has also been granted. Yes, we even get back what we rejected.
>
> For "mercy and truth are met together. And righteousness and bliss shall kiss one another."[5]

Here is a person like us, who sensed that all the decisions and choices he had made in his lifetime had been only his own to make. The complete responsibility for his life had seemed to be in his own hands the whole time. But so graciously he was reminded otherwise. In the startling tastes of turtle soup, baked pheasant, and priceless wine, life's curtain was pulled back for a twinkling. And reality blazed forth: Another is in control, complete control. How blessed we are!

The infinite one is above and beyond the limitations that we think our choices weave for us. Our decisions, especially the bad ones, seem to hedge and harbor our freedoms as we attempt to control the course of our lives. Nevertheless, God is the author of choices and decisions. In some inscrutable way, His is the power to redeem whatever He chooses to redeem.

Poet Dylan Thomas understood that we are not as free and in control as we may believe when he wrote his exquisite but sad lines:

> Oh as I was young and easy in the mercy of his means,
> Time held me green and dying
> Though I sang in my chains like the sea.[6]

Yet the chains that bind us are bonds of love. For God saves us from the control we seek to exert over all things in our lives.

Radio commentator Paul Harvey recently spoke of high schooler Kevin, a star football defensive back and prodigious baseball player for his school team. It was reported that Kevin had been in a car wreck, to everyone's great concern. The doctors dealt successfully with his new injuries, but discovered an old one far more serious. Kevin had been playing with a broken neck for years. At any time, during all those years of ball, a wrong hit, a twisted slide into second, and Kevin would have been paralyzed by a sharp bone fragment severing his spinal cord. Harvey commented: "Kevin will be eternally grateful for that car wreck."

Thank goodness, we are not in control. We often feel that weakness is a scourge and that to give up control would reveal a flawed character. This is typically why people seek counseling, to clear up a weakness. Yet the way of love is in helping us embrace our so-called weakness and learn to live with it. In a sense, we can celebrate our weaknesses, for grace enters our lives at the points where we are most wounded, most confused, most unable to do for ourselves. At these times, if we let ourselves, we can experience the omnipotence of God and receive His love.

> It is when things go wrong, when the good things do not happen, when our prayers seem to have been lost, that God is most present. We do not need the sheltering wings when things go smoothly. We are closest to God in the darkness, stumbling along blindly.[7]

Embracing the Role of Loss

So it is with believable fiction—demanding happiness, requiring control—that we effectively squeeze out any room for grace. If we can make ourselves happy by appointment, then we do not need the joy that could break in at the oddest moments. If we are constantly busy, there is no space for resting in the divine presence; if we are always in control we can pretend to limit the limitless.

There is another way. We can welcome loss as a distant cousin; he can hurt us but teach us. He brings a dimension to our lives that challenges us to live better, with more awareness, as we encounter at least four new challenges:

Accept the "Holiness" of Loss

Where there is sorrow,
there is holy ground.[8]

One of our friends, Allen, lost a child through SIDS (Sudden Infant Death Syndrome). He told us his story:

We woke up on a Saturday morning and kind of laid in bed, waiting for Lee to begin crying for his morning meal. We thought he was oversleeping, but when we went into the room to check on him, we discovered him blue and cold. He had just stopped breathing in his crib during the night.

How do people cope with such sudden, devastating loss? Surely they cannot glibly repeat the popular, sentimental aphorisms like "God must have wanted another little angel to sit on His lap" and then go on their way with life, as though little had changed. Yet even people like Allen speak of an aspect of such losses as being an invitation . . . a piercing summons to reach out for the meaning of divine sovereignty. To be sure, some make it the reason to turn completely away from God or religion or even the idea that something in life is holy. But Allen says:

I spent days on end in a fog. I couldn't think, couldn't do much but weep, moan, sigh all the time, with a big hard heavy lump of lead sitting on my chest. But I did begin to take long walks on a trail that followed along the river near our home.

And I tried to talk to God, to pray. But nothing coherent would come. No rational words came to me. If someone had tried to record what I was saying, it would have made no sense.

Certain thoughts are prayers.
There are moments when,
whatever be the attitude of the body,
the soul is on its knees.[9]

But I was absolutely sure some kind of holy communication was happening, some form of sacred interaction between me and the

Almighty. And it wasn't a form of love particularly, it was just the sense of smallness of the human being—of *my* smallness, of my utter dependence on the sustainer of the universe. I felt as though I was on my knees during that whole time, uttering silently, deeply: *Holy, Holy, Holy, Lord God of Hosts.*

And I knew I could not turn away from this terrible, enduring relationship. I can't say I knew that it would turn to love again. But all during those first months, everything was tinged with holiness and sovereignty and awe.

I think that's how the children of Israel must have felt when they approached the smoking, thundering mountain of God's presence after Moses received the Commandments: a strange blend of abject fear; they needed to run, but they needed to keep looking, too. Because the source of dread was at the same time their only source of life.

> For He wounds, but He also binds up;
> He injures, but His hands also heal.[10]

To grow in Christian maturity is to give up, give in, relinquish our lives to the One who can remake them. Thus we can speak of a sacredness that is piercing and severe in every event in which something is taken out of our hands.

In C.S. Lewis' *The Lion, the Witch and the Wardrobe*,[11] the person of Christ is represented by Aslan the Lion. As the children in the story go through the woods to find Aslan, they contemplate meeting him with a certain mixture of excitement and dread: "At the name of Aslan each one of the children felt something jump in his inside. Edmund felt a sensation of mysterious horror." Lucy wonders what it will be like to come face-to-face with him. She asks: "Is he—quite safe?" The reply she receives is,

> Safe? . . .
> Who said anything about safe? 'Course he isn't safe.
> But he's good. He's the King, I tell you.

We want love, especially divine love, only as a gentle panacea. But it won't submit to that. It roars and bares its teeth. It is just too powerful to be safe, too holy to be merely pleasant.

Receive the Benefits of "Emptiness"

Often the complaint is that we are empty. And we have spoken of a "love vacuum" that people attempt to fill in destructive and addictive ways. There is another way here as well, another blessed paradox of the search for love: The emptiness we have been speaking about in this book is less a thing to be overcome or wiped out than to be embraced. We can aspire to friendship with our deepest longings rather than keep them as enemies to our contentment. We can enter the wide-open spaces of our emptiness rather than trying to fill them up. For our emptiness is the place where God dwells.

The Bible tells us that in the very beginning of the Creation, the earth was "formless and empty" (Gen. 1:2). Biblical scholars tell us that the Hebrew words in this passage picture an existence that was in disarray—anarchic, meaningless, void of order and reason. Yet, look around you and observe what has resulted . . . truly a creation of love.

Thus emptiness implies the potential for fullness. If it is fullness that we seek in our lives, then, of course, we must allow some emptiness, or at least embrace it when we come in contact with it. What, in practical terms, is this emptiness? It is any occasion, situation, or event that feels as though it needs to change if we are to be happy—but which, if embraced, will force us to create new meaning for ourselves—in other words: will force us to grow. When loss and depression are allowed to do their creative work, we benefit. When we fill up our emptiness we lose its potential gifts.

> I am the Lord your God. . . .
> Open wide your mouth
>   and I will fill it.[12]

Some of the ancient kings apparently placed jewel-gifts in their honored visitors' mouths. What a way to be greeted! And an empty mouth would bring the greatest blessing. For in such circumstances, only emptiness *receives*.

Learn to Live with Imperfection

The demand for perfection in ourselves and in others keeps us from admitting something that feels like a serious loss when we give it up: imperfection is the story of our lives and of our world.

I came across this quotation in a quotebook once:

> " . . .Uh, huh. . . . Yeah. . . ."
> —Miles Davis

Why would someone put that in a book of quotes? What meaning could it possibly have? Then I began to think that I knew what Miles was talking about: a sense of perfection that sometimes breaks in to highlight our constant struggles with imperfection. You know what Miles was talking about too, don't you? The IT of perfection? The late, great trumpeter reached it sometimes with the cool, husky tones of his intricate jazz. And he knew it.

When has Uh-Huh transported you into a different world? Maybe you were once lucky enough to lurch into the most perfect golf swing, feeling the soft thud of ball on sweet spot, as though your arms were at one with the club, the ball crackling off into the distance. Uh-Huh. Or you watched the delicate ballet accompanying a perfectly fielded grounder to short—over to second for one, then a midair pirouette . . . and over to first for two. You sat back and knew that something in harmony with heaven had just lifted your vision.

Really, you may not have to look very far to find perfection today. Not if you are aware, open-souled toward your world. You may catch the joy of the perfect jazz riff on your car radio. Or maybe you'll stop to shoot a basket or two with the neighbor boy and find, after all these years, you can still enter that "zone" where the little hoop gets so big you couldn't miss it with your eyes closed.

Yes, we can stumble into those moments and rejoice in them. But here's the problem: Life doesn't let us embrace perfection steadily. We'd like to cuddle up and melt into it, but we only touch it at the rare, serendipitous moment. When IT bumps into us head-on, those blessed intrusions, we are called to recognize the grace of it. But we are also called to recognize that those moments are rare indeed.

The Apostle Paul was a rabbi well schooled in the rigors of religious argument. He would have freely engaged in the rambunctious sessions of jot-and-tittle haggling over theological fine points that characterized rabbinical training in those days. He certainly had his perfectionist tendencies, as anyone who reads through the exquisite logic of Romans, for instance, will quickly acknowledge. Yet this very penchant toward perfectionism in the face of his limitations (a physical "thorn in the flesh" being an obvious example) was no doubt for him—as it so often is for us—the cause of Paul's obvious depressive episodes. Feel the undercurrent of despair in the face of sinful compulsions:

> I do not understand what I do. For what I want to do I do not do, but what I hate I do. And if I do what I do not want to do, I agree that the law is good. As it is, it is no longer I myself who do it, but it is sin living in me. I know that nothing good lives in me, that is, in my sinful nature. For I have the desire to do what is good, but I cannot carry it out. For what I do is not the good I want to do; no, the evil I do not want to do—this I keep on doing.[13]

Yet Paul was a preacher of resurrection and redemption. The one who in Romans 8 proclaimed the restoration of the entire creation knew he could not put on personal perfection in this life. Yet he could find a way to rejoice in the very fact of his weakness. As poet Richard Wilbur wrote,

> What can I do but move
> From folly to defeat,
> And call that sorrow sweet
> That teaches us to see

The final face of love
In what we cannot be?[14]

Paul's thorn was never removed, as far as we know. But it did serve him well, bringing him to the limitless love of God.

Believe in the Blessing of Depression

That's a quote from Martin Luther. He said it in German, of course, and Walter Trobisch, in *Love Yourself*, tells us something quite interesting about the German word for depression, *Schwermut*. Apparently the first part of the word, *Schwer*, can mean "heavy" and "difficult." The second part, *Mut*, means "courage." Thus, one way to understand depression would be to call it the courage to be heavy, that is, heavyhearted. Or we might say that it is the spiritual fortitude to stay in contact with what is difficult in our lives and to face it, in spite of the sadness it will produce.

Trobisch goes on to quote the poet Rainer Maria Wilke as an example of this principle. Wilke was writing to a friend suffering depression:

> You must not be frightened if a sadness rises up before you larger than any you have ever seen; if a restiveness like light and cloud-shadows passes over your hands and over all you do. You must think that something is happening with you, that life has not forgotten you, that it holds you in its hand; it will not let you fall. Why do you want to shut out of your life any agitation, any pain, any melancholy, since you really do not know what these states are working upon you? . . . Just remember that sickness is the means by which an organism frees itself of foreign matter; so one must just help it to be sick, to have its whole sickness and break out with it, for that is its progress.[15]

Acknowledging and resolving our losses helps our love receptors heal, so they are functional when opportunities to love come again. As our friend Allen healed from the loss of his son, he was prepared to love the infant he held in his arms four years later. Perhaps if Allen hadn't grieved, he would never have moved on to have enough courage to be responsible for another infant again.

❑　　　❑　　　❑

Time Out

How Do I Deal with Loss in My Life?

During some quiet sessions of self-reflection, consider doing a survey—and analysis—of the periods of loss you've experienced in your life so far. Here are some steps and questions to get you started:

1. Make a list of the losses you've experienced, from your earliest memories to the present.

2. Go back through your list and place stars by the most significant losses. Perhaps these will be the ones that have hurt you the most. You may still feel the hurt deeply.

3. As you observe your list, ask yourself:
   ❏ *How have I reacted and responded during these times of loss?*
   ❏ *What insights about myself come through, in light of my responses?*
   ❏ *What did I miss out on because of these losses—things that would have been good? How did I grieve these things (or not grieve them)? How do I/can I still grieve them?*

4. In hindsight, can I see any "benefits" to experiencing these times of loss?
   ❏ *Was I graciously spared from experiencing any "bad" things?*
   ❏ *What personal growth (new strength, courage, patience, wisdom, etc.) resulted?*

5. How am I different today because of these losses?

6. How can my losses influence my prayers during the weeks ahead?
   ❏ *Laments to offer God (suggestion: read and meditate on Ps. 13)*
   ❏ *Petitions to offer God (suggestion: read and meditate on Ps. 17)*
   ❏ *Praise to offer God (suggestion: read and meditate on Ps. 30:1-5)*

❏   ❏   ❏

Can You Trust Happiness?

The alternative to embracing our loss—the normal experience of human existence—is to pull back from all of the fullness of life for fear the little bits of joy we cling to might be taken away. John Steinbeck brings this point home, in a poignant way, in his novel *The Grapes of Wrath.*[16] A family of poor field workers, the Joads, were pushed off their Oklahoma tenement. They decided to load everything onto their rickety old truck and head to the green fields of California to find work and happiness. In their fertile imaginations, California was a paradise, a Garden of Eden of opportunity. Listen to old Grandpa talk about what a plentiful, bountiful, heaven this California must be:

> Jus' let me get out to California where I can pick me an orange when I want it. Or grapes. There's a thing I ain't never had enough

of. Gonna get me a whole big bunch of grapes off a bush, or
watever, an' I'm gonna squash 'em on my face an' let 'em run offen
my chin.

So . . . this poor "Oakie" family is all geared up to start the journey to the
Promised Land. Yet in spite of all the excitement and the feelings of antic-
ipation, another emotion eats at the edges of their minds. It comes through
in a conversation between young Tom Joad and his mother:

"Tom, I hope things is all right in California."

He turned and looked at her. "What makes you think they
ain't?" he asked.

"Well—nothing. Seems *too* nice, kinda. I seen the han'bills fellas
pass out, an' want folks to come an' pick grapes an' oranges an'
peaches. That'd be nice work, Tom, pickin' peaches. . . And it'd be
nice under the trees, workin' in the shade. *I'm scared of stuff so nice.*
I ain't got faith. I'm scared somepin ain't so nice about it."

Tom said: "Don't roust your faith bird-high an' you won't do no
crawlin' with the worms."

"I know that's right," [she said]. "That's Scripture, ain't it?"

No doubt, we need to develop our capacity to trust the prospect of
happiness.

Every good thing that comes into our lives carries within it the power to
make us fear its loss. Yet, at those distressing times when we lose our grip on
the things we think will save us, there is something beyond our fear. It is the
recognition that loss can carry hope along with it: the hope that what is
taken away will be replaced by something even better (though we couldn't
imagine what it might be). If we live in love—in God's love—this hope is the
truth of our existence. For our good is His greatest happiness.

If we can only open up and trust it.

Opening Up Your Love Receptors (Part 1: With People)

Both happiness and depression are fueled by the same source: the capacity to feel, to allow ourselves emotion, and to experience the full range of life.

—Lesley Hazleton

A minister friend of ours had been invited to conduct a funeral for a couple whose only daughter had died. The family did not have a church, and so our friend was a virtual stranger to them. As they were riding in the same car together, headed to the grave site, the man turned to his wife and said: "Please tell me how to feel about all this. Tell me how to act. I don't know what to feel, and I don't know what to do. Help me!"

How do we humans become so closed up? How do we get to the place where we can't even feel our own grief—or know any of our feelings without having them explained to us by someone else?

The Physiology of "Closed-up" Living

Do you recall our discussion in chapter 3 about the "brain chemical connection"? It will give us a picture for envisioning the concept of love

125

receptors here. Remember that the effects of adrenaline can be blocked with medicines called beta-blockers. Each cell has what might be called keyholes in it, shaped differently to receive different chemical "keys." Adrenaline affects two keyholes, the alpha-receptors and the beta-receptors. When adrenaline goes to these different keyholes it produces different effects in the cell. At the beta-receptor site, adrenaline causes an increase in heart rate and blood pressure while dilating the lung's bronchial tubes for better breathing. At the alpha-receptors, adrenaline causes blood vessel constriction, increased blood pressure, and heightened awareness.

We said that certain drugs block these receptors. A beta-blocker drug is a medicine that fits—like a key in a lock—into the beta-receptor site, but it doesn't unlock the lock. In a sense, it fools the cell, blocking that receptor so adrenaline can't fit there. So we fool the cell by giving it a chemical to take up a receptor site (which does not produce the reaction the chemical adrenaline would). Now no other key can fit in that site, even though the correct key is available. In other words, the adrenaline is ready to act, but can't, because the receptor site is already filled.

❑　　❑　　❑

Adrenaline Going into Receptors

Types of Responses

Increased Heart Rate
Faster Breathing
Increased Blood Pressure

▼ = Adrenaline
\/ = Receptor

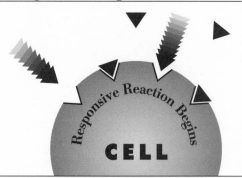

Adrenaline with No Place to Fit

Types of Beta-Blockers

Inderal
Tenormin
Corgard

▽B/ = Beta-Blocker

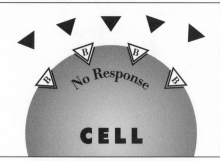

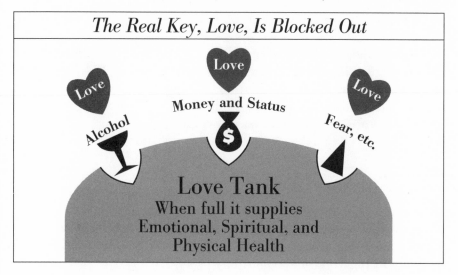

What we're talking about here, by analogy, is the fact that we have "love receptors" in the same sense that we have receptor sites in our cells ready to receive chemicals for physical functioning. The love receptors' sole function is to bind to love and present it to our mind and spirit. Everyone has these love receptors, but often they are filled with various kinds of "blockers" instead of love.

This is why we can speak of a "love-blocked person," someone who cannot receive love. Although love is out there, just as adrenaline is available to my nervous system, my receptors may be filled with other things, like alcohol, for instance. Alcohol goes to the receptors, but it doesn't create the desired effect. It creates a feel-good feeling for a short time, but after that comes the typical feel-bad feeling—"I feel bad over things I did." And I feel bad physically too.

There are people who spend to feel good, to try to feel that feeling that love should give them. Or people act out sexually by having affairs or various "conquests"—trying to get the feeling that only true love can give. Or they overwork instead of being able to receive love. So these are some of the blocks we place in our love receptors, the things that eventually bind us into addiction. Actually, any action or substance that makes us *temporarily feel good* can block our love receptors.

Of course, the blockers do not have to be obvious. A primary blocker, for example, is fear. Like the man at his daughter's funeral, we fearfully close off our feelings. If we dared to show what is really inside, we fear that two things might happen: (1) we may lose control; (2) we may be rejected. These possibilities seem too overwhelming for us. We remain blocked with fear and separated from the love we need.

So we're maintaining that all of us have these receptors, this ability to receive love, but that we rarely open them to the real thing. We've allowed so many blockers to fill our God-created receptor sites that we require a monumental transformation process. Step by step, we must begin opening and loving, learning to live our lives more fully.

❏   ❏   ❏

Time Out

It's important to see that just as beta-receptors can be blocked—*physically* blocked by certain medicines—so love receptors can be *emotionally* blocked by things we think and do compulsively.

The question we need to ask ourselves, then, is:

❏ *What is it that is blocking my love receptors? (Note: It may be more than one thing.)*

This is the very first step in learning to receive love, because it is necessary to STOP using the false "keys" (the blockers) and START using the real thing—love.

❏   ❏   ❏

How to "Open" Those Receptor Sites

How to begin? In order to break the love-block we have to do several things that will help us gradually remove the false keys blocking out love. We open the receptor sites by becoming aware of and learning what love is and where to find it. And then we begin to soak it in like a sponge. All of this is a gradual process, a journey that begins with the first small steps.

We have already covered several of the *broad steps* in this process in this Part II section of the book: In chapter 5 it involved exchanging inner lies for God's truth. Next, in chapter 6, it required embracing the potential growth that comes through loss. This chapter and the next will cover six of the more *specific steps*. Then chapter 9 will follow up with the culminating task: to commit to self-nurture as the basic approach to life.

Step 1: "Soften" (Risking Vulnerability)

A ship in harbor is safe,
but that is not what ships are for.[1]

Staying emotionally safe requires interpersonal secrecy. And keeping secrets can be hazardous to your love life. Writer Keith Miller said that learning to keep a secret is an important step in becoming a distinct individual, but it does not make a person able to be intimate and loving. As a matter of fact, being able to keep secrets may make us lonely and isolated.

I have said to people all my life, "Love me, please, love me." And some did, *but I did not believe them because I knew they didn't see the real me crouched inside.* I wondered whether they would love me if they knew my "secret, bad thoughts." Finally, I realized that my only hope was to find out—to let someone see me as I really am, bad thoughts and all.[2]

The point is, all of us need to soften like that, in the smallest of ways, as a primary step in opening up our love receptors. After all, if people don't know the real you, then any love that comes your way *will feel as if it belongs to somone else.* I [Brian] recall a time on a Sunday morning when I had to stand up at the end of a worship service and make an announcement. My wife Debi and I, the previous day, had had quite a riff, and I had been a jerk. But the pastor had just preached a convicting sermon on how to treat one another in marriage. I felt as though he was talking directly to me. So when I stood up to make the announcement, something in me wanted to reveal a bit of my guilt and also my sense of encouragement that I could change. I said, "Well, I can tell Debi's been giving the pastor some suggestions for sermon topics again."

Everybody laughed, and I suppose it was kind of funny. But this minute piece of self-revelation made a difference. Debi and I were able to talk things through later. And I'm aware that I had an opportunity, in that moment when I stood up, to let down my pride a little and admit my guilt feelings.

In the midst of fear and conflict come these brief opportunities to "soften"—and truly we must take them. The price is too great to let those amazing moments pass us by, as shaky as we feel when they confront us. They are gracious nudgings to let down and say: "Let's stop the charade; here is what I'm feeling right now. . . ."

One of the most powerful portrayals of the destructive effects of shutting down such opportunities is in Arthur Miller's play *Death of a Salesman*.[3] It's the story of Willy Loman, an aging traveling salesman, who is bowed down by the years of pressure that have come with his job. Willy travels 700 miles a week in his old Chevrolet, puts in long hours tramping through stores, hoping for big sales. He maintains the highest of expectations for himself, especially the goal of being "well liked" wherever he travels, and of making big money someday. But, at the apex of middle age, he is failing to live up to his incredible standards, though determined that no one will know it.

Eventually Willy comes to believe that his only hope resides in the fortunes of his two sons. He can vicariously live out his dreams of success through their successes in life. Bif, especially, once the high school football hero, once so well liked, has all the potential to take the world by the tail. Surely Bif can vindicate Willy's sad existence.

But after winning the city championship football game, Bif dropped out of life for fifteen years. (He had become disillusioned with his father's hypocrisy, having discovered that Willy was having an affair.) But the failure of Bif to be "well liked" as an adult—or to even settle into a profession— literally drives Willy crazy (and to eventual suicide). He sinks into great contempt for his son Bif as self-hatred, pride, and fear consume him. It is his secret life, which no one is aware of, that he unconsciously hates most of all.

The point here is that there are numerous places in the play where Willy could have made a new start with his family, but it would have taken some courage to "soften." In one scene, Willy has a supreme chance to change the direction of his worsening relationship with Bif by responding with vulnerability. In the scene, Bif gets down on his knees before his father, seeking atonement:

BIF: Dad, I'll make good, I'll make good. *Willy tries to get to his feet. Bif holds him down.* Sit down now.
WILLY: No, you're no good, you're no good for anything!
BIF: I am, Dad, I'll find something else, you understand? Now don't worry about anything. *He holds up Willy's face.* Talk to me, Dad. . . .

What would it have taken for Willy to change everything—in that instant—for the sake of love? Just the slightest loosening of the muscles where Bif's hand rested? Just a turning of his eyes to meet his son's gaze with a morsel of compassion?

Have you been in that moment? Such a small thing is required of us in those pregnant pauses, but what power we are given to make or break a relationship in that instant of eternity! We hold in our hands the moment of choice—for softening or hardening—that makes all the difference in the world for our loving. Do I apologize or remain angry? Do I offer a compliment or let the silence linger? For Willy, a hug would have said everything: "Son, whether we have anything else in the world, we have our love. I love you no matter what you are . . . or do . . . or say. It's enough."

But Willy never softened. Fear held him captive.

And pride killed him.

No doubt Willy wanted to maintain the image of being "well liked," the one thing he so much wanted for his sons. But the saddest part is that all along, he had opportunities to become vulnerable. The same kind of opportunity that comes to us when our spouse lashes out once again . . . and we have a brief choice to escalate the battle or pull back and reveal our hurt. The same opportunity when our teenage son insults us . . . and we must decide whether to reach into our old bag of tricks to find a more cutting rejoinder, to up the ante. . . . Or choose instead to reveal, in some small way, how scary it feels to be a parent, how fearful the possibility of failing at it.

Masterfully, playwright Miller traced the slippery descent into love-block. Each time Willy dashed those sacred opportunities he became a little bit more hardened and a little less capable of loving and being loved. Pride filled his love receptors.

So the first step in our opening up is seriously to ponder: *What is that thing in me that must turn, or melt, or somehow be dismantled, before love can flow in and heal my wounds and draw me closer to others?* Perhaps your marriage relationship will be the place to start.

> You're both being had in these no-win battles. Somebody's got to make a move for honesty.
>
> "Jill," you say, "we're getting farther apart every time we fight. You're out to win by putting me down. I'm out to win by putting you down. We both lose. I don't care who wins. I just want to be close to you."
>
> There's surprise all over her face.
>
> "That's what I really want, too," she says.[4]

When we are hurt we can begin to recognize that closing up creates a kind of protective shell. It does keep us from pain, but it is the same shell that blocks out love. In the end it causes much more pain than the protective shell prevents. Therefore it is better to be truthful with others, with ourselves, and with our God.

> Surely You desire truth in the inner parts;
> You teach me wisdom in the inmost place.[5]

Learning to be vulnerable is a process, a series of events leading toward wholeness. It requires a conscious decision to put down the weapons we use to push people away so that we can begin sharing from the depth of our souls. Such vulnerability leads to truthfulness, which gradually leads to self-acceptance. As we learn to accept ourselves, we slowly begin to receive not only other people's love for us but also God's love for us. But it's scary. And we have to say, "Well, I shared that little bit and that was OK. Next time I can show a little bit more of myself and see how that goes." And we're not going to be good at it, either, not at first. We're going to feel silly, unnatural. The more we do it, though, the easier it becomes.

One of our clients named Bill tended to be a jokester growing up. He was always trying to get people's approval by being fun-loving and a happy person. "Gee, Bill is always upbeat, he's always happy," people would say. Even though there were days when he might be unhappy, he still had to have that happy mask on. As he tells it. . . .

Then I heard a story that made great impact on me and helped me open up with people. It's a story about a man who went to a psychiatrist. The man was extremely unhappy, sad, and he began pouring his heart out. So the psychiatrist was looking for some practical suggestions to give him. He said, "I hear there's a clown act in town. I heard that this clown is really funny and he really makes you laugh and feel good. You ought to go and see that act."

Very sadly the man looked up at the psychiatrist. He said, "Sir, I *am* that clown."

I think that is a beautiful illustration of how so often we can put on a happy face, we can run from any form of vulnerability, simply to hide our fear and sadness. We are afraid to show anyone that we do have thoughts that are ugly, that aren't pure, that aren't good, because if they saw us as we are, they might not love us.

We all have this fear to some extent, and only personal growth—risking vulnerability—will move us beyond it. The Lord asks us to be truthful to Him. If we choose that path in our lives, then we can be truthful to ourselves and to others.

Step 2: "Unblock" (Choosing Forgiveness)

Forgiveness is the balm that restores the love receptors to their full capacity. If it is through vulnerability that we soften our love receptors, then it is through forgiveness that we unburden them, freeing them from the sludge of bitterness.

Forgiveness corrects love-block in two ways. First, it works by restoring our hearts to God by asking forgiveness for our own sins. We need to ask God to forgive us for how we have not loved well. We ask forgiveness for the many ways we have blocked the flow of love in our lives. We also ask forgiveness for the ways we have refused to offer our own love.

Second, and most surprising, forgiveness is the healing power when others have damaged our love receptors through abuse. Perhaps the most descriptive illustration of this is a little girl who is sexually fondled by her father. She is born with a need for love. She is born dependent on her father to supply those love needs. When he uses her body for his own sexual pleasure, her love receptors become damaged. She begins to believe that it is wrong of her to love, that if she didn't want love, perhaps these horrible betrayals wouldn't have happened to her. Forgiveness helps her realize that she was completely a victim of her father's sins. It helps her restore the truth that her longings for love were legitimate and that it was her father who damaged her love receptors through his abusive sin against her. Through forgiveness her life can be restored. Her father, sin, and victimization rules her life without forgiveness. Through forgiveness she is free to live and love.

Consider the biblical Joseph. Having become "ruler of all Egypt," he eventually confronts the brothers who had sold him into slavery as a boy. They wonder just what Joseph will do, now that all the power is in his hands, for they had come to him with their father to avoid starvation.

They said, "What if Joseph holds a grudge against us and pays us back for all the wrongs we did to him?"

So they sent word to Joseph, saying, "Your father left these instructions before he died: 'This is what you are to say to Joseph: I ask you to forgive your brothers the sins and the wrongs they committed in treating you so badly.' Now please forgive the sins of the servants of the God of your father." When their message came to him, Joseph wept.

His brothers then came and threw themselves down before him. "We are your slaves," they said. But Joseph said to them, "Don't be afraid. Am I in the place of God? *You intended to harm me, but God intended it for good.*" . . . And he reassured them and spoke kindly to them.[6]

I [Joe] was struggling at one point with why I had to go through some painful things in my life. My question became, "God, where are You? Don't You love me?" And God seemed to direct me to the verse where Joseph says to his brothers, "You intended to harm me, but God intended it for good." Not only do I know that verse, but it's personal, it's part of me. I was able to forgive those who had wronged me. But it didn't necessarily help them; it helped me!

So often we view forgiveness as being for the other person. We say, "I will never forgive him," as though we are holding him to some form of punishment to be endured until we release him. No, we are the ones enduring; we endure the ravages of bitterness closing up our hearts.

Forgiveness is for *me*. And if I harbor an unforgiving spirit, then that is a part of me that God cannot have, a part in which God's love cannot reside. So it is for ourselves that we attempt to release our bitterness. Forgiveness, in this sense, is primarily a selfish act, perhaps the only selfish act that is perfectly justified, because we are commanded by God to do it.

For if you forgive men when they sin against you, your Heavenly Father will also forgive you. But if you do not forgive men their sins, your Father will not forgive your sins.[7]

We simply must forgive. Why? Because those who hurt us are only human, just like us. And all of us together stand in need of forgiveness.

As we forgive people, we gradually come to see the deeper truth about them, a truth our hate blinds us to, a truth we can see only when we separate them from what they did to us. When we heal our memories we are not playing games, we are not making believe. We see the truth again. For the truth about those who hurt us is that they are weak, needy, and fallible human beings. They were people *before* they hurt us and they are people *after* they hurt us.[8]

We are *not* commanded to forget, of course. But eventually releasing our bitterness may bring us to a point of choosing to forget, as well. Forgiveness cancels the debt: "He doesn't owe me anything anymore." This is the opposite of holding on to our anger at the one who has hurt us.

One thing I do: Forgetting what is behind and straining toward what is ahead.[9]

Lots of things are worth forgetting, aren't they? How many hurts have you received in your lifetime? How many nasty looks? How many intentional slights and relational bruises? Do you hold them in your mind, ready to unpack at a moment's notice? Or do you store them in your body as aches and pains, ulcers and hypertension, and trumpets of anxiety that can break the concentration for the task at hand?

Suppose we choose to forget the things that are no longer worthy of the marvelous recall-powers of our minds and bodies? Suppose in the midst of our day we take a moment to push those memories aside, refocusing on the present and our opportunities right now to love and be loved?

The amazing thing about the swirling, clamoring pains of the past is that when we attend to the present, most of those old hurts gradually become less important, certainly less powerful. And sometimes they become undeserving of any remembering at all.

It seems that some cultures are better at all of this than others. Perhaps they value the benefits of forgetting—some might call it the virtue of equanimity—more than we do. Numerous stories circulate in the East that lift up this quality of soul-healing forgetfulness, and perhaps we could learn from them.

No, we are not calling for a mindless, doormat-like acceptance of abuse. But surely we can do better at *choosing to live our own lives* while confused or vindictive people do this or that on the periphery, so much of it beyond our control anyway. Not all of it must affect us. None of it need make us bitter. And certainly much of it can be forgotten, to our great benefit.

❑   ❑   ❑

Time Out

Bitterness Self-Evaluation

Is there any bitterness clogging your love receptors? Where is forgiveness the next step for you to take?

One way to become more aware of the effects of unforgiveness in your life is to do a "parade of faces." In a few moments of solitude, take some time to let the faces of your world pass before you in succession: your family, relatives, friends, neighbors, coworkers. All of the people that have made up your relationships world, past and present. The people may be living or dead. But let them come to mind for a few minutes.

When the "parade" has passed, THINK—

❑ Which faces seemed to clamor for your attention, over others? Why?

❑ Which were looking at you with gentle faces? Which had countenances of anger, fear, bitterness, or hatred?

❑ To which faces would you attach any feelings of anger or bitterness in yourself?

❑ Which faces touched a part of you that hurts? How, specifically, has this individual hurt you?

If your brother sins against you, go and show him his fault, just between the two of you. If he listens to you, you have won your brother over. —Matthew 18:15

Now, PLAN—

❑ According to Jesus, if we have been hurt, it is our responsibility to take action with the goal of mutual forgiveness. Jot your ideas about what could be done to heal a relationship in the near future:

_____

_____

_____

After you have attempted a reconciliation, THINK—

❑ To what extent have I forgiven and let go?

❑ In what ways am I still holding on to bitterness? How can I tell?

Five Things to Remember about Forgiveness

It is important to keep in mind a few practical points related to forgiveness. They can save us much heartache.

It's Not a Feeling, but a Command. Too often, we mix up forgiveness and feelings, thinking that, "Well, I haven't felt like I've forgiven," or "I don't feel as though I *want* to forgive, so I can't practice it without hypocrisy." Yet forgiveness is not a feeling. Feelings can come as a result of forgiveness, but basically, it's a command.

> If you forgive men when they sin against you, your Heavenly Father will also forgive you. But if you do not forgive men their sins, your Father will not forgive your sins.—Matthew 6:14-15

> Then Peter came to Jesus and asked, "Lord, how many times shall I forgive my brother when he sins against me? Up to seven times?" Jesus answered, "I tell you, not seven times, but seventy-seven times." —Matthew 18:21-22

> If you hold anything against anyone, forgive him, so that your Father in heaven may forgive you your sins. —Mark 11:25

> Do not judge, and you will not be judged. Do not condemn, and you will not be condemned. Forgive, and you will be forgiven.—Luke 6:37

It's a Process. Some people get caught up in thinking that forgiveness is always a one-time event. There are times when little irritations come along, when forgiveness can indeed be a one-time event. For example, I may be able to forgive a friend for hurting my feelings when he makes an unthinking hurtful remark. We simply move on from that. But other events cause deeper pain and demand that forgiveness become a more involved process. At those times—and most times—forgiveness isn't something that we can just conjure up; it's a process in which we have to work through feelings and issues.

First of all, we'll go to God and say, "Lord, I want to be obedient in Your command to forgive. I don't feel like forgiving. I don't want to forgive. I hurt. I'm angry. I'm bitter. But I want to ask You to help me begin that process and work through these feelings."

Next would be to ask God to help you understand what truly needs to be forgiven: the denial, anger turned inward, anger turned outward. All of which involves genuine grief and a movement toward resolution, a point at which we release what feels like our right for retribution. It may take days, months, even years before we are able to say to God, "Vengeance is Yours, Lord. You take it."

One of our favorite quotes comes from the book *As for Me and My House* by Walter Wangerin. He describes forgiveness this way:

Forgiveness is a sort of divine absurdity. It is irrational, as the world reasons things, and unwise.[10]

A logical mind says that we've got to get even with people and be able to get our payback. But forgiveness is a release of that. Grace and mercy come into the picture. With the help of God, and the grace of God, and the love of God, I can forgive.

It Doesn't Require Ignoring the Sin. I remember once working with a young lady in the hospital. Her father was a pastor, and he would sexually molest her every Sunday after church. This went on for a number of years. I was fairly recently out of school, and I remember saying to myself, *How do you really approach a person, who has been so heinously abused and sinned against, about the issue of forgiveness?* The Lord revealed to me something that really seemed to help her—that God hated the sin that was committed against her worse than she did. And that we're never to forgive the sin. We're always to hate the sin but forgive the sinner.

So often, we have been confused in thinking that if I forgive, it means that what happened really wasn't so bad or that I really wasn't hurt by it. We'd prefer to make an excuse for the act, and go on.

But forgiving is harder than excusing, because to forgive we must face squarely the pain of the wrong done to us. We must also have the courage to hold the other person accountable. This kind of forgiving means entering into a relationship, determining to treat the other as a worthy human being—worthy of our full attention and involvement. To excuse, on the other hand, minimizes the other as being not quite valuable enough to take up our energies. We simply choose to ignore her and go on our way. Yet my fearful decision to approach this person could possibly become the start of a new friendship, the enduring quality of which might pleasantly surprise us both, years later.

It Doesn't Automatically Fix the Relationship. We may believe that if we have truly forgiven it means that the relationship will now be thoroughly repaired. That's not necessarily true, since at times the other person isn't repentant, isn't willing to admit the wrongness in his or her own actions. They continue being hurtful, spiteful, self-destructive. We still need to forgive them, but that doesn't necessarily mean that we jump back into an ongoing relationship.

There is forgiveness, and then there is reconciliation. They are two different things. Forgiveness is a unilateral process; it only takes one person to forgive, not both parties. If somebody has abused you, then you can do the forgiving even if that person is dead or no longer present in your life. It's a unilateral process.

But reconciliation does require the consent of both parties. Sometimes we come to a point of forgiveness and want to have reconciliation, but the other person has not changed and remains unwilling. So reconciliation cannot take place at this point. Now we are called to develop patience. And we get on with our own life.

It May Apply to God Too. So often we get angry at God for things that we perceive Him as having done or allowed to happen. Lewis Smedes, in his book *Forgive and Forget* relates this story:

> A tailor leaves his prayers and, on the way out of the synagogue, meets a rabbi.
>
> "Well, and what have you been doing in the synagogue, Lev Ashram?" the rabbi asks.
>
> "I was saying prayers, rabbi."
>
> "Fine, and did you confess your sins?"
>
> "Yes, rabbi, I confessed my little sins."
>
> "Your little sins?"
>
> "Yes, I confessed that I sometimes cut my cloth on the short side, that I cheat on a yard of wool by a couple of inches."
>
> "You said that to God, Lev Ashram?"
>
> "Yes, rabbi, and more. I said, 'Lord, I cheat on pieces of cloth; you let little babies die. But I am going to make you a deal. You forgive me my little sins and I'll forgive you your big ones."[11]

Are we assuming that God has done something wrong? No. But that may be our perception—either conscious or unconscious. We may need to tell Him that. We need to let God off the hook for a wrongly attributed event. No doubt we are trying to control God when something painful happens and we say, "Wrong, God!" When we become angry with God, perhaps it's because we want to *play* God. We want to be in control and say, "I don't like what You let happen, and You didn't do it right. It should have been *this* way." Confused thinking, perhaps. But it's something in the relationship that needs to come to the surface. God will not be threatened by our narrow perceptions.

I [Joe] had a patient who was terribly abused as a child, a young professional guy who was emotionally, physically, and sexually abused by his mother. I remember the guy saying, "I will never forgive her."

He was adamant as he talked through these feelings. He wasn't at a place where he could come to forgive at that time. He was still in that period of intense anger. As time went on, he shared with me and said, "You know, I feel like this anger is just turning into bitterness. It's hurting me." So, we talked about that, about how his anger and bitterness was hurting him. It wasn't hurting the other person; his mother was dead. And then he eventually came, in tears, to the point of forgiveness. This was a weight on him that he felt being lifted as he began forgiving.

God looks at our hearts and knows where we are. He knows how we've been hurt. But we must be courageous enough to begin dealing with the hurt, for unresolved anger will turn sour and become bitterness.

❑   ❑   ❑

Step 3: "Receive" (Cultivating Awareness)

The third specific step in opening our love receptors with people is to pay attention to the love flowing toward us each day. Love is around you. Look for it in the little things, in each present moment. The problem has not been that love wasn't there; we just haven't recognized it.

Too often we focus on the big picture of our goals, our needs, our wants. We forget the little picture of our present moments as they come to us.

> We are all dreaming of some magical rose garden over the horizon— instead of enjoying the roses that are blossoming outside our windows today.[12]

Notice how people treat you, the very next person you meet. When she says: "Did you have a good weekend?" she is loving you. When people are spending time with you they are loving you. When someone shares a part of himself with you, he is loving you. When the rain falls on your garden, the Lord is loving you. Things like that happen to us daily, though we write them off as meaningless and instead

> . . . learn to shuffle through leaves on a golden day without wonder, or to stare at a bleak landscape or at birds in flight without longing. We learn to mute the joy we feel at special moments of rapture. We learn to disengage from life, at the gain of lessening grief, and at the cost of lessening life. . . . We smog our vision, flatten our path, drug our sensibilities, and siphon off our energies in dull routines such as jogging and cocktail parties and cable TV.[13]

However, it is the times when we are being loved by the people around us that make us more aware of God's love for us. Through such attentiveness, we will become aware of His kindness, of His hand being active in our lives every second of every day in everything that we do. As writer Frederick Buechner said: "The word that God speaks to us is always an incarnate word—a word spelled out to us not alphabetically, in syllables, but enigmatically, in events."

Felt through all this fleshly dress
Bright shoots of everlastingness.[14]

A few years ago, a popular wall poster showed a beautiful scene of red and purple wild mountain flowers. It was captioned: *When I look, let me truly see.* In every moment of our daily routine we can keep alert, for we may see love in so many places if we look with eyes truly open. Yes, bend down to smell the roses. Look up at the sky and be graced with its incomparable blueness. Or let a midnight thunderstorm resonate in your chest and fill you with awe.

What a thing it is to sit absolutely alone in the forest at night, cherished by this wonderful, unintelligent perfectly innocent speech, the most comforting speech in the world. . . . Nobody started it, nobody is going to stop it. It will talk as long as it wants, the rain. As long as it talks I am going to listen.[15]

Pay attention to the silences that come after a conversation or after you turn off the TV. Melt into them and savor them, for they are sacred spaces to know the love of God.

I say that we are wound
With mercy round and round
As if with air.[16]

Look around you and see how you share in all of God's creation. Look at the beauty all around that was created just for you. It is important to do that every day, wherever you may be. As you begin to get in touch with all the loving people who have been around you remember that they too are also created by God. It is not a problem that God has ever stopped loving us or had not been loving us all these years, it is the fact that we did not know how to accept, or sometimes even recognize, His love for us.

A greater poverty than that caused by lack of money is the poverty of awareness. Men and women go about the world unaware of the beauty, the goodness, in it. Their souls are poor. It is better to have a poor pocketbook than to suffer from a poor soul.[17]

We are so often distrustful of others, assuming they have a hidden agenda that will hurt us. As we become more open to the pervasiveness of love in our world, we can let down our guard a bit. We can begin to see small kindnesses—or any time spent with us—as acts of love. Some of the smallest overtures, things we may naturally brush aside as trivial or unimportant, are acts of love toward us that can build us up and transform our perceptions of the day. It is up to us to see these things and accept them.

When we first wake up and come to consciousness in the mornings, we can ask ourselves: *How will I choose to interpret my world today?* Will it be a world full of demons and dragons, as I approach each encounter ready to be attacked or put down? Will I enter my day assuming the worst, unconsciously beckoning beastly confrontations, ever expecting to be unloved, confirming my suspicion that the world is basically a hostile place?

Or will my world today be filled with nobler assumptions—beget by a mind-set that sees the good, that approaches each human encounter as a dance with the innocent? Will I recognize that most people are doing the best they can, many hurting, and many, with every word and gesture toward me, simply making a plea for understanding?

Opening Up Your Love Receptors (Part 2: Toward God)

Are we related to something infinite or not?
That is the telling question of life.

—Carl Jung

For I tell you this: one loving blind desire for God alone
is more valuable in itself,
more pleasing to God and to the saints,
more beneficial to your own growth,
and more helpful to your friends,
both living and dead,
than anything else you could do.

—The Cloud of Unknowing

Have you ever stood in front of a masterpiece at an art museum and thought, *My, that's a beautiful painting?* It's certainly lovely at first glance. But the more you study the painting, the more that painting comes alive to you—the more enriched you are, the more you see in it, and the more you understand about it. As we continue to open up our love receptors—risking vulnerability, forgiving and being forgiven, becoming aware of all the love around us—the same kind of process takes place: life becomes progressively more beautiful and meaningful to us. It's an upward spiral.

Relationship with God

The process must involve a relationship with God. And it is indeed a process. Like getting married or starting into any other relationship, over time we learn more about God—who He truly is, how to enjoy His presence, and what it means to worship Him. So let us continue the steps of "unblocking," with emphasis on our relationship to God.

Step 4: "Know" (Discovering the True God)

Only a few years back I [Brian] began to realize that how I envisioned God was unscriptural and probably idolatrous, because it was not an accurate vision of who God was. This really made impact when someone asked me: "What does God look like when you pray?"

That's when I thought about it, and I saw my old staircase imagery, the staircase with red carpet on it. The carpeted staircase has a low platform, and four other stairs, and a throne. Whenever I prayed I would see myself standing on that platform looking down the stairs in some sort of shame—instead of looking at God. When this mind-picture came to my full conscious awareness, and I shared it with Debi, we began praying that God would help me understand the meaning of this imagery for me.

I never fully identified the shame that prevented me from seeing God and looking at God, but I began asking God to change that image of Him in my life, the image of an unapproachable God who looks down at me with unkind eyes. Eventually, I began recognizing, first of all, the reality that Christ is seated at the right hand of the Father constantly interceding for me. So, that image of Christ praying for me, twenty-four hours a day, seven days a week, began to encourage me deeply. How much more can God love you than to be interceding for you each second of every day?

> Who is He that condemns? Christ Jesus, who died—more than that, who was raised to life—is at the right hand of God and is also interceding for us.[1]

"People see God every day," said Pearl Bailey. "They just don't recognize Him." How true! All of us have a God-image—a sense of who God is and what He is like. This image develops early, influenced by everything that happens to us as we grow, both the good things and the bad. And though we may have plenty of theological "head knowledge" about God, our deep sense of who He really is may be somewhat distorted. Then we fail to recognize Him in the grace-points of our lives.

Talking about God Is Difficult

The reason for our distortions is that *God can be known, but not fully comprehended.* Finite minds, of course, cannot expect to fully understand or "explain" the infinite God. Even our best attempts at theology fall short; our theologies are not God, merely imperfect attempts to describe Him. Listen to one theology professor's struggle with this:

> Sometime during my first few weeks at seminary, I got into a discussion with two seniors. I suppose they were trying to figure out my theological orientation. Was I conservative? liberal? When they asked, "What do you think about God?" I stunned them with the response "I don't like to talk about God."
>
> What I meant was—after all I did spend three years at seminary talking quite a lot about God—I feel trapped between the necessary and the idolatrous. . . . As humans, we are caught between necessity and idolatry. We need our words and images if we are to talk with each other about God. But when talking about God, let us proceed with caution, removing our shoes, lest we succeed only in creating a god who is no God at all.[2]

Clearly, we must learn to distinguish between our image of God—what we think and say about God—and the true nature of God Himself. This involves a lifetime of discovery, and it is absolutely necessary. For, as A.W. Tozer said: "The essence of idolatry is the entertainment of thoughts about God that are unworthy of him."

How does this relate to our love-receptor discussion? The point is that many of us, perhaps unconsciously, stay closed up to God, to some degree, because we have made a caricature of Him—or a straw man, if you will—that is secretly *not* to our liking. For some of us, God is the One who . . .

Let my brother get hit by a train
Punishes me for bad thoughts
Is far, far away from me and my insignificant problems
Stands by helpless while people suffer
Is just like my dad (or uncle, or grandfather, or mother . . .)
Ruins my fun
Others (fill in your own):_____.

Such distorted images may have developed because of disappointments early in life, judging and punishing parents, or any number of experiences. The result is that we pigeonhole God with an unworthy image, then reject that unworthy god, either actively (by declaring our "free-thinking human-ism") or passively (by becoming submissive, depressed, or just going through the motions of meaningless religious habits).

❑   ❑   ❑

My "Picture" of God

Our image of God lingers under the surface unless we consciously attempt to bring it to awareness. These three steps may help you do that:

First, take a moment to see what you are envisioning when you pray. Spend five minutes in prayer. Jot down your thoughts and images.

❑ Who/what were you directing your prayers to? Could you draw a picture of the image?

❑ Where were you?

❑ Where was God?

Second, choose one of these "unreal gods" (suggested by J.B. Phillips)[3] that comes closest to a God-image you either have now, or have had at some time in the past:

❑ Resident Policeman: He is our conscience
❑ Parental Hangover: God as the image of our earthly father
❑ Grand Old Man: old-fashioned and naive
❑ Meek-and-Mild: God as "Baby Jesus," soft and sentimental
❑ Absolute Perfection: Demanding 100 percent; unbending
❑ Heavenly Bosom: a comforting escape
❑ God-in-a-Box: He is obviously a Baptist, Lutheran, Methodist, etc.
❑ Managing Director: controlling the cosmos; uninterested in our "little" problems
❑ Second-Hand God: based on book and film portrayals of "life"
❑ Perennial Grievance: doesn't fulfill our expectations and plans
❑ Pale Galilean: a negative, no-fun killjoy.
❑ Other:

Third, reflect:

❑ What may be some reasons that I have this particular God-image?

❑ In what ways might my image be a distortion of the God revealed in Scripture?

❑ What "replacement imagery" could I begin to practice in order to bring my God-image into closer alignment with the true God?

❑   ❑   ❑

How do we come to know God? It's important to see that knowing God is a relationship that encompasses more than the intellect. It is a relationship to be experienced on many levels.

> You do not think of God; you experience him.
> He seems closer to you than the blood
> that surges through your veins.
> From the cellar of your soul
> you call him Father.[4]

If our lifelong journey is to know God better and better down through our days, then perhaps we might begin by trying to discern more insight about His revealed nature, along with confronting distorted images that block us, or hold us back, from full communion. An entire book could be written on this theme (in fact, a good one is Larry Stephens' *Please Let Me Know You, God* referred to earlier). But let's just consider five "truth statements" about God and their typical accompanying distortions. None of the statements are meant to be dogmatic assertions about God's true nature, for we take the insight about human finiteness seriously. But the statements can serve as challenges to each of us—to discover whether they are indeed verified by our own study of Scripture and our own reflections on our life experiences with God.

God Is Demanding (Distortion = a "Nice," Unassuming God)
We start out by admitting something that may not be very popular: Our first encounter with God is usually God's judgment upon our life, the consciousness of our sin. Martin Luther said: "Dread is God's greeting at the first, just as when we see how the lightning shatters a tree or slays a man." This is not a "nice guy," docile, "How-do-you-do?" God cares too much for us, pursues us too passionately, ever to be a mere passive bystander along the sidelines of our history.

The famous short-story writer Flannery O'Connor dedicated many of her story themes to showing us the pursuing, demanding kind of grace that God uses with us, an insistent prosecution that will not let us go. In her story *The Enduring Chill*[5] the main character, Asbury, is a twenty-five-year-old

young man who has given himself to "Art and Culture." He left his
hometown, which he always viewed as hopelessly backward, to spend time in
New York becoming a writer. But he became ill and had to return home to
the "sticks" with his mother and sister. He believes he is going to die and
takes perverse pleasure in his coming martyrdom for ART. For at least he
will never have to give in and admit his heritage; he is above it all and will
die in noble devotion to his own higher principles.

When his mother calls for the neighborhood minister, Asbury angrily
refuses to see him; the local religion is far beneath him. He has risen above
archaic notions of God and scoffs at her for suggesting the meeting. Instead,
he wants an enlightened, modern Jesuit priest— "[Asbury] would talk to a
man of culture before he died."

But the unexpected happens. A priest arrives, but he does not engage
Asbury in a nice conversation. "The Holy Ghost will not come," he tells the
young man, "until you see yourself as you are—a lazy ignorant conceited
youth!"

Later, Asbury discovers a deeper need within him than his pursuit of art
and culture can fulfill:

> He felt as if he were a shell that had to be filled with something but
> he did not know what. . . . There was something he was searching for,
> something that he felt he must have, some last significant culminating
> experience that he must make for himself before he died—make for
> himself out of his own intelligence. He had always relied on himself
> and had never been a sniveler after the ineffable. . . .

Eventually, when Asbury is told that he has undulent fever—a malady
that will not kill him but that will keep him perpetually weak and often
bedridden—he is *horrified* to discover that he is in the process of conversion.

> The boy fell back on his pillow and stared at the ceiling. His limbs
> that had been racked for so many weeks by fever and chill were
> numb now. The old life in him was exhausted. He awaited the
> coming of new. . . . He saw that for the rest of his days, frail, racked,
> but enduring, he would live in the face of a purifying terror. A
> feeble cry, a last impossible protest escaped him. But the Holy
> Ghost, emblazoned in ice instead of fire, continued, implacable, to
> descend.

What a gripping—though unusual—picture of conversion. Is it without
merit? Certainly, it is not a nice picture, or a particularly soothing one. For
Asbury, like us, is dealing with a God who is in pursuit, demanding his
attention. This is not a nebulous, all-pervading spirit that awaits our bidding
and meekly joins in the fun when we invite Him to our party. This is the God

who makes us uncomfortable because we need to wake up. He is the exhilarating presence who brings us to the precipice of eternal life, shows us our sins, and bids us leap into His arms. From this wooing God, the "hound of heaven," a response is demanded.

> There comes a moment when the children who have been playing at burglars hush suddenly: was that a *real footstep in the hall?* There comes a time when people who have been dabbling in religion ("Man's search for God"!) suddenly draw back. Supposing we really found Him? We never meant it to come to that! Worse still, supposing He had found us?[6]

God Is Love (Distortion = a Manipulative, Scheming God)

Now we are ready to speak of God in the more traditional way. The point, however, is that though we know God is love, *we so often assume He loves us only for what we will become* through His transforming power. So we stay closed until we can "clean up" for Him.

No. God loves sinners.

One of the most common mistakes people make is thinking they have to do all kinds of Christian work in order to receive (that is, earn) God's love. They try to make their lives presentable. They try to make themselves lovable. The premise is, "If I could just get my life straightened out, then I could fill this love hunger." Like the woman who fixes her hair before going to the beauty parlor! Quite the opposite is true: you must receive God's love in order to straighten out your life. Indeed, it is only *because* we are lost that salvation is even possible, for Jesus said: "I have not come to call the righteous, but sinners to repentance" (Luke 5:32).

> When Christianity speaks of God's love for sinners, this is explained as meaning that what God really loves is not so much the sinner as what can be made of the sinner. . . . How very different from the divine love revealed in Christ! When Jesus says, "I came to call sinners," a call to repentance and amendment is certainly included. But this does not mean that love is the means and amendment the end. Love is always an end in itself, and the moment it is degraded into a means to some other end it ceases to be love.[7]

Of course, the ultimate gift of love is the Incarnation and the Crucifixion. Few of us see the Crucifixion as an act of God's love; we see it purely as a redemption, not love. Yet Christ has suffered the humiliation of crucifixion as an act of love for each of us personally. He had been with the Father throughout eternity, but He broke into time to become one of us, to die alone, separated from the love He had always known.

If God is love, and He is as John says, then everything that He does is an act of love. The challenge to us, then, is twofold: (1) to recognize daily the loving acts of God in our lives, and (2) to make a conscious effort to receive and personalize each and every act.

As Christians we were important enough for God to send His Son who suffered the humiliation of dying on the cross for our sins so that we can live eternally with God in His glory. This should make us feel more loved than anything else we could experience on earth.

So, it is of primary importance that we stop telling ourselves that because we are unworthy and unlovable God cannot love us. Actually, it is *because* we are unworthy and unlovable that God *does* love us! We have fellowship with God, not on the basis of our righteousness—as most religions claim—but on the basis of our sin. Max Lucado takes this point further by suggesting that in some unfathomable way, God's pure, unmotivated love is a loving of Himself.

> Moms: Why do you love your newborn? I know, I know; it's a silly question, but indulge me. Why do you?
>
> For months this baby has brought you pain. She (or he!) made you break out in pimples and waddle like a duck. Because of her you craved sardines and crackers and threw up in the morning. She punched you in the tummy. She occupied space that wasn't hers and ate food she didn't fix.
>
> You kept her warm You kept her safe. You kept her fed. . . . Why? Why does a mother love her newborn? Because the baby is hers? Even more. Because the baby is her. Her blood. Her flesh. Her sinew and spine. Her hope. Her legacy. . . .
>
> She knows babies don't ask to come into this world. And God knows we didn't either. We are His idea. We are His. His face. His eyes. His hands. His touch.
>
> We are Him. Look deeply into the face of every human being on earth, and you will see His likeness. Though some appear to be distant relatives, they are not. God has no cousins, only children.[8]

God is love and His love is "unmotivated." It was not generated in any scheme for our improvement (though that will come!) or plan based on rational calculation. Our reason tells us that God seeks fellowship only with those He finds to be good. Christianity tells us the opposite: God wants to fellowship with the sinner.

God Is Responsive (Distortion = a Remote, Uncaring God)
I [Joe] was struggling with a problem in my life and wondering: *how much does God really love me?* I was in the middle of reading, just starting a new

section of a book, but I was really struggling with this problem and couldn't concentrate. I put the book away, and for forty-five minutes sat there meditating and thinking about this issue. I just couldn't come to closure on it. I couldn't understand it, and I was frustrated and upset.

Anyway, I picked the book back up, and the new section of the book was about grace. And there, on the first page, I saw not only my question—verbatim—but also the answer. (I'm getting chills talking about it even now.) I remember reading this lightning bolt of insight, directed to the heart of my confusion, and I thought, *I can't believe this; it's bizarre.* I went in and told Jo Nell, "You're not going to believe this."

Now she's been a Christian a long time. She looked at me, shrugged her shoulders, and said, "That's grace!" But I, in that instant, realized, as I never had before, just how much God loves me. That He knows when I'm struggling, and what I'm struggling with. *He knows what book I'm reading and what page I'm on.* It was one of the most awesome times of growth—it caused a great surge of growth in me in terms of trust, in terms of understanding and savoring God's love. I still love to think about it today: God interacting with me on the most intimate, mundane level.

Many people feel that God is, at best, involved in their lives from a distance. However, God is always approachable; He cares about every moment of our existence no matter what we are doing.

Why, then, do we use God like an insurance policy? When all else fails we cry out for His help. Perhaps we feel that, yes, He knows about us but that He is too busy to be involved or care much about our insignificant concerns. This could not be farther from the truth. God knows each of us individually and He sees us as individuals. He sees each of us as a wonderful, unique creation, and He knew us before our lives began.

> Before I formed you in the womb
> I knew you, before you were born I set you apart.[9]

God's grace is His love for us *in action.* Yet so often even Christians see the things that happen to them as mere serendipity. Stop for just a moment and reflect on your own life. How often have you narrowly escaped something harmful or even tragic, and how often have you almost missed something wonderful? Do you recognize these things not as luck, but grace? If we were more aware we would often see that God's hand has been upon the situation through its entirety. He is involved and responsive. Every time something happens, He is there loving us.

God Has Feelings (Distortion = a God Who Can't Relate)

Many of us assume—though we might not consciously admit it—that God is "bigger" than feelings. So we stay closed up to Him, unable to share our deepest feelings with the One who seeks our most intimate communion.

The old theological doctrine of God's "impassibility" (He is not moved by feelings) may need to be rethought. Surely God experiences sorrow, anger, grief, joy. Surely He is touched by our infirmities, pained by our world's evil. In His Son He experienced the full range of human feeling, suffering, and even death.

Abandonment is usually the culprit when we experience God as feelingless. It is hard to trust God if we're putting Him on a scale with an earthly parent who was emotionally or physically absent. Our feelings aren't reflected back to us then, and the "mirroring" of emotions is crucial in helping a child form his identity.

> Children need mirroring and echoing. These come from their primary caretaker's eyes. Mirroring means that someone is there for them and reflects who they really are at any given moment of time. . . . Abandonment includes the loss of mirroring [and] remains important all our lives.[10]

When Mom or Dad is absent at a time when those mirroring eyes are so crucial, a child will still crave the sense of blessedness no matter how old he is. Like the biblical Esau, who wailed "Bless me—me too, my father!" the abandoned child continues to cry out in his lifelong search—for an earthly nurturer . . . and a heavenly one.

The Nobel Peace Prize winner of 1986, Elie Wiesel, was sent to a Nazi concentration camp when he was only sixteen years old. Though he survived with two of his sisters, his mother, father, and youngest sister died in the camps. Wiesel has spent a lifetime "doing theology" related to the struggles of war prisoners, trying to make sense of the God who allows suffering. He tells this story in a BBC interview,[11] about something he witnessed in the camps: Three pious and learned Jewish men came to their wits' end with the months of suffering and starvation. They had watched so many of their fellow countrymen waste away and die—but they had doggedly held to their faith in the goodness of God. However, they were now coming to question what kind of God they worshiped.

One of the men stood up in the middle of the barracks and said something like: "Let us put God to the test, put Him on trial for His sins. Let us see how He will defend Himself for all this suffering!" A great debate raged. And they did put God on trial, for three long days. When it was over, the verdict was given: "Guilty!" And then, the men met briefly again and agreed with one another: "It is now time to go back to our daily prayers." They would stay in relationship with their God, even a "guilty" God.

But Wiesel adds another comment to the story. He says that he would like to write a play someday about this trial of God. But he would introduce a new character—one who defends God. "He would be the only one who takes God's side," says Wiesel, "the only one who says that God's ways are justified, even in Auschwitz. . . . And I would say that that character is Satan." For there is nothing worse than to ignore God, assuming that He does not care, that He does not feel what we feel and grieve with us. "For a Jew to believe in God is good. For a Jew to protest against God is good. But indifference to God? No. You can be a Jew *with* God or *against* God," says Wiesel, "but not *without* God."

Our calling is to *be in relationship* with God—a God who understands us and knows our sufferings. We are thus called to love God.

And we are allowed even to hate God.

But to ignore God is abominable, for it cuts off the relationship completely.

Several years ago my wife Jo Nell and I were working out in the yard and she hurt her back pulling up a weed. She continued to have minor problems with it until about a month later—she bent over and herniated a disc . . . and couldn't straighten back up.

We went to a neurosurgeon friend of mine, who tried to treat her conservatively with bed rest and anti-inflamatory medications. But she began losing the function of her leg and, even after the required surgery, continued to have problems walking. She developed a foot drop—a condition that occurs when the nerve from the back controlling the foot is damaged. Compensating with the good leg made her walk strangely. And she had constant pain.

Needless to say, Jo Nell began to get down about this. She couldn't do the things she used to do and as a young woman, she began to feel old and useless. I had to take over a lot of the chores around the house. She slowly slipped into a depression, wondering: *How could God let this happen to me?*

She discussed this with a wise friend of ours, who asked her: "Have you told God about this?"

"Well, to tell the truth, I didn't feel comfortable admitting to God that I was angry at Him about all of this."

"Do you think you could tell Him anything that He doesn't already know?"

Jo Nell immediately had what we call in our household a "lightbulb reaction," a sudden moment of spiritual insight. Shortly thereafter, she was driving one day in the car and tearfully screamed out her anger at God. The business was finished after that. Her anger was released, her depression lifted.

"Looking back, I can see that the experience has made me a stronger person," she says. "But more than that, the recognition that God can handle any of my feelings—all of them— has added so much to my walk with Him."

The deepest sense of God's love often comes to us as we bare our aching souls to Him. In this case, God seemed to say, "Jo Nell, it does not matter how you are feeling when you come to Me. I know the feelings you have; I feel them too. And *your passion for this relationship pleases Me.* I will love you unconditionally." To approach God in anger, with our deep need laid open, is to engage in an appropriate form of divine-human contention.

So Jacob was left alone, and a man wrestled with him till daybreak. When the man saw that he could not overpower him, he touched the socket of Jacob's hip so that his hip was wrenched as he wrestled with the man. Then the man said, "Let me go, for it is daybreak." But Jacob replied, "I will not let you go unless you bless me."[12]

God Enjoys Our Joy (Distortion = God, the Celestial Killjoy)
I saw a cartoon that showed Moses speaking, just returned from Mt. Sinai with the stone tablets of the Ten Commandments in his hands. He's reporting to his people about his encounter with God on the mountaintop:

"It was hard bargaining—we get the milk and honey,
but the anti-adultery clause stays in."

But must a life of faith be a series of hard-bargaining rounds, as this cartoonist believes? It's true that some things are clearly wrong and a number of "anti" clauses must stay put (the real Moses would never have questioned that!). Yet some people view God as quite disappointed when His creatures seem to be having a little fun.

That's a contrast to my sense of who God is. For example, I've been surprised to find out how much joy flows from the pages of Scripture—pure fun: singing, dancing, shouting, playing, making music. Surely God smiles at our joy. He built it into us, and it will flow out from us, spontaneously, if we can just remove the barriers of fear and worry. Perhaps it would help if we could begin to view His commands as simply an invitation to live a happier life.

Loving God Is an End in Itself

Perhaps we stay closed up to God because we assume we need a "reason" to love God. We wait for it; and when it doesn't come, according to our preconceived formulas, we give up on the idea.

One thing that can help is to consider the marriage and human-love imagery in the Bible. Read through the Song of Songs, for instance.

How beautiful you are, my darling!
Oh, how beautiful! Your eyes behind your veil are doves.
Your hair is like a flock of goats descending from Mount Gilead.
Your teeth are like a flock of sheep just shorn,
    coming up from the washing.
Each has its twin; not one of them is alone.

Your lips are like a scarlet ribbon; your mouth is lovely.
Your temples behind your veil
    are like the halves of a pomegranate.
Your neck is like the tower of David,
        built with elegance; on it hang a thousand shields,
        all of them shields of warriors.
Your two breasts are like two fawns,
        like twin fawns of a gazelle that browse among the lilies.
Until the day breaks and the shadows flee,
I will go to the mountain of myrrh
    and to the hill of incense.
All beautiful you are, my darling;
    there is no flaw in you.[13]

Speaking of our divine love affair, Sallie McFague writes in *Models of God:*

Beyond fear of judgment and punishment for sins, and beyond relief and gratitude for forgiveness, lies loving God for God's own sake because God is God, attractive, valuable, lovely beyond all knowing, all imagining.[14]

Fellowship with God, then, can never be pursued as a means to some other end. If we have set our sights on something else, no matter how good and worthy that thing might be, then God ceases to be the object of our desire. To seek a "reason" for intimacy with God in something else is, for all practical purposes, a denial of intimacy with God. To open our love receptors to Him means taking a step of trust—to trust that God's love for us, and our love for Him are just *there.* Because that is the way God is.

Because God is . . . love.

❑   ❑   ❑

Time Out

Reflections on My Experience with God

We do have an intellectual relationship with God—the things we think about Him. But we also *experience* God. Sometimes these two aspects of the relationship are quite disconnected. A little reflection can help.

Reflection questions . . .

❑ What times in my life so far would I label as the most "sacred" times? How did I experience God during those times?

❑ What themes emerge from those sacred experiences? What insights about my unique relationship with God—how He works with me? calls me? guides me?

❑ How could my insights about my experience with God influence my thoughts about God?

❑ How could these reflections transform the way I will relate to God in the future? What my expectations will be? How I will pray? How I will seek guidance?

❑   ❑   ❑

Step 5: "Be" (Practicing the Presence)

The next step brings a deeper spiritual dimension to the journey. Rather than launching into action at the first sign of healing, perhaps it would be good to take some time out—to learn to "be" in God's presence. After all, we cannot program our journey into love. Whatever good happens in our lives will be a work of divine grace. It will come to us as we put ourselves in the place where we can be blessed. Therefore, we may need to rediscover a lost art that has always been at the heart of true spirituality: the ability to embrace quietness, solitude, and meditation.

> It is a sad commentary on the spiritual state of modern Christianity that meditation is a word so foreign to its ears. Meditation has always stood as a classical and central part of Christian devotion, a crucial preparation for and adjunct to the work of prayer. No doubt part of the surge of interest in Eastern meditation is because the churches have abrogated the field. . . . Let us have the courage to side with the biblical tradition and once again learn the ancient (and yet contemporary) art of meditation. May we join with the psalmist and declare, "As for me, I will meditate on thy precepts" (Ps. 119:78).[15]

How will you respond to this call, so eloquently stated by Richard Foster? No one can prescribe, in specific terms, how you should approach this goal of learning to be with the Lord. God relates to us all in a very personal and unique relationship, and meditation is just one way we experience the holiness and love of God. However, here are some suggestions as you test what may be new waters for you.

Enjoy Being the Object of God's Delight. In learning to be with God, we come just as we are, not defended, not cleaned up. All of our feelings toward

Him we bring before Him, all of our longings, fears, joys, and griefs. We do this when we begin to recognize that He wants us for no other reason than to love us. It will take time to know and believe that God has no other motive. If there is indeed a service for us to perform on His behalf, or a command to obey, it will only be done in sincerity when it flows from a heart already secure in perfect acceptance. Since He is more interested in the condition of our hearts than in our accomplishments, even serving God is a privilege given to us out of love. For who could suggest that God might somehow need our help?

We often feel that we are wanted for some other reason, as though God is a nagging spouse who only wants something from us. James Dittes points out how disheartening this can be in a human relationship.

He recalled his wife's response when he had impulsively called her the other day from the office just for a midday chat and telephone hug. Her response, an eager and delighted "I'm so glad you called," had given him just what he had wanted, and had lifted his soul. But immediately the rest of her sentence had crumbled it. Why was she glad he called? "If you would bring some milk on the way home, it would save me a trip out . . . I didn't want to call you, but. . . ."

She wants him in her life! What he most craves: Wants! Him!

She wants him as chore boy—what he most hears. Be a quietly useful, on-call problem solver, the good Scout, the good boy. . . .[16]

God does not seek us to make us into mere chore boys. No human being is burdened with divine ulterior motives. The motive is the same for all of us: to save us, to make us whole, to live in fellowship with us forever. We may well distinguish between the "saved" and the "unsaved"; however, from God's perspective we are all being pursued with the same, unconditional love.

Where can I go from Your Spirit?
Where can I flee from Your presence? . . .
If I rise on the wings of the dawn,
    if I settle on the far side of the sea.[17]

The primary characteristic of God's love is its unchangeableness. When we are unable to feel God's love, it is we who have changed and moved away from Him. Nevertheless, He continues to love us. There is nothing we can do to change that. This is agape love, an unconditional, ever-present love. We can simply enjoy being its object.

"What do you do during the day?" a friend asked an elderly Scottch woman who lived alone. "Well," she said, "I get my hymn book and sing. Then I read the Psalms, meditating on God's greatness. When I get tired of reading and cannot sing anymore, I just sit still and let the Lord love me!"[18]

Savor the Agenda-less Moment. It seems a reasonable idea that we must keep ourselves constantly on the go. Think about the anxiety that wells up in most of us when we either decide, or are forced, to do nothing at all, to have no agenda. How long can we stand it?

In the International Trans-Antarctica Expedition, six men, each from a different nation, started out in July of 1989 to trek across Antarctica by foot, dogsled, and skis. This was the first human attempt to do so without vehicles. For over 200 days the men braved the most severe weather known, including constant howling winds and temperatures reaching below -40° F. Eventually they completed a 3,741-mile route.

One of the adventurers was Japanese representative Keizo Funatsu. On the 218th day of the expedition, in a horrendous blizzard, Funatsu walked out a few feet from his tent to feed his dog team. He became disoriented in blowing snow and, after wandering 300 feet from the tent, could not find his way back. Eventually he lay down to await discovery, becoming completely buried by snow in a matter of minutes. Carving out room to breathe, he waited for his searching friends to find him. Later, he wrote in his journal:

> When I was in my snow ditch I tried to enjoy the opportunity. . . . I thought to myself, "Very few people have this kind of experience, lost in the blizzard; settle down, try and enjoy this." . . . With the snow and quiet covering me, I felt like I was in my mother's womb. I could hear my heart beat—boom . . . boom . . . boom—like a small baby. My life seemed very small in comparison to nature, to Antarctica.[19]

For thirteen silent hours, Funatsu understood that to do *anything* would have been fatal for him. He must simply be, not do.

Few of us have been buried alive in a snowy grave. Yet we can learn from the experience of one who has. For we have countless opportunities "simply to be," if we will take them; we need not wait for the drastic blessing of a forced entombment.

The benefit of just being, rather than constantly doing, is that it allows us to engage in what the Middle Ages monk Brother Lawrence called, "practicing the presence." The Lord of the universe is present with us at all times. But how often are we present to Him?

Opening ourselves to the reality of God's constant presence requires a readiness to lay down all the "important" things we have to do and to think about. Some of us can only handle short periods of pure presence. It is a process of attention that must be developed over time, as Brother Lawrence said:

I worshiped him as often as I could, keeping my mind in his holy presence and recalling it back to God as often as I found it had wandered from him. . . . And yet, I must tell you that for the first ten years I suffered a great deal.[20]

This "holy inactivity" may mean moving back from your work desk for a moment just to say, "Now I am with You, Lord" . . . and staying that way for as long as His presence can be "tolerated." Others may carve out a bit of time to sit on the porch stoop and just be in God's loving arms for a few moments. Still others will take a brief walk with no particular destination, consciously knowing that Jesus is with them.

Our agenda-less moments are sacred spaces because the one who dwells in us has the agenda already planned. It is not primarily a plan of action (for when it is time for action, if we are open, He will produce through us all that needs doing). Rather, it is a way of revealing to us the thing we keep so buried in all our activity: the whispered truth, "I am so close; and I am in love with you." Do you hear it?

Listen for the Lord. Rarely do we receive a bonfire sermon, blazing direct from the gates of glory. Rather, we must learn how to "see" God in the tiny dots of light scattered into our days. Henri Nouwen speaks of the spiritual life not as our search for God—for God is always seeking us—but rather as the steady attempt to take up a stable address where God can find us. We must learn to be still and listen, to be "home" so that someone's there to hear and to answer when Jesus knocks.

God's voice often comes through our intuition, His still, small voice within us. It is a sound that can't quite be explained with our rational minds. Yet it is a sense of "rightness" when we have made a decision, a quality of conviction when we have sought the truth, a sense that something "feels like it fits," though we can't prove it. A deep and gentle tugging.

Intuition may carry emotions with it, but ultimately it supersedes emotion. It is an internal suggestion, a veiled hint that comes through people, events, books, or art. And God compounds the message in various ways, not just once.

What is the key to hearing this voice? We can let our prayer lives move off center. We can try being with God for a quarter of an hour, waiting in silence. We can learn divine listening, attending to people, events, and circumstances for the words of wisdom they may whisper. In our retreats to quiet, we can begin to name the things that seem to be saying yes and no to us. We can remain open to the possibility that within them is God's voice, for, as A.W. Tozer said, "Whoever will listen will hear the speaking Heaven." He went on to say:

This is definitely not the hour when men take kindly to an exhortation to *listen,* for listening is not today a part of popular religion.

We are at the opposite end of the pole from there. Religion has accepted the monstrous heresy that noise, size, activity and bluster make a man dear to God. But we may take heart. To a people caught in the tempest of the last great conflict God says, "Be still, and know that I am God," and still He says it, as if He means to tell us that our strength and safety lie not in noise but in silence.[21]

❑   ❑   ❑

How Jesus Listened to His Father

Just looking through the Gospel of John, we find numerous examples of Jesus staying close to His Father, constantly "listening" for guidance and encouragement.

❑ Jesus gave them this answer: "I tell you the truth, the Son can do nothing by Himself; He can do only what He sees His Father doing, because whatever the Father does the Son also does. For the Father loves the Son and shows Him all He does. Yes, to your amazement He will show Him even greater things than these. . . . By Myself I can do nothing; I judge only as I hear, and My judgment is just, for I seek not to please Myself but Him who sent Me."—John 5:19-20, 30

❑ Jesus answered, "My teaching is not My own. It comes from Him who sent Me. If anyone chooses to do God's will, he will find out whether My teaching comes from God or whether I speak on My own. He who speaks on his own does so to gain honor for himself, but he who works for the honor of the One who sent him is a man of truth; there is nothing false about him."—John 7:16-18

❑ But if I do judge, My decisions are right, because I am not alone. I stand with the Father who sent Me.—John 8:16

❑ I am the good shepherd; I know My sheep and My sheep know Me—just as the Father knows Me and I know the Father—and I lay down My life for the sheep.—John 10:14-15

❑ Do not believe Me unless I do what my Father does. But if I do it, even though you do not believe Me, believe the miracles, that you may learn and understand that the Father is in Me, and I in the Father.—John 10:37-38

❑ For I did not speak of My own accord, but the Father who sent Me commanded Me what to say and how to say it. I know that His command leads to eternal life. So whatever I say is just what the Father has told Me to say.—John 12:49-50

❑   ❑   ❑

Envision His Reality. Here we speak of the legitimate use of imagery in our prayers. What is in your mind when you approach the Lord? I [Brian] once envisioned myself approaching the throne of God, walking up on Christ and God conversing, and they were saying, "Hey, We were just talking about you. Come on in." That imagery encouraged me to begin seeing prayer as an inviting, positive thing, rather than a chore. I began having a visually personable understanding and connection with God. My prayers no longer seemed just to go up somewhere with nothing in my heart that I was connected to.

About this time, I began praying with another image in mind. It actually came from the old Peter Pan play, where Peter had a shadow that was a black, kind of mesh cutout that Wendy had to sew back on because Peter Pan had lost his shadow. The shadow symbolized for me the Holy Spirit, who is whispering in Christ's ears the prayers that are too deep for groaning while He is constantly interceding on my behalf to the Father. Does this sound silly to you? I share it only to say that when we do start to have intimacy with God, our mental imagery becomes important.

For me [Joe], the reality of God comes through to me as "Abba, Daddy." I can go sit right on God's lap at any time in my day. I'm one of His kids, and I can come right to the throne and just be. He says, "Come on. Sit up here and talk to Me. I'm interested in you. I love you, son."

Paul tells us in Ephesians 2 that we are seated in the heavenlies with Christ right now. And so, being "up there" already, I can just go and talk to my Dad. The mental imagery of God wanting to spend time with me—the creator of the universe saying, "Joseph, come here. You're special; you're important," is so powerful for me.

❑   ❑   ❑

Time Out

Christian Meditation

Some people question the use of meditation, seeing a similarity to the practice espoused by Eastern religions. However, we can clearly distinguish between the two types. In other religions, such as Buddhism and Hinduism, the purpose of meditation is to still the mind in order to empty it of all content. One goal is to divorce oneself from mental concepts in order, presumably, to achieve direct contact with reality. Other goals involve ridding oneself of ego-desire as a means of merging with the World Soul or emptying into the Great Void. Ultimately, Eastern meditation is meant to bring the experience of enlightenment, or *satori*—the sudden recognition that we are one with all things, including God (in effect, that we *are* God).

How different is the biblical purpose of meditation! Here we do indeed calm ourselves, becoming quiet in God's presence. But any "emptying" is *for the distinct purpose of filling up*—with God's Spirit, truth, guidance, and love.

There are numerous ways to approach meditation. But one way to start is by linking times of silent reflection to Scripture reading. For example, after a few minutes of relaxing your muscles and calming your mind, take any passage of Scripture that has some sense of "place" to it, and put yourself into the scene. Be on the shore with Jesus, or at the mountaintop with Moses. Perhaps you could start with the beautiful images in Psalm 23. After each phrase, let the words and images of this biblical poetry sink into your being (see the italicized suggestions; picture them; add your own). Pause frequently and let God speak through His Word.

> The LORD is my shepherd, I shall not be in want. *(I am a lamb held in the arms of the Shepherd just now . . .)*

> He makes me lie down in green pastures, He leads me beside quiet waters, *(I am at rest in a sunny meadow of calm and peace with You, Lord . . .)*

> He restores my soul. He guides me in paths of righteousness for His name's sake. *(I bask in this sense of restoration, strength, goodness, and divine care . . .)*

> Even though I walk through the valley of the shadow of death, I will fear no evil, for You are with me; Your rod and Your staff, they comfort me. *(Jesus is here with me now; His hands are on my shoulders . . . I am comforted by His closeness. . . . All my problems and fears are His now. He is bigger than they are.)*

> You prepare a table before me in the presence of my enemies. You anoint my head with oil; my cup overflows. *(Soothing, healing oil flows down over me . . . from the Lord.)*

> Surely goodness and love will follow me all the days of my life, and I will dwell in the house of the Lord forever. *(I am surrounded by warm, bright light . . . in God's loving presence . . . in His house. I sit*

still . . . and know that He is God. And that He loves me.)

For specific examples of guided meditations for use in prayer, see Eddie Ensley, *Prayer That Heals Our Emotions* (San Francisco: Harper & Row, 1988). Ensley writes:

> When we open our hearts wide to God's caring, the deeper roots of our nature find the permanent soil of an infinite love. We find in the cellars of our souls an ocean of infinite rest that gives meaning to our seemingly endless activities. There is a place within where the sea is always calm and the boats are steady, and Christian meditation takes our awareness to that place. The Kingdom of God, Jesus said, is within us .[22]

Step 6: "Give" (Offering Praise)

In so many of the old, epic movie scenes, you see it: The servant enters and walks down the marble-columned hall to the steps of the throne. He stops in front of the august personage and slowly bends at the waist, letting his body display the state of his heart. He bows low and stays that way for many moments. Here is complete servanthood, loving respect, and even a healthy fear for Pharaoh, or Caesar, or King Henry.

There is something to be said for the healing power of such worship. The "good life" surely must include a recognition that my many blessings have not come to me merely as a result of my innate brilliance or ingenious planning. Life does not work that way; in fact, perhaps the whole meaning of our lives revolves around our response to this heaven-sent invitation: to perfect the art of praise. Both our blessings and our crises summon us to bow before a sovereignty that (we secretly know) commands recognition as the ground of our very existence.

> God, who has made us, knows what we are and that our happiness lies in him. Yet we will not seek it in him as long as he leaves us any other resort where it can even plausibly be looked for. While what we call "our own life" remains agreeable we will not surrender it to him.[23]

It is good, then, to take time for worship in our days. In moments of stillness, we can focus our minds and bow our bodies to the honor of the only Being that deserves our reverent adoration. When we get distracted from that essential purpose, no doubt God notices—

> You gave Me no kiss . . .
> You did not anoint My head with oil. . . .
>
> —Jesus

Consider the story of the woman at the well in this regard. It doesn't matter how strong we are or how close to God we feel, we know that throughout our lives we must continually go back to the well of Christ to quench our thirst for love and spiritual life. All of us continue going to the wrong wells to find the water of life. We get caught up in our sinfulness and our foolishness. We grasp for the next thing we think will satisfy us. These things, when all is said and done, often leave us more empty than before. For now we need something else, something bigger, better, more exciting. Without worship, we are caught in the web of our own tiny longings and preplanned fulfillments. With our eyes turned inward, we miss out on the glories of God and His creation.

> Glory be to God for dappled things. . . .
> All things counter, original, spare, strange;
> Whatever is fickle, freckled (who knows how?)
> With swift, slow; sweet, sour; adazzle, dim;
> He fathers-forth whose beauty is past change:
> Praise him.[24]

Recall the old joke about the man whose wife complained that he never told her that he loved her. He says to her, "Well, I told you on our wedding day that I loved you, and if that ever changes, I'll let you know." Do we sometimes treat our God that way? "God, I accept You, and if that ever changes, and I don't accept You anymore, I'll let You know. In the meantime, let's live our separate lives." Yet when we worship, we are lifted with love. And the blessed paradox operates: in giving praise, we receive so much more in return.

But Is It Real for You?

Nathanael West's satirical story *Miss Lonelyhearts*[25] tells about the writer of an advice-to-the-lovelorn column. The writer is actually a man, a minister's son, who has left behind his childhood faith. Each day he reads a pile of letters that spill out human pain and misery. He hears the laments of hurting people through this correspondence—sickness, divorce, lost jobs, and lost loves. Frustrated and frightened people, all trying to survive life's daily perils, open their hearts to him with their deepest secrets.

Miss Lonelyhearts finally determines to stop reading these letters. He just can't go on. He realizes that "Christ is the answer," the only one who can bring healing to these letter writers. But he feels that he ought to steer clear of what he refers to as "the Christ business."

Yet the burden is too much. Miss Lonelyhearts becomes ill, but senses that his view of faith has something to do with his sickness. Recalling his boyhood in his father's church, he remembers that when he affirmed the name of Jesus Christ, he knew a power within himself.

At this point, Nathanael West interjects a memorable line, offering his understanding of Miss Lonelyhearts' sickness: "He had played with this [Jesus] thing, but had never allowed it to come alive."

Have you allowed Jesus to come alive in your life? Or, have you merely "played with this thing"?

Start Where You Are

There is a sense in which we, as love-seeking humans, are like the colanders sitting in our kitchen cabinets. When we begin receiving love, becoming filled with it, we begin to leak it out. We go to the well of Christ, we become filled, and His goodness flows out of us to others. Overflowing with love, we can bring love to other people, be it our children or our spouses, our friends or neighbors. The process starts with our decision this very moment to take the next step.

And no preparation is needed for the next step, other than to take it. Everything we've been talking about in this chapter (and the previous one) takes place in the routine of daily living, with each small step we choose to take—with each decision to reveal, to unblock, to be, to receive, and to give. As popular writer Thomas Moore says in *The Care of Souls,* "Spirituality is seeded, germinates, sprouts, and blossoms in the mundane. It is to be found and nurtured in the smallest of daily activities."[26] What one activity or attitude could become for you, today, a seedbed of spiritual growth?

Choosing Self-Nurture

Self is hateful.

—Blaise Pascal

God does not merely confirm worth; He creates it.
Shall we then not love what God Himself
has created and made valuable?

—Unknown

As we learn to let God love us (and begin loving Him), we can also turn our attention to the other directions the stream of love can flow in our lives: our love toward ourselves and our love toward our fellow human beings.

We want this love in our lives, but love takes work. I think one of the best explanations of this fact shines through in the definition of love offered by Dr. M. Scott Peck, in his book *The Road Less Traveled.*

> [Love is] a form of work or a form of courage. Specifically, it is work or courage directed toward the nurture of our own or another's spiritual growth. We may work or exert courage in directions other than toward spiritual growth, and for this reason all work and all courage is not love. But since it requires the extension of ourselves, love is always either work or courage. If an act is not one of work or courage, then it is not an act of love. There are no exceptions.[1]

Love, then, is an *active process* requiring our own action and energy.

How often I have wished to wait passively for something to happen, wondering why there was such loneliness in my life, not realizing that receiving love and loving others would require an act of risky courage. The Apostle John said it best when he proclaimed, "Little children, let us not love in word or speech but in deed and in truth."

The Call to Active Loving

Love is clearly a call to action; it is about work—whether we are loving ourselves, loving others, or hoping to receive another's love. We will focus on actively loving others in the next chapter. But for now let's explore the concept of self-nurture a little further.

Love and self-nurturing go hand in hand. Most of us, throughout our childhood and adult lives, have been caring for others and have rarely been encouraged to care for and love ourselves. Later on we enter relationships expecting our deepest needs to be met by someone else. This is what "true love" would feel like for us: linking up with a super-attentive-affectionate personal love-giver, endowed with the perpetual capacity to meet our every need. Especially when we're the most needy. Comedian Jerry Seinfeld satirized the idea, though it hits many of us close to home:

> For me, the best part of a relationship is when you're sick. And the best time to be sick is in a relationship. If I have to get married, you know all those vows, "For richer or for poorer, for better or for worse" . . . all I need is the sickness part. That to me is the most important one. "Do you take this man in sickness?"
>
> The rest of the time go out, have a ball, do whatever you want—but if I get the sniffles, you'd better be there.[2]

Of course, it is impossible to find anyone who will meet our every need, even in marriage. Our spouse may be just as needy and have the same expectations of us. And instead of fulfilling our dream of finally receiving love and nurturing, we end up locked in a nightmarish cycle of escalating demands: "You *must* love me more than this!"

Actively Loving Ourselves

A better way is to form the habit of inner listening. Some have called the process "focusing," or "centering," but it simply means taking the time to regularly identify our true needs. It sounds simple, but it is a radical undertaking for which very few have the courage. To do it well, we must incorporate times of solitude, or some form of personal space, to listen for the clamoring hungers inside us. We have spoken of just "being" with God; we must learn to be with ourselves, as well. Over time, our childlike inner voice begins to whisper: *This is how I need, this is what I want, this is where*

I hurt, this is what I yearn for, this is the grief I've held for so long.

At first these "spoken" needs of our hearts will sound foreign to us. For we so rarely listen for them; we have so infrequently unmuzzled that voice of the truth-of-our-lives, which only timidly speaks up when given the opportunity. Yet, over time, we can become familiar with what it tells us about who we really are. And we can begin recognizing for ourselves the ways to pursue our own nurture with gentle self-care. Somehow we have come to see our own neediness as either weakness or selfishness. But we all have needs. To identify and meet them is the beginning of self-care. Consider these five suggestions as possible self-nurture starting points.

Honor Your Deepest Longings. Christian apologist C.S. Lewis spoke of *sensucht*, or "sweet longing," referring to our great, unquenchable desire for "something more" in our lives. We plan a vacation imagining how it will refresh us and renew our vitality for work. We look forward to it with great relish. When we do finally walk the beaches, climb the mountains, sit all afternoon in the hot tub, we find that the vacation does fulfill its promise— but only for a while. Too soon we must return to our real world, and soon enough the mundane breaks through and thrusts us back to reality . . . and our longing for the next vacation.

Or we seek a "special someone" to love and be loved by. We envision the relationship healing our old wounds of rejection and self-doubt. And the romance of it does do those things for us—until we become used to one another. We pull back and recognize that not even *this* longed-for relationship will bring us lasting, unbroken contentment. We do have our periods of joy, of course, but not a solid, settled happiness-for-good. As Lewis put it: "Our Father refreshes us on the journey with some pleasant inns, but will not encourage us to mistake them for home."

What shall we do, then, with this God-given, built-in longing? To honor it means to accept it as a part of our lives that will not be completely satisfied until we are Home. To reject it is to find ways to dull its pain. We do so with actions that are quite unkind to ourselves, from harboring bitterness, to overworking, to indulging in crude forms of escape.

A crucial aspect of loving ourselves is to refuse to close off the part of us that yearns for security and satisfaction. It is to let the *sensucht* draw us gradually, joyfully, and painfully, to its sweet Source, the Lover who makes us complete. When we fall into addictive or compulsive behavior (when the closing off occurs), when love's call becomes too painful, we can gently remind ourselves that we are not Home yet. This is not the best of all worlds.

Recognize That Nothing Needs to Change. Change is the purpose of our quest, but we need not change a thing to begin loving ourselves better. Brian and I have a friend who, when he was a teenager, started feeling lumps in his body. He was sure he had some form of cancer, since his father had been taken from him a few years earlier with that dread disease. "I remember going to our family physician and finally getting up the courage to show him what I thought were deadly testicular lumps, and he assured me everything was normal. Yet I remained convinced for several years afterward that my life would be a very short one, just like Dad's."

Some of us do tend to go around with a picture of ourselves as flawed. It's as if a giant X-ray machine were attached to our bodies, scanning the self and continually finding parts that should be surgically removed. And the belief is this: I will never be happy until I get rid of my "unacceptable" symptoms, feelings, compulsions, or bodily attributes. That feeling of something wrong gets ingrained in our psyches far too early in our lives.

The happy alternative is to embrace the whole ME. I have made a part of me my enemy and sought to destroy it, but now that part does not have to go away for me to embrace self-acceptance. It may be a "symptom" or "nerves" that I demand to heal. Yet this "it," which is me, does not have to disappear for me to get on with life's adventure.

There is not a fight by me against IT. This is me—all the parts. No part needs to be cut off or shamed or rejected. Each part is to be honored. If it is truly a bad, or sinful part, then love will find a way to transform it. Again, the change I seek is a growth in love with God and others. But I embark on the journey "Just as I Am."

Make Mistakes without Shame. Thinking about all those mistakes today? Rather than wallow in guilt, probably the best thing we can do now is to reframe our mistakes.[3] Guilt keeps our minds focused on the original error and so compounds that error, over and over again, perhaps for an entire lifetime of self-shaming. Self-love becomes virtually impossible.

Reframing mistakes means determining to view them in ways that dissolve their devastating characteristics. Instead of seeing them as terrible disasters, we begin to view them as normal and natural results of our courage to make decisions and take risks. We realize that we can and will make mistakes, but we refuse to allow them to call into judgment our personal self-worth. In other words, we reject the shame that can attach to mistake-making.

A mistake can serve as a welcome call to slow down and look more closely at the direction we're traveling. What adjustments can I make? How can I avoid this in the future? What shall I do now to rectify the matter as a responsible human being? My mistake need not grow into a moral frame-up in the court of personal self-condemnation. Like any other human experience, I can invite a mistake to become my teacher.

Set Personal Boundaries. Someone has said, "There is no such thing as a well-adjusted slave." If that is true, then loving and nurturing ourselves means determining to be our own persons. What does that require? First, it means *learning to say no.* Years ago a book was published with the title *When I Say "No" I Feel Guilty.*[4] It sold well because it examined a virtually universal experience: the fear of setting personal boundaries in our relationships by simply speaking clearly and directly. Think of all the requests made of you during a typical day. How many of them should rightfully be turned away in the interests of your duty to care for yourself?

❑ "Will you please fill in at the finance meeting tonight at church?" *Yes!* (Boy, am I angry for having to miss Billy's soccer game on such short notice!)

❑ "I'm afraid we're going to have to charge you for a new cable." *Oh, all right.* (But you broke it yourself! If you ask me, you ought to replace it free of charge.)

❑ Realtor, over the phone: "Oh, and would you mind describing your ethnic identity for me?" *OK.* (Now what in the world does that have to do with house hunting?)

❑ "I'd love to go out with you. How 'bout it?" *Sure!* (This guy sure gives me the creeps.)

We wear ourselves down with the frustration and anger of the dishonest yes. In cases like this, and countless others, how could we love ourselves better? By setting boundaries with a simple declaration: "No."

Second, setting boundaries means *refusing to be a victim.* Dr. Wayne Dyer, in *Pulling Your Own Strings,* presents some of the ways we actually "ask" to be victimized. We do it with words or phrases that swirl around in our private thoughts or crop up in our speech.

❑ I know I'm going to lose.
❑ I get upset whenever I have to confront someone.
❑ The little guy never has a chance.
❑ I'll show those guys that they can't dump on me.
❑ I hope they won't get mad at me for asking.
❑ They'll probably think I'm stupid if I tell them what I did.
❑ I'm afraid I'll hurt their feelings if I do what I want.
❑ I can't handle this alone: I'll get someone who isn't afraid to do it for me.
❑ They really shouldn't do this; it's not fair.[5]

How many of these self-victimizations sound familiar to you? Self-nurture calls us to confront the false realities we have engineered, even in our own minds. We can change those self-victimizing mind-tapes. The fact is,

I may win, after all.
I can confront without "losing it."
Sometimes even I (the little guy) make out pretty well.
It never hurts to ask.
Everybody does silly things once in a while.
People actually expect me to do what I want.
I can attempt to handle this alone.
True, sometimes life isn't fair. I don't expect it to be.

Third, we must begin to *say what we want*. No one can argue with a clear statement of "I want _____." Certainly, someone can deny giving us the thing we want, but he cannot level the charge that merely wanting something is inappropriate. A want simply is. It is a state of being, not an argument, not even a request. It is a report of our personal condition at the moment: "Something feels missing inside me right now." Who could argue with that kind of report?

If someone should say: "But you really shouldn't want *that!*" we can simply acknowledge that we are not yet at the stage of evaluating the rightness or wrongness of our wanting. We can always decide to move on in the process to that stage, and we may even invite a friend along for the ride. But for now, the initial step is to be able to report, in fact, that I *do* want *that*.

Consider how this form of self-nurture might revolutionize our prayers as a more honest approach to God. Suppose Ralph, a Christian, desires to indulge in pornography. Further suppose that, as soon as he felt this desire within him, he turned to prayer. What should he say to God? Should he say: "Lord, You know that I don't want to do this"—when, in fact, he very definitely *does* want to do it?

What might happen with a more honest owning of his true desires? Suppose Ralph admitted: "Lord, more than anything else, in this moment, I want to look at pictures of naked women." Would that be shocking news to the Lord?

Yet it's true that Ralph has deeper desires even than that. He wishes, for example, to be a dedicated disciple of Jesus. He wants his life to be an example of Christ's love and purity. He wants to be faithful to his wife, even in his thoughts. All of these sincere desires, though, have been pushed to the back of his consciousness in this moment of intense wanting. So as the lust of the moment crashes in, will he be helped by trying to hide his want from himself and his Lord? Or by trying to fight it (the "fight"—willpower—being the fuel that addiction feeds on)?

Actually, his chances of avoiding the victimization of temptation and addiction are improved with his decision to say what he wants, even to God, in all candor. For when all is out in the open, he may well recognize what a poor substitute for real life is the momentary fantasy he feels tugging at him. To bundle up those desires and push them down, time after time, means they will likely flood out in uncontrollable fury some time in the future. (For evidence of this, consider the rather frequent news reports describing media preachers who "suddenly" fall into sexual sin.)

Develop Personalized Means of Self-Nurture. The specific ways we determine to love and care for ourselves will be quite particular to our own unique personalities. What things nurture you? How well are you doing at making sure those things are in your life?

❑   ❑   ❑

Time Out

How Well Am I Taking Care of Myself?

We will typically ask people, "What do you like to do?" Some people respond: "I like to go to the mall, walk around and look at people." Or: "I like to take a bath."

So we'll say, "Can you do that once a day? Can you do something like that? Can you spend twenty minutes reading a book, if that's what you like to do?"

How about you? Do you regularly engage in some pleasurable activity, just pleasurable for you and not doing something for somebody else? That's self-nurture. Here are some other questions to ask yourself about how well you take care of yourself:

❑ How much rest and sleep am I allowing myself each day? Explain:

_____

_____

❑ What forms of exercise do I engage in regularly? Explain:

_____

_____

❑ How would I describe my eating habits? Am I getting the best nutrition, or frequently binging on fast foods? Explain:

_____

_____

❑ How much "personal space"—alone time and free time—do I have in my days? Explain:

_____

_____

❑ What friendships am I enjoying? Explain:

_____

_____

❑ What "creative outlets" do I have in my life right now—things I do that make my life interesting, and that tap into my special abilities?

(Examples: *I take calligraphy classes at the junior college; I spend some time woodworking on Friday evenings; I listen to classical music at lunchtime.*) Explain:

_____

_____

❑ How would I rate my ability to set personal boundaries in my life right now? Explain:

_____

_____

❑ How have I been cultivating my relationship with God—doing things that nurture my soul?

(Examples: *I spend a few minutes in Bible reading after the kids leave for school; I pray as I'm driving to work; I sit in silence with God just before starting my chores.*) Explain:

_____

_____

❑ What other things do I need in my life in order to be whole, healthy, and growing? (Examples: *I'd like to get back to playing my guitar; I need more art in my life, more color; I need some time away from the kids; I need. . . .*) Explain:

_____

_____

❑   ❑   ❑

Knowing the Difference: Self-love or Selfishness?
Someone might say: "Aren't we supposed to love God and not self?"

Is it true that "self is hateful," as Pascal once suggested? Should we hate ourselves, in order to have a deeper spirituality, a sense of closer relationship to God?

Or can we distinguish between appropriate self-love and sinful selfishness? I believe we can, if we recognize that the thing we love—ourselves—has no value apart from the value that was created for it by the Creator. In other words, God has not loved us because of our inherent worthiness to be loved. Rather, He Himself has created something valuable, something worthy to be cherished. If He has created our worth, should we not fear to disdain it?

We can make such distinctions intellectually, of course. But that does not guarantee our avoidance of a perverted self-love. As writer Jane Austen once said: "I have been a selfish being all my life, in practice, though not in principle." Self-deception lurks at every turn. Thus, we must admit: we take a risk in loving ourselves, knowing it can lead us dangerously close to the precipice of narcissism.

In Ephesians 5:29 Paul says, "After all, no one ever hated his own body, but he feeds it and cares for it, just as Christ does the church." Yet many people, particularly some Christians, continue to feel that it is somehow wrong to love and take care of themselves. They feel that if they are not doing something for someone else then they are not serving God properly. According to Paul, however, we are to love ourselves as Christ has loved the church. I can think of no greater love than the love Christ has for His flock, and we are to love ourselves with this same powerful love.

The church father Augustine (A.D. 354–430) once said:

> Two cities have been formed by two loves: the earthly by the love of self, even to the contempt of God; the heavenly by the love of God, even to the contempt of self.[6]

Yet I believe even this great saint came to see that there must be a form of self-kindness that frees us to receive God's grace. Augustine had spent years hating himself because he felt powerless as a young man to control his sexual lust (he lived with a woman out of wedlock for years). But once the grace of God burst into his life, he was able to let go of his self-loathing.

Augustine also proclaimed: "God is always trying to give good things to us, but our hands are too full." Sometimes what our hands continue to grasp so tightly is the sad, mistaken belief that we are too sinful even for God to love. Surely it is a challenge to *learn simply to receive*.

The Challenge of Active Receiving

By emphasizing the active nature of love we properly stress the danger of mere passivity. The only positive aspect of passivity is this paradoxical truth: the natural seeking we do—the work of love—must be nurtured, yet ultimately love can only be received as a gift.

Unfortunately, people expect love to just blossom in their lives, not investing the time and energy to, in a sense, prepare the soil of the heart. No wonder they become discouraged so quickly when they fail to find the love they need.

The passive aspect of love is our acceptance of it. But unless we are encouraging the yearning, our passivity will end up denying us the thing we need. God's love does not have to be earned, but it does have to be actively accepted. There is a difference. The story of John Wesley demonstrates how active seeking led to being graciously grasped by the love of God.

The young Anglican priest had set out from England to be a missionary among the American Indians in Georgia. He experienced some success there as a preacher, but felt primarily defeated. He was recalled to England after only two years because his visitation practices were considered "too censorious."

On the voyage back to England, Wesley's boat was threatened by a severe storm, and he became deathly afraid, writing in his journal: "I went to America to convert the Indians, but oh, who shall convert me?"

Later that same year . . .

In the evening I went very unwillingly to a [church] in Aldersgate Street, where one was reading Luther's Preface to the Epistle to the Romans. About a quarter before nine, while he was describing the change which God works in the heart through faith in Christ, I felt my heart strangely warmed. I felt I did trust in Christ alone for salvation. And an assurance was given me that He had taken away my sins, even mine, and had saved me from the law of sin and death.[7]

Wesley was surprised by love, but he also had been—and continued thereafter to be—actively in pursuit of God's love in his life. The overwhelming love of God initially caught him unaware and warmed his heart. Love had been his aim, but he knew little of its power until it found him. The great paradox, once again: We choose, but find that we have been chosen already.

And here is the crux of the problem for so many adults. When we have not learned the process of receiving love as children and are unable to accept other people's love and process it into ourselves, we become frustrated. We feel that it should happen automatically and we are not willing to expend energy—as the true seekers always do.

If we were frustrated as children in trying to obtain love we would just simply stop looking for it. It is this inertia that creates the love vacuum. Yet receiving anything—even a gift—requires a reaching out, action, and energy. We must open our arms.

Opening Our Arms to Love

"Love me. Please love me!" This is the cry of every heart. Yet the problem is not that we are not being loved, it's that our arms are not open to receive that love.

I believe it is possible to learn how to access and take in the love that is around us every day and incorporate it into ourselves. As Leo Buscaglia says: "Love is a learned emotional reaction. It is a response to a learned group of stimuli and behaviors."

There is a way, then, to begin placing ourselves in love's path. It is not a guarantee that we can produce what we want. And of course, even without doing a thing, love may enfold us at any time and warm our hearts. But a commitment of time and energy will help prepare the way. Consider these steps:

Face Past Pain. We must face the past, pain and all. It is especially important to be realistic about how our love needs were met, or not met, as a child. How shall we go about this? The first step might be to find a counselor to help us explore our past with our eyes on childhood deprivations. However, some people begin by doing this "pain work" on their own. Allen reported this experience:

> Sometimes I would just feel a lump in my throat, or a heaviness in my chest, during an afternoon at home. It was like I wanted to be sad but didn't really want to let myself feel it. I'd want to eat or go rent a movie, or do anything but stick with that feeling. I think I feared that a bunch of crud wanted to come to the surface all at once.
>
> Many times, I'd hold it in and it would just go away if I distracted myself enough. But sometimes I'd go in the bedroom and lay down and let the feeling come up to see what was there. Usually, if I paid attention to it long enough, it would bring pictures to my mind, kid-scenes of being alone, or of being put down. Mostly I had this picture of myself as small and weak and basically helpless.
>
> I'd even get down on the floor and kneel with my head bowed, because it often felt like I was in a corner, with people looking at me, making me ashamed. And this incredible hurt welled up.
>
> I started doing this a lot. I dreaded these feelings, but I also *wanted* to have them because it felt like the most honest thing I had done all week.
>
> I would almost always cry for a while. Sometimes, I'd really wail.

As strange as it may sound, the more we allow this type of bubbling up of pain, the more we are fearfully drawn to it. Why? Because it is honest. To be in contact with the truth of our childhood deprivation, as painful as it may be, has an edge to it that tells us we are *alive*. And this life—with its joys and tears—is always better than the dullness of denial. Over time we become generally happier in our lives—the paradox of pain. For we have softened our souls and opened up not only to pain but to love.

Everything in us tells us that to feel pain is bad. "Don't do it!" But the truth is that the way out of pain is through the pain. Don't get me wrong, it is not easy to do this work of grief. It may well be the hardest work of all.

> To fight aloud, is very brave—
> But *gallanter*, I know
> Who charge within the bosom
> The Cavalry of Woe.[8]

To cry out with tears, sobs, groans is not self-pity but self-care. Mourning allows us to move from a place of despair, where we are totally alone with our pain, to a place of freedom where we trust there is no place or time where pain may assault us that the loving, healing, transforming grace of God will not encompass us.

> In the midst of winter,
> I found within me an invincible summer.[9]

❑   ❑   ❑

Time Out

We often hold our emotional pain in our bodies in the form of muscle tension. So take a moment to do a quick "Feeling-Tension Inventory." Just pause for a moment, take a couple of deep breaths, and begin checking out your body.

❑ Where do you sense tightness, discomfort, or pain?

❑ Place your hand down by your abdomen and breathe. Get a sense of what you are feeling down in that area. Are you unsettled, not at peace?

❑ Put your hand over your heart, and just allow yourself to feel what's going on in your heart. Are you tenderhearted? Heavy-hearted? Is your heart aching?

❑ Place your hand at your throat and along your jaw muscles. Are you swallowing back hurt, anger, sadness, fear? Are you clamping down on your feelings? Do you wish to "snap" back at someone, or "bite their head off"?

It is good to take time regularly to ask ourselves: *Where is the anger in my body just now? the hurt? the sadness? the fear?*

❏   ❏   ❏

Overcome Denial

True psychological and spiritual growth can only occur through the sharing and confronting of past and present pain and problems. The problem here is that it is very difficult to admit that one was not loved as a child. Denial is very powerful. As we have shown, at some level it is easier to have high blood pressure than to admit you weren't loved.

Writer Joanna Powell compiled quotes from numerous famous men who spoke about their relationships with their fathers. Many of these men did have the courage to face the pain of their childhoods.

> I can't even imagine a father who is nice or kind or good. Whenever I think of a child, I always think of somebody afraid. Whenever I think of a wife, I always think of somebody afraid. I'll never be writing about the Waltons or a Cosby-like family, because they simply did not exist in my universe.[10]

Does everyone have a childhood like that? Of course not. However, the possibility of love calls us to explore the truth of our lives. Many of us have put on rosy-colored glasses to view our pasts. And time, rather than healing all wounds, has simply covered them with perpetually tender scar tissue.

Accept What Is Given As Enough

I believe we can find more tangible evidence of love in our lives if we look at the circumstances and accept them for what they are. Love may be as simple as someone wanting to spend time with you, a friend calling on you to check on you or just to talk. Take in and savor every act of love, just as it is. If we are always looking for more, we will stay unhappy. Learning fulfillment in what God provides is a great gift. As the Apostle Paul said, "I have learned to be content whatever the circumstances."

"But I'm so lonely most of the time."

Yet even loneliness itself can be the gracious means of greater love for us. If we are willing to honestly accept our state of aloneness, it can become an opportunity to reach out to others in similar circumstances.

> There is a tendency in each one of us to deny loneliness. We want to live life independently, no leaning on other people. But a nagging sense of loneliness keeps getting in the way. Sometimes it becomes so severe we can hardly think about anything else. I believe God created us incomplete, not as a cruel trick to edge us toward self-pity, but as an opportunity to edge us toward others with similar needs. His whole plan for us involves relationships with others:

reach out to the world around us in love. Loneliness, that painful twinge inside, *makes* us reach out.[11]

It is so important to accept what is given to you as enough—when people want to nurture you or be with you and spend time with you. It is our decision to accept those people loving us that will fill our love needs.

Accepting what is given to us will become more automatic over time, but at the beginning it requires a lot of concentration and hard work. It must be a daily exercise in our lives if we are to succeed. We'll actually be on the lookout for circumstances in which people want to nurture us and we'll accept that for what it is: somebody loving us. It may be as simple as someone taking us seriously or listening to our concerns, dreams, and desires. When we start to look at it this way we can find in our daily lives an almost overwhelming presence of love.

Risking for Love

Everything we have been saying requires some risk. We have seen that love is a gift, but it is by no means a passive encounter. Thus we speak of the "work" of love.

To be loved, and to love, needs courage, the courage to judge certain values as of ultimate concern—and to take the jump and stake everything on these values.[12]

And so this is the challenge: to risk change. It is easy to stay the way we are, for change requires energy, courage, and even pain sometimes. However, being unfulfilled and unhappy should be reason enough to seek change. The possibilities of psychological well-being and spiritual growth are even better reasons. Growth, however, only comes through identifying problems and then confronting them.

It is not God's will for us to remain separate and lonely but to be in communion with others and with Him in true love. This is our goal and this is our challenge, but *we must take the jump and stake everything on it if we are to succeed.*

PART THREE
Healing Others

10

Loving Your Neighbor

What does love look like?
It has the hands to help others.
It has the feet to hasten to the poor and needy.
It has the eyes to see misery and want.
It has the ears to hear sighs and sorrows.
That is what love looks like.

—Augustine

Inside of every human being God exists
and waits to be detected
so that He may thrive.

—Louis Evely

Practice random kindness
and senseless acts of beauty.

—Bumper Sticker

An old story tries to describe the difference between heaven and hell. It seems that a potential resident of one or the other destination was given the opportunity to visit both of the places to compare their accommodations. St. Peter first took this man to hell. There he saw laid out before him a banquet table that stretched into eternity. The table was piled high with the most

183

delicious-looking foods. Yet the diners sitting at the table were suffering terribly, apparently in the last throes of starvation.

"Why are these people starving?" the man asked.

"Look closer," said St. Peter.

The man looked and saw that the only eating utensils available were long, pointed sticks tied to the unhappy banqueters' hands. It was impossible to bring the food up to their mouths.

Then St. Peter took the visitor up into heaven. There, to his amazement, the man saw a similar banquet table, stretching forever, with a throng of healthy, joyful, and obviously well-fed people eating and celebrating. They too had long slender utensils in their hands.

"Why are these people not starving, just as the ones we left below?"

"Look closer," replied Peter.

And when he looked he saw that the banqueters were reaching out, lifting the food not to their own mouths, but to the lips of their brothers and sisters sitting across from them.

Reaching Out

Clearly an apocryphal story; however, it makes a valid point about love: It is not a thing to be used for our own purposes alone. Love is meant to be raised from our hearts and lifted out to others as we form relationships with them. God is in relationship with us, and He calls us to this relationship to love us; thus we are able to love Him back. The natural extension of this relationship is to reach out to the rest of God's creatures.

You don't live in a world all alone. Your brothers are here, too.[1]

In chapter 2 we spoke of the problem of codependency and made the point that it hinders personal growth when we hand over to others the responsibility for our lives. We lose our true self and begin to feel we have no choices; our lives become controlled by those we hope to please or attempt to "save." So we must seek a greater degree of independence.

Yet it is possible to go too far. Some people feel they must be *completely* independent to be happy. They spend much energy "doing their own thing." They go out of their way to show that "I am my own person"; or that "I did it my way." They end up isolated and lonely. For it is unrealistic to think that we can live a life with no dependence at all. Molly Haskell summarized the problem in a magazine article entitled "Can You Be Too Independent?" She directed her words to women, but they apply to anyone who is afraid to risk appropriate dependence in a relationship:

Running away from love, as from any permanent alliance, is never far from the forefront as a national sport. . . . It may be that as women our dependent, love-addicted selves continue to hover over us like shadow limbs. It is perhaps the sense of this, the temptation to fall back, that underlies the strenuous refusals of young women to countenance or enter into any relationship that smacks of dependence. The fear is that it will feel *too good,* like drowning in a warm bath. But it may also be that we are conceptualizing as an "unacceptable" dependency what is in fact a source of power: the ability to acknowledge dependency and at the same time recognize the force of love.[2]

Can loving and being loved be a *source of power?* I believe it can. Love empowers us to become all that we can be. And for a Christian, it gives us *the means to empower others to become all they can be.* For the call to live a loving Christian life is far from a summons to become a people-avoiding hermit. It is rather an invitation to transform the world with "a vision-of-what-you-might-become," offered to one person—one neighbor, one relative, one friend, one coworker, even one enemy—at a time.

Loving God in Others

God chose to become incarnate in the flesh of human beings. Do you recognize the staggering implications of this? In a sense, whenever we long for a relationship with a fellow human being we are reaching out for God as well, for we seek fellowship with His living, breathing creation. And just the reverse is true: When we seek God we cannot ignore His creatures, expecting to have the Creator for ourselves without relating to His creative works placed all around us. Listen to how Jesus spoke to those who thought they could love God and not His people:

> I tell you the truth, whatever you did for one of the least of these brothers of Mine, *you did for Me. . . .* Whatever you did not do for one of the least of these, *you did not do for Me.*[3]

Someone has said that though God does not need our sacrifices He has chosen a representative to receive them: our neighbor. Thus our neighbor becomes for us the unseen Christ.

You may think we state the case too strongly. However, you have surely seen the power you have to bring out the saintliness in another . . . or to bury it more deeply. We have a friend who recalls seeing all of this at work when he was in his high school band decades ago.

The band director, Mr. Givens, had to choose a new drum major from among the members. Now, being the drum major in this particular band was a big deal. The accomplished group of musicians, who wore the redcoat uniforms of British Grenadiers, was going to the Macy's parade at Thanksgiving and would be seen on national TV. Whoever led the Grenadiers down through New York's Times Square would have a position of high honor. Everybody wondered: Who would Givens choose?

He chose Larry, a senior saxophone player whom we might call, nowadays, a kid "at risk." Larry was from a broken home, he'd had some scrapes with the school authorities, his grades were not good. Worst of all, he cut up a lot in band rehearsals and had received numerous detentions. But Mr. Givens saw something in Larry. Something that, if given a chance, just might blossom. He decided to risk the band's reputation—and his own—on a potential failure.

And Larry blossomed. Perhaps no one had ever said to him, either in word or action: "You have something in you akin to greatness, and I will not let you slide by without tapping it and letting it flow out." But it had been said in no uncertain terms when the huge baton was thrust into Larry's hand, and Givens said, "It's your show, guy!"

> The true light *that gives light to every man*
> was coming into the world.[4]

Let's assume for a moment that this verse means there is an ember of God's light in everyone we meet. Would that be stretching it too far? We do know, at the very least, that all humans have a built-in recognition of God's moral will.

> Indeed, when Gentiles, who do not have the law, do by nature things required by the law, they are a law for themselves, even though they do not have the law, since they show that the requirements of the law are written on their hearts, their consciences also bearing witness, and their thoughts now accusing, now even defending them.[5]

So we meet people with holy truth-embers glowing within them, perhaps so deep down they have little conscious awareness of it. Here in this person before you, then, is the potential of God's love ready to burst into the flame of belief and discipleship . . . or to slowly die out and grow cold. We are speaking by analogy here, of course, but let's continue with this suggestion: *We have tremendous power to fan holy flames—or douse them—with the quality of our human contacts.* We dare not take our life-and-death influence lightly.

> It is a serious thing to live in a society of possible gods and goddesses, to remember that the dullest and most uninteresting person you can talk to may one day be a creature which, if you saw it now, you would be strongly tempted to worship, or else a horror and a corruption such as you now meet, if at all, only in a

nightmare. All day long we are, in some degree, helping each other to one or other of these destinations. . . . There are no ordinary people. You have never talked to a mere mortal.[6]

We are the product of the things that have influenced us over the years. We could say that every experience in our lives—everything and everyone with whom we have come in contact—has acted as a chisel cutting away the statue that ends up being our whole life. And so, consider what others in your world are: *they are, in large part, exactly what you have made them.*

Love the World As God Does
Every Christian knows John 3:16,

> For God so loved the world that He gave His one and only Son, that whoever believes in Him shall not perish but have eternal life.

But in what way, and to what extent, does God love the world? One indication that we may doubt God's love of the world is the way we split off our so-called "spiritual lives" from the rest of our lives. We go for a walk in the woods and smell the flowers, delight in the sun filtering through rows of pines, observe the brilliant pink and gold of a sunset. And we love this world.

How rarely do we connect these things to our relationship with God! That is for church and prayer meeting. Yet it might be well to ask: if Jesus were walking beside us would He have any words of appreciation for what He observed with us? Could we imagine Him commenting on the shades of yellow in the flowers, or the jasmine smell in the air? If "all things were created by Him and in Him all things consist," would He nevertheless wish to ignore the beauties of this world and consider them merely "secular" distractions? But He told us to look at the flowers:

> Consider how the lilies grow. They do not labor or spin. Yet I tell you, not even Solomon in all his splendor was dressed like one of these.[7]

The same must hold true for the ugliness of the world. If the world's beauty is loved by God, does not the world's pain move Him to compassion? Should it not move us, as well? Many people know the story of Kagawa, the Buddhist man who converted to Christianity years ago. I don't know where this quote from his writings came from, but it is truly powerful:

> God dwells among the lowliest people. He sits on the dust-heap among the prison convicts. With the juvenile delinquents He stands at the door, begging bread. He throngs with the beggars at the place of alms. He is among the sick. He stands in line with the unemployed.

Therefore, let him who would meet God visit the prison cell

before going to the Temple. Before he goes to church let him visit the hospital. Before he reads his Bible let him help the beggar standing at his door.

We may prefer to think that God dwells only in heaven and relates to us only on a spiritual plane. But we can broaden our concept of the spiritual, for everything that God creates is spiritual—even the material world. And is not every relationship of love and compassion in this world a spiritual relationship?

The point is that we are called to heal others by loving them as God loves them, with unconditional love as our response to God's unconditional love of us. And we do it in the real world that we touch and see, in all its beauty and horror, as the highest of spiritual endeavors.

Probably the best description of unconditional love was written by Paul in his first letter to the Corinthians, where he says,

> Love never gives up.
> Love cares more for others than for self.
> Love doesn't want what it doesn't have.
> Love doesn't strut,
> Doesn't have a swelled head,
> Doesn't force itself on others,
> Isn't always "me first,"
> Doesn't fly off the handle,
> Doesn't keep score of the sins of others,
> Doesn't revel when others grovel,
> Takes pleasure in the flowering of truth,
> Puts up with anything,
> Trusts God always,
> Always looks for the best,
> Never looks back,
> But keeps going to the end.[8]

This is the kind of love we ought to strive for in our relationships. This is also the kind of love that is readily accessible to us, since it is offered to us freely by God. The more we learn how to accept this free gift, the more freely we will be able to offer it to others. Not only do we begin to receive healing in the warm influence of this love, we begin to facilitate healing in others as well. Giving and receiving love is one of the most important things we can learn in life. It should be one of the most important aims of our lives.

Consider how well we are doing this in the church today. We wonder whether to risk reaching out to those in "questionable circumstances" or preserve our reputation by maintaining a holy distance. But would creating such a distance really be a holy action? Charles Colson summarizes its possible consequences:

> Whether the church is willing and able to step up to its biblical responsibility is still to be decided. It may be the greatest question we face. For if we fail even the simple test of responding to human needs in our own community, what possible claim will we have to assume a role of genuine moral leadership in society?[9]

Be Alert for Needs

In light of what we have been saying it is time to ask ourselves: How available am I, ready to hear and prayerfully respond to the needs of those around me?

Can we become more available? One way would be to begin *watching for signs of people in distress today.* When our eyes are truly open to see, they will be flooded with numerous, subtle indications from those around us that "support is needed here."

What a relief it can be to a hurting person to have a friend, coworker, or neighbor inquire sincerely, "What's on your mind today?" or "How are things going with you at the moment?" Gently stick with the question after the formalities are exchanged ("fine," "OK," "can't complain") and you will find the needs pouring your way.

You have made yourself available. Now you can offer help, comfort, and those wonderful words of encouragement: "I'll be praying for you," or "Is there anything I can do?" Those words will not ring hollow, as worn-out cliches, when people find that you are staying in touch, inquiring about their progress, asking about the ongoing state of their hearts. Today any of us can open our inner eyes to see who is looking back with a plea for help. It is such a practical thing, a down-to-earth choice we make to offer what is needed in this very moment.

No, we need not *like* the potential recipient of our kindness. We can go beyond liking to loving. As writer Frederick Buechner said,

> Liking them may stand in the way of loving them by making us overprotective sentimentalists instead of reasonably honest friends.[10]

How do we do it? As creatively and generously as possible!

Booker T. Washington was born a slave. Later freed, he headed the Tuskegee Institute and became a leader in education. In his autobiography, he writes:

> The most trying ordeal that I was forced to endure as a slave boy . . . was the wearing of a flax shirt. In that portion of Virginia where I live, it was common to use flax as part of the clothing for the slaves.

That part of the flax from which our clothing was made was largely
the refuse, which of course was the cheapest and roughest part.

I can scarcely imagine any torture, except, perhaps, the pulling
of a tooth, that is equal to that caused by putting on a new flax shirt
for the first time. It is almost equal to the feeling that one would
experience if he had a dozen or more chestnut burrs, or a hundred
small pin-points, in contact with his flesh. . . . But I had no choice, I
had to wear the flax shirt or none. . . .

My brother John, who is several years older than I am,
performed one of the most generous acts that I have ever heard of
one slave relative doing for another. On several occasions when I was
being forced to wear a new flax shirt, he generously agreed to put it
on in my stead and wear it for several days, till it was "broken in."[11]

Experience the Goodness of Reaching Out

Love leads us to discovery. It teaches us about who we really are and also
about the possibilities of who we can be. Love also teaches us about others in
at least two important ways: about our connection to other people, and
about the role of our own pain in other people's lives.

Gain a Sense of Connection. People who come from dysfunctional
families often complain that they do not feel connected to other people.
They feel as though they are on the sidelines of life as life is passing them by,
but they do not really contribute or participate. They are just observers. It is
this feeling of disconnectedness that leaves people unfulfilled.

Have you ever stood at a perfectly still, clear lake or pond and watched a
soft breeze send silent ripples over it? When the surface ripples with the wind
it reflects fragment-pictures of the surroundings: sun, clouds, trees, birds . . .
and other people near—each of them with their unique joys and sorrows.

This is the way we usually approach our lives: fragments of experience
coming our way, pulling us into momentary attachments and leave-takings.
And our hectic schedule tempts us to think we are completely separate from
everyone else, perhaps in competition with them most of the time.

But the miracle of clear, calm water is that when the wind dies down, we
can look straight down through aqua transparency and see the still bottom
as a single masterpiece of wholeness. As you become vulnerable and share
more of your true self with others, you will experience love and acceptance
and incorporate love into yourself. You become connected to others in a
masterpiece of wholeness that is planned by God (its full expression being,
indeed, only within His own body):

Consequently, you are no longer foreigners and aliens, but fellow citizens with God's people and members of God's household, built on the foundation of the apostles and prophets, with Christ Jesus Himself as the chief cornerstone.

In Him the whole building is joined together and rises to become a holy temple in the Lord. And in Him you too are being built together to become a dwelling in which God lives by His Spirit. . . .

We will in all things grow up into Him who is the Head, that is, Christ. From Him the whole body, joined and held together by every supporting ligament, grows and builds itself up in love, as each part does its work.[12]

In light of this passage, I do not believe a sense of human connection is complete without the acceptance of God's love. For it is through God that we are all connected and it is through God's love that any of us are able to love each other. God's love is the source of all love, because God *is* love.

The best place to find people-connectedness, therefore, is in your church. We suggest if you are a woman that you find several women who are loving and nurturing people that you feel you can relate to. Consider forming a share group that might meet weekly. If you are a man, we would suggest the same thing with a group of men from your church. Remember that if you come from a dysfunctional family you did not see love, particularly self-love, modeled for you. It is probably very foreign to you and that is why it is so important to seek out loving people.

I [Joe] am treating a woman now who has never experienced love in a relationship. I've placed her on antidepressants, and with counseling she has come a long way; she has started forming relationships again. Her problem has been that when she finds someone to relate to, she begins to smother that person. She wants to have all of him/her, all the time, afraid he/she is going to leave her. We're dealing with her abandonment issues, but what we're also dealing with is how to share in a relationship a little bit at a time.

Building a relationship is like building a house: you don't just show up one day and the lot is cleared, and the next day the house is standing there. First you pour the footings, then you put in the foundation, and then you add the framing, and so on. That's how a relationship grows. We don't share all at once everything about ourselves, flooding the other person in one massive tidal wave of emotional release. Sharing in vulnerability must start slowly and build over time. If we do too much too soon, it can turn someone away from us.

Heal Others through Your Pain. Who shall we find to love? Bernie Siegel suggests finding some ninety-five-year-olds:

They know all the answers, because they've lived through everything that can happen. Whenever I have somebody who's ninety or ninety-five in my office I introduce her (or him) to whichever medical student is being my shadow that month. I walk in and say, for the student's benefit, "I guess you've had a tough life." And the answer is always, "No, I haven't had a tough life. That's why I'm ninety-five."

"But," I say, "didn't your house burn down?" Yes. "Business go bankrupt?" Yes. "Child run away from home?" Yes. "Youngest son die?" Yes. "Husband die?" Yes. "Second husband die?" Yes. And then she'll say, "Gee, I guess I have had a tough life."

But people like this have learned that the only way to make sure you never outlive all the people you love is to find new people to love. This is always possible, because God has given us a never-ending source of people to love. Through our pain we can find others to love and to heal.[13]

Loving others through our own pain is no easy task. It may demand things of us that we would not naturally choose to give. Yet it may accomplish things for which we would never even decide to work. For once we've been loved, we don't *work* to love, *we actually become love*. This means that when we give, it is a self-sacrificial offering. It may even lead to the ultimate sacrifice, as it did for Jesus and has for so many of His followers down through the ages. What do I mean? Consider this modern-era example:

Not many years ago, five strong, idealistic young men landed their float plane in Ecuador's Curaray River and docked it on a quiet stretch of sandy beach. They were missionaries. And they had courageously determined to be the first white men ever to make peaceful contact with the Auca Indians—natives who had lived for centuries isolated in the equatorial jungles. The Aucas were considered a "savage tribe," dangerous and unpredictable. But, as the young men would have told you, "They needed the Gospel."

The events of that day are rather sketchy. But one of the men, Jim Elliot, kept a diary, so we can put together the pieces. It seems that their first contact with the Indians was successful—at least on the surface—as they met with one man and two women. They even took the man for a ride in their plane.

Two days later, however, many men from the village came back and confronted the newcomers. The two groups faced each other there on the beach, apparently not knowing exactly what to do or even think. Not able to communicate, they no doubt stood and stared for a while.

But then something changed. Whether it was fear, or misunderstanding, or just a sudden rush of hatred . . . the Indians take up their bows and begin launching arrows. The young men are wounded. They struggle back to the plane. There they have rifles and bullets. There they can defend themselves.

But Jim Elliot does not pick up his rifle. "We couldn't do it," he writes. "We had decided just to shoot the guns into the air." They had come not to bring death to these people, but the message of God's love.[14]

Not one of the men survived that day.

But they opened the way. If we go to the tribe today (now called the Waorani), we will be embraced by Christian brothers and sisters—hundreds of them. And the love of God abounds.

We are, indeed, called to more than the mere giving of the love we graciously receive. We will *become love* for those around us, if we let God's work in us flow unhindered. Then, what cannot be accomplished through our servanthood? For love is the greatest power in the world. It can surmount every obstacle, smash every barrier, turn any tragedy into victory. Would we be too far from the truth if we said that, without a doubt, love will always find a way? That it cannot be stopped once you just give it a chance?

11

Loving Your Children

Give a little love to a child
and you get a great deal back.

—John Ruskin

We begin life needing everything from our parents . . . most of all, unconditional love and acceptance. And we continue to have a basic need for unconditional love all of our lives. Nowhere is this more clearly acknowledged than in the pages of Scripture, where such unconditional love shines forth like a beacon light. Consider the Apostle Paul's prayer, for instance, when he asks that we all come to know and experience this love of infinite dimensions:

> I ask [the Lord] that with both feet planted firmly on love, you'll be able to take in with all Christians the extravagant dimensions of Christ's love. Reach out and experience the breadth! Test its length! Plumb the depths! Rise to the heights! Live full lives, full in the fullness of God.[1]

Paul is saying: experience Christ's love in its fullness. *You will never be the same as when you are filled.*

Love Tanks . . . and the Love Vacuum

The Creator built us with the capacity to receive "extravagant" love, and we either take it into ourselves or suffer from its lack. This is wonderfully illustrated in the book *Love Is a Choice* by Drs. Hemfelt, Minirth, and Meier

195

in their description of love tanks. A love tank is the storage place for love inside each person. All love comes from God, and in the ideal family both parents are regularly accepting and processing this love into themselves. They share love and intimacy freely with each other and so their love tanks are nearly full. When they have children, they are not trying to fill their own love tanks from their children. Instead, they can fill their children's tanks (because at birth those tanks are nearly empty).

But the "ideal" family is, of course, extremely hard to find. Many families today are dysfunctional, with one or both parents suffering love tanks that are at best partially full, but more commonly, nearly empty. They have reached adulthood untrained in the art of receiving love, thus their love tanks are never filled and they journey through life as needy people. As a couple's neediness increases they both try to draw love from each other without giving to each other. A relationship like this is doomed to failure. They are trying to siphon off the love from each other's tanks rather than voluntarily replenishing each other by giving love.

Often such parents will go to their children expecting to find love there. They reverse the God-given order that parents are to give love and nurture to their children. And their children—instead of having their tanks filled during childhood—become drained of any love. Never having learned to receive love, they approach adulthood empty and bitter. Deep down they feel damaged and can spend an entire lifetime searching for something they don't know how to find. They have a basic distrust of life.

We call this situation a love vacuum because when our God-given need for love is not met a huge void develops in us and in our relationships. Although most people cannot identify that their loneliness and isolation is created by this unmet need for love, they do experience an emptiness and pain deep within them. It is this loneliness and pain that causes people to search for something to fill this love vacuum. People spend their lives ingesting food or other substances to fill it. Or they obtain possessions, or perform certain activities, to fill up the space where love should thrive. Yet none of these substitutes can even come close to taking the place of love.

Yet a child's love tanks can be filled . . . and refilled again and again. One of my [Brian's] earliest memories takes me back to my sixth birthday. A party was planned but my father was out of town on a business trip. He intended to make it back for the party, though, and I remember being so excited that my father would be there. But when the party started . . . no Dad. Talk about disappointment! I wouldn't have known how to describe the feeling then, but I can recognize now that I needed my dad to be there in order for me to feel right with the world, to feel loved and accepted.

All of a sudden, there coming through the door, in the middle of the party my dad shows up. I still remember exactly what he brought for me. He gave me a softball bat, a softball, and a Lassie book—a Lassie Golden Book.

As I sit here at my desk, I can turn around and look back at my bookshelf and I have that Lassie book placed very carefully up on my shelf. My kids aren't allowed to look at that book without my being with them. It's that special to me, this symbol of my father's love for me. Because my dad showed up in time for my birthday party.

Discipline: Safety Vs. Overprotection

We can't provide a whole course on parenting in one brief chapter. However, we can suggest some of the ways that the theme of this book intersects with parent-child relationships. Primarily, what we're talking about here is *raising a balanced child*. For a child to be able to receive love, he has to be able to trust that he is safe. That is the main task of parents, to provide safety through the growing-up years.

The Safety Factor

In order to trust, he has to be disciplined, for discipline is what makes a kid feel safe. It sets the limits, the boundaries, that mean "I am loved around here."

All children are asking two basic questions of their parents, all the time. First: "Am I loved?" They need to know that every time—in every circumstance—the answer will be "yes," through the safety of consistent discipline. The second question they are asking is, "Can I have my own way?" For the most part, if foolishness is bound up in the heart of a child, and the responsibility of a parent is to confront and transform foolishness into wisdom, then much of the time kids need to hear, "No, you can't have your own way." They need to hear "YES, you are loved." And they need to hear "You are so loved that on occasion I can and will say NO to you, when I feel your request is unreasonable or unsafe." Knowing when to say no, knowing when to say yes. That is the task of love presented to every parent.[2]

We worked with a fourteen-year-old boy and his father. This young man's father was unable or unwilling to discipline his son with the appropriate "Noes." In a counseling session one day, the boy, in the most honest and down-to-earth revelation, told his father exactly what he was wanting. He said, "Dad, if I had a boy acting the way I am acting, I would put me on the back porch in a sleeping bag and leave me out there all night long. And I'd say, 'When you start acting right, you can come back in and be a part of this family.' "

This was a fourteen-year-old telling his father: "Please discipline me! I do not feel safe here; I'm out of control." Basically, what he is saying is, "Dad, I really want you to care enough to discipline me. I want to see you stand up and I want to know that when I hit against this brick wall it's not going to move. Love me!"

Of course, there is the other kind of parent, who wants to dictate every decision the child will make, leaving no room for testing things out and growing through mistakes and failure. Those children often end up rebelling in powerful, self-destructive ways. Having had no freedom for so many years, they burst out into various levels of anarchy.

Part of discipline is being age-appropriate. When the child is two, most of the times you are going to be saying "No," and you are going to be making all of the decisions. By the time the child is fourteen, there are more and more times when it becomes appropriate to say "Yes." And the teen begins having much more input into the decisions being made. Eventually, when he is eighteen or twenty years old, and he has to make all of his own decisions, he has some practice at doing it and some confidence in his own skills.

We can use the letter "V" to illustrate the idea here. At the bottom of the point, when a child is a newborn, they have very little decision-making capabilities. All decisions have to be made for them.

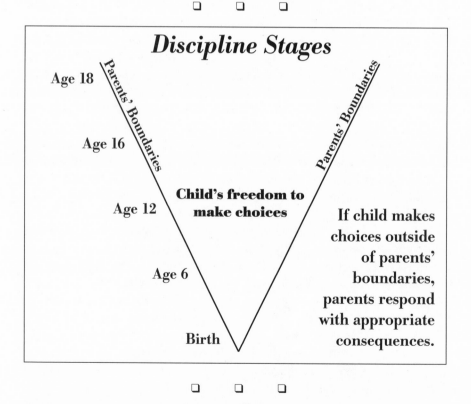

As you move up the V, so to speak, the outside of the V represents consequences, the inside of the V represents decisions that the child is able to make. As they move up the V to the point of it being eighteen, you broaden their ability to make decisions *and to be able to fail with those decisions.* Then, when they step outside of the V, that's when the consequences show that they have stepped too far and they are going to be in serious trouble. That's when you bring them back inside. As they grow, children should be given more and more opportunity to make their own decisions. But until they are on their own, they'll still have boundaries. If they cross the V and step outside of it, there is going to be a consequence.

The Danger of Overprotecting

Some parents wonder whether they say no too often. To these parents, theologian-writer Vanessa Ochs suggests a series of self-reflective questions, such as: What are the *real* risks in this situation? What might mitigate these risks? What is in it for my child if she takes these risks? Whose problem is this anyway—mine or hers? ("Am I reacting to my being a wall-flower at a dance? What wounded us may never happen to them.") Suppose I compare the *genuine risks* with the *genuine benefits?*

> When protection turns to overprotection, regardless of how we rationalize, regardless of how and why it was motivated . . . it has serious, long-term consequences for a child's self-esteem and sense of well-being. . . . [It is] an insidious form of child abuse. You are locking a child's horizons in the closet. The difference is this abuse is caused by an enormous amount of love.[3]

Alice was a thirty-eight-year-old female who came to me because of anxiety and chest pains. After a thorough physical exam with no significant findings, I decided to do an exercise stress test. Though Alice had been careful not to tell her parents about the test, she was mortified to find them waiting for her that morning outside the treadmill area at the hospital. She was angry because she desperately wanted to be on her own, but her parents still treated her like a child.

Concerned parents? Let's look deeper. Alice originally moved to New York to get away from her parents, but as is so often the case in codependent families, she was not able to completely leave home. Although she had left physically, she had not left psychologically and spiritually. She soon ended up moving back to an even more entangled relationship with her folks than she had left several years before. The relationship was cemented by the fact that not only did she work for her parents but they insisted on paying all of her bills. They retained almost complete control over their grown daughter. She considered herself to have no choice in the matter.

These parents, in the name of love, are actually not loving their daughter at all. They are fostering an unhealthy kind of dependence that

Alice could not escape. She felt helpless, as if she were being consumed.

Instead, child-rearing can be like flying a kite. You start with a little bit of string and let it out slowly. If you let out too much, the kite will fall to the ground. If you don't let out enough string over time, the kite never gets to soar. The idea is to let out enough line, to get the kite high enough to where it is flying on its own, flying real well . . . and then you let it go.

Are You Overprotecting Your Child?

Here are some age-specific indications of parental overprotection, along with some possible solutions:[4]

The overprotected child:

❑ Usually refuses to play with peers; would rather be with a parent.

❑ Looks to the parent(s) to solve problems with siblings, friends, teachers.

❑ Depends on parent to pick out clothes and get dressed.

❑ Could be characterized as "clingy."

Some signs that you are overprotective:

❑ You are virtually the only parent who still escorts your child to school or waits for the bus.

❑ You find fault with your child's friends and parents.

❑ You are quick to justify doing things for your child that other children are doing for themselves.

Ways to start letting go:

❑ Notice responsibilities and skills your child's peers have been given. Could your child do these things as well?

❑ Pay attention to the risks your child's peers are permitted. Are your prohibitions making your child feel delicate, accident-prone, or like a baby?

❑ Listen closely to what your child asks to do. Consider what motive for personal or social maturity may be behind it.

❑ Remember that school is your child's territory. Don't expect to be told everything.

❑ Help your children find solutions to their own problems. And don't make a nonissue into a big deal.

❑ Maintain time and places for your child to be alone. Everyone needs privacy.

Do for You . . . in Order to Do for Your Children

Letting kids make decisions at the appropriate time is so important. But what many parents may fail to realize is that good growth in children flows from the parents' prior ability to work on their own growth issues. Parents must be disciplined themselves, for example, in order to convey and model good discipline for their children.

Also, we can't develop our child's love receptors if we are not working on developing our own. The receptors are there in the newborn, and they are open. They need to be developed and nurtured. Discipline and the giving of authentic love is what nurtures those receptors and stimulates them so they'll continue to be open. The overly permissive child's receptors are not being stimulated. She is being given the message, "I don't care about you; do whatever you want." That child will eventually find other things to put in her receptors. Or the other child, who is raised in an overly strict environment, hears, "I'm not smart enough or good enough to make my own decisions." If his love receptors are not nourished, he will find drugs, alcohol, sex, to put in those receptors.

When we're talking to people who have a problem receiving love, and they have children, one of our primary goals is to show them *how to avoid passing on that problem to their children.* This requires two basic steps: (1) We must *do for ourselves* in order to become better parents; and (2) we must *do for our children* the things that will open their love receptors and keep them developing.

What You Can Do–for Yourself–to Become a Better Parent

If there is anything that we wish to change in the child, we should first examine it and see whether it is not something that could better be changed in ourselves.[5]

Yes, good parenting starts with self-examination. Here are three foundational requirements for "love-block recovering parents" to work on, things that will have the secondary benefit of developing their children's love receptors:

Love Your Spouse. In a healthy marital relationship, unconditional love flows from God to the husband and wife and is accepted heartily. That love replenishes their tanks and passes easily to their children. In this kind of relationship the children learn very early how to receive and process love.

In a relationship where this is not happening, the husband's and the wife's love tanks again become empty. If the mother and father can't share love between themselves, they will typically go to their children for what they lack. They will reverse the relationship and let the children parent the parents. They will develop an unhealthy attachment for one or more of the children. The kids think they are real lucky at first. But don't be fooled. They will pay, because they are going to be sucked dry. Everybody in that system gets in trouble.

Actually, one of the most common forms of passive abuse today is from lack of love between the parents. When the husband and wife live together for convenience or are "staying together for the children," but there is no intimacy and love in the relationship, the children quickly see this and suffer its consequences. This is passive abuse in that the children never have modeled for them true love or intimacy. How is it possible that they could ever learn anything about love when it is not being modeled by the people they hold in highest esteem?

"I saw Mommy kissing Santa Claus . . . "

Perhaps this old song should be the national anthem of childhood, for it expresses one of the most joyous things that can happen in a child's life. Did you ever get to see that kiss? If you are wondering at this very moment how best to encourage your child, why not walk up to your spouse right now and give him or her an affectionate hug and kiss? Let little Billy see the love flowing in your home.

Feel Your Feelings. This is needed in order to make "feeling feelings" OK in the family in general. But it starts with you. First, we need to make time for focusing, allowing the pain of imperfect love to have its rightful place in us. Naturally, we need to be careful in exploring this kind of pain by ourselves. The hurt, anger, and grief involved need to be "processed," that is, released slowly, in a controlled environment, and allowed to have their say with appropriate impact. There are times when we need to be with a friend, a pastor, a Christian counselor, to think through, and feel the effects of such issues.

But in general, in counseling we encourage people to feel the feelings they are feeling as a way to begin the process of healing. Pain has been festering for years, leaking out its poison in the form of broken relationships and addictive behaviors. Once we open that up and get that pain out and talk about it and grieve it out, then that kind of wound does not have to continue affecting us the rest of our lives. One of our friends, a writer, journaled this process over the years. Here is an entry he made on a day when fear rose to the surface:

I have a lot of fear today. What is my fear trying to say? Maybe it can teach me about what's happening inside.

A childhood scene emerges: I'm playing in the front yard of our old frame house on 57th Street. Twilight descends. As a chilly breeze lifts my hair, I can see the lace curtains cascading out through open windows, looking like ghosts trying to escape the living room.

I'm through playing in the yard now. And I suppose I'm too little to imagine that my house might be empty when I go inside. But it *is* empty. So I clack through the shadowy rooms, wide-eyed, leather saddleshoes on hardwood floors.

Where is Mommy? Where did Daddy go?

I race up the back stairway to the old couple living on the second floor. But no one answers my little fist's rap-tap-tap on the door. . . . Overhead a couple of moths click against the bare lightbulb. It's dusty up here, and the dust drys out the back of my throat. Hard to swallow.

Panic! My first heart-ripping encounter with ALONE. I'm scared.

I have suffered panic attacks since then, too. Talking with my friend, I asked: "When is this going to let up?" She said: "Invite your fear inside; find out what it will teach you." I can see that my only defense is having no defense at all—complete and total acceptance of this feeling of anxiety. It will draw me into a better, calmer place if I follow where it leads.

As we allow it to happen, feelings bubble up at the most unexpected times. We cannot plan for this, for we have held in the feelings for so long that they surge up for validation at the least loosening of our grip. Perhaps this was the experience Lord Tennyson spoke of when sadness whelmed up in him in a "happy" field:

> Tears, idle tears, I know not what they mean,
> Tears from the depth of some divine despair
> Rise in the heart, and gather to the eyes,
> In looking on the happy Autumn-fields,
> And thinking of the days that are no more.

We can't go back and change the days of our past; those days truly are no more. But we can let their sadnesses become an acknowledged part of us. Yes, and we can "find out" about our fears, our angers, our joys. Rather than numbing the feelings, we can heighten our awareness. To defend against fear or any other so-called negative emotion is to give it a power it doesn't deserve.

Bundling up our feelings is like harboring an abscess, and our children will feel the impact of our sickness. In physiological terms, an abscess is an infection in a closed space. You can take all the antibiotics in the world, but it's not going to make that abscess better because the antibiotics can't get to it. The only way to cure an abscess is open it, what we call I&D (incise and drain). Once you open it and let it drain freely, it gets better on its own. It may produce a scar. But you're not going to be sick anymore.

Another word of caution, though. Sometimes what an abscess will do is come to the surface on its own. It becomes so large that it bursts on its own. You don't want that to happen. That's dangerous, because festering emotions can burst out in panic attacks, severe depression, and raging behaviors. But if we can bring these issues up slowly, process them with someone who knows how to help us, we drain those feelings . . . and the wounds heal.

One question Christians sometimes ask: How can a person—who sincerely wants to survey the past for personal pain and deal with it—avoid the "false memory syndrome"?

Many times in counseling sessions we'll start out with prayer, asking God that if there is any pain in this person's life that they need to deal with, that He would show them that. There is such a thing as false memory syndrome, in which counselors influence people to relive certain things that actually never occurred. But we can ask the Holy Spirit to bring to mind the things we need to face. It is the Spirit's job, after all, to "convict of sin" and direct us, and all our pain flows from some lack of conformity to God's will, things we have done or things others have done to us. With the required precautions, God can use our memories as part of our healing process.

Learn to Play Again. If we are to become better acquainted with our true self, what some have called our inner child, it will mean not only coming to grips with our sadness but also rediscovering our innate playfulness. The blessed paradox of doing our pain work is that in releasing our grief we at the same time release our childlike capacity for wonder, joy, laughter, and even silliness. What a joy this can be for our children—to have playful parents.

When did you last sit at a playground and watch children play—just to experience what it is like for them? Many of us grew up too quickly. Others had no chance to be a kid at all, taking on the parenting task at the earliest age. With such a lost childhood, we need to go back and experience it as adults.

One counselor uses "play therapy" in this process: having adults draw pictures, play games, make clay sculptures. One of his clients was struck by the fact that he didn't know how to do somersaults.

When we play, when we are finally able to go out and just get lost in joy and fun, we know we are healing. I [Joe] think of my kids, Joseph and Jenna, watching our cats and horses. They will watch and see the animals do something silly and they will fall on the floor laughing. My daughter, Jenna, wanted to make a video to send to the "America's Funniest Home Videos" program. We have a horse that likes to play with balls, so we rolled a soccer ball out to it, and somehow that horse just stuck its leg out and kicked the ball back to us. It wasn't that big a deal until we saw it on tape later. We were screaming with laughter. We couldn't believe our soccer-playing horse.

To be able to watch an animal have fun and really enjoy it, that is your inner child coming to the surface. If your initial feeling upon being invited to do something like that is: "Oh, that's stupid; that's a waste of time," perhaps that is the indication that you should go for it!

> The more people have studied different methods of bringing up children, the more they have come to the conclusion that what good mothers and fathers *instinctively* feel like doing for their [children] is the best after all.[6]

What You Can Do–for Your Children–to Open Their Love Receptors
We have said that we must do things for ourselves to better prepare our love receptors for our effective, loving parenting. But we can also begin doing things for our children—immediately—to keep their receptors opening and developing. It may help at this point to make explicit what we have been addressing from many angles throughout this book: That learning to receive love is a developmental process that occurs in stages, beginning at the earliest age.

❑　　❑　　❑

THE DEVELOPMENTAL STAGES OF LEARNING TO LOVE

Stage One Intact and open love receptors.

Stage Two Environmental forces impact the love receptors.

Stage Three Conditional acceptance and/or abuse: love receptors become blocked. The love-block.

Stage Four Compensating for blocked receptors by seeking to "fill up" on other things.

Stage Five Finding healing and restoration/opening of love receptors. A lifetime of learning to let go of "counterfeit loves."

Stage Six Giving love: strengthening of love receptors in self and others.

❏ ❏ ❏

How shall we encourage this developmental process in our children? Here are some suggestions:

Cut Down on the Shaming

I [Joe] was examining a mother who had a young child in my office. While I was examining her, the little boy was exploring around, picking up things, looking at things—and the mother was constantly turning around to yell: "Stop that! What are you doing? Don't you know that this is an office?"

Clearly the child was embarrassing his mother. She sensed she was out of control, so she was shaming her child. "You know better than that! You shouldn't touch things! What's wrong with you?" Finally, I had to stop her and say, "Look, first of all, this child isn't doing anything that any other normal child wouldn't do—exploring a new environment. And second, I have kids, so this doesn't bother me at all. And third, let's look at why you're doing this to your kid." We talked about normal behavior, normal discipline, and how not to shame. No one had ever taught this young mother how and when to discipline.

I [Brian] was kind of a neat freak about keeping our basement garage cleaned out. One day as I was cleaning the garage, I ran across my father's old bowling ball, the one he hadn't used in years. I knew it was something that was just in the way, so I decided that it needed to go.

I would always put the garbage in big plastic trash bags, but I knew this ball wouldn't work in one of those bags because it couldn't be picked up without breaking the bag. So I decided the way to dispose of it was to put the ball out in the woods behind our house. That way it would be out of the way, we'd be rid of it, and it wouldn't be any problem.

Well, the bowling ball actually rolled down into a neighbor's yard behind us. They found it and saw that it had my father's initials on it. Calling him up, they said, "Hey, we found your bowling ball in our backyard." And did I get teased by the rest of the family!

"Brian's just throwing bowling balls out in the woods!"

"How many squirrels did you knock down, Brian?"

"Did you score a turkey?"

When I was in my counseling training program, I shared that story with my teacher, Larry Crabb, and he said, "Yes, what you really wanted to have happen was for a parent to come alongside you, put their arm around you, and say, 'Hey, you're very creative in trying to get rid of that bowling ball. You had a dilemma on your hands. You had a problem. You had a bowling ball you didn't know how to get rid of. And creatively you chose to dispose of it in the woods.' " He affirmed the good part of what I had done, rather than shaming the "strange" part. I believe we can do that with our children too.

Increase the Instances of Unconditional Loving

Every time a child does some kind of wrong behavior, that is an opportunity for a parent to show unconditional love. In other words, we don't reject the child, we reject the behavior. But we still love that child.

That is a challenge for parents. Most of the time, kids do things a certain way, usually not the way we would do them. But every action they take is a "teachable moment." It is an occasion for us to show appreciation for their creativity, to correct the behavior—if necessary—and to affirm our unconditional love for them.

> There is always one moment in childhood
> when the door opens and lets the future in.[7]

Focus on Process Too

Our children need our time. I think that is where we, especially dads, can tend to struggle, not being able to allow the time that we have with our kids to be *a process of fun*. If we are doing something with our kids, we are often in an accomplishment mode, more focused on some predetermined goal. We miss the process and the relationship that comes through the process. Both of our wives have had to teach us this.

One day my [Brian's] four-year-old daughter Rachel was watching TV and she said, "Dad, what does it feel like to have a cream pie thrown in your face?" I said, "Honey, I don't know. I've never had that experience before. Why don't we go and find out?" We got in the car, drove to the store, bought whipped cream and some pie pans.

It was raining outside when we arrived home, so we got in the bathtub with our clothes on. Then we filled up these pie pans with whipped cream and took turns smashing them in each other's faces. I remember that as we were winding down, I was thinking: *OK, that goal is completed, check it off. What's next?*

As soon as I had that thought, I started cleaning up the mess. But my wife Debi stopped me and said, "Honey, don't miss the process." You see, Rachel still wanted to sit in the tub, play in the whipped cream, throw it on each other, and still have fun with it. I was just thinking, we accomplished the goal, let's move on to the next thing.

Women may be better at the process part than men. I [Joe] know my wife is so much better at that than I. And yet, I think kids need to learn what it is to be goal-oriented too. They need that balance. That is why God gives us a father and a mother. Jo Nell can get on the floor and lie around with the kids and just be lost in something, and Jenna has taught me about enjoying the doing. She truly knows how to have fun doing anything. But children also have to learn that accomplishing things is (1) important, and (2) can also be fun.

My son Joseph and I do a lot of things out on our farm. It is something we have in common. We really enjoy working with each other. At times when we are kind of drifting apart or if our relationship is having trouble, I will make a point to say, "Let's go out there, let's go do this," and we always come back with our arms around each other. Our relationship is renewed. So accomplishing when you play is important, also. It teaches a child that work is not always work. Work can be fun. You can enjoy, you can be accomplishing and enjoy.

Give Appropriate Touch

"One touch is worth ten thousand words." I don't know who first said that, but it's true, isn't it? After all, what works best when you need consoling? A few choice words of pithy advice? A well-stated admonition? A systematic review of the reasons why you might feel downhearted?

It's likely that none of these methods will reach in and soothe your aching heart the way a wordless touch can. Warm contact helps heal the part of us that does not respond to mere reason. Words certainly have their place in our relationships. But there is a time and place too for the wordless touch.

> A little four-year-old girl became frightened late one night during a thunderstorm. After one particularly loud clap of thunder, she jumped up from her bed, ran down the hall, and burst into her parents' room. Jumping right in the middle of the bed, she sought out her parent's arms for comfort and assurance. "Don't worry, honey," her father said, trying to calm her fears. "The Lord will protect you."
>
> The little girl snuggled closer to her father and said, "I know that, Daddy, but right now I need someone with skin on!"[8]

A child's self-image can blossom under a caress to the cheek, a warm embrace of the shoulders. A specific message to dads is that it is OK to hug your children. In fact, it is imperative that you do. So often dads are less demonstrative in terms of the physical side of love. If you want your kids to hug and show affection, then it comes from you. You set the tone. Sometimes parents will back off and act almost childish in saying, "Well, I'm not going to initiate it. If they want it, they will have to come to me." It is wrong for a parent to come to that point, because the parents need to be constantly reaching out to the child.

If it is inappropriate for the child, he will tell you. If she doesn't want you to hug her in public, she'll tell you. If he gets to be fifteen or sixteen, and he says, "Mom, don't kiss me in front of my friends," that's OK. But the child will tell you. But I think it is necessary, especially during those teen years, that you continue to hug your child, that you continue to show them physical love. Let them tell you what they are comfortable with.

Part of "touching" is the look we give—our focused attention and eye contact. It gives or it takes, as actor Marlon Brando came to understand:

> Most of my childhood memories of my father are of being ignored. I was his namesake, but nothing I did ever pleased or even interested him. He enjoyed telling me I couldn't do anything right. He had a habit of telling me I would never amount to anything. He was far more emotionally destructive than he realized. I was never rewarded by him with a comment, a look or a hug. . . . I loved him and hated him at the same time.[9]

"Convey God" with Your Life

It is our privilege to introduce our kids to God and God's love. We do it, initially, just with the lives we live.

> The child will receive an inherited vision of God. . . . There are two ways that God can be presented. One is very healthy; it will affirm a child and invite him or her to live more fully. The other is unhealthy; it can only threaten a child and diminish his or her prospects for life. In this second, distorted (as it appears to me) version, God loves us only *conditionally*. He loves us if, and only if, we make ourselves pleasing to him by obeying all his laws. However, if we fail—in thought, word, or deed—he will immediately withdraw his love. . . . It is a pretty heavy load to lay on a young mind and heart. If children later reject belief in this God, they are certainly one step closer to the truth.[10]

If our God is loving toward us, we will have the resources to love our children with His love. It is of course essential to involve our children in the life of the church, to be in age-appropriate Sunday School classes that teach the Word of God.

One of our favorite things to do on Sunday in the car after church is to find out from our children what they learned about in Sunday School. They always know we're going to ask them that question, so they pay close attention to the lesson. They repeat that lesson back to us. It is such a joy to hear them learning Bible stories. It is sad to see an adult new Christian, who has missed out on all those stories, have no clue as to what the Bible says. Those stories are so powerful.

Essential in developing and nurturing love receptors has to be the Word of God, putting the Word of God in the heart of children. Consider the work of the Bible Memory Association (BMA) in this regard. They have Bible memory material for children starting them as early as three years of age. Another way we can nurture those love receptors is through song—singing to our kids and teaching our kids songs. Music is a very vital, healthy way to nourish and cherish and stimulate those love receptors.

All of this happens at church, but it can be an integral part of home life too. Studies now show that children raised in churchgoing homes—with families who have devotional time, Bible reading time, prayer time—are much more stable and seem to thrive better than kids who are without these sources of spiritual nurture.

Be Willing to Admit Mistakes

The amazing thing about kids is that they are very resilient and they also have the ability to forgive easier than adults do. They don't necessarily block up their love receptors and stay angry the way adults do. They are still kind of pure in their love. One of my son Joseph's most endearing qualities is his willingness to forgive. No matter how often I blow it with him, when I ask he is always ready to forgive.

Children are resilient, and if their love receptors have not been developed they can be developed over time. And then as grown adult children, if they see you working on your issues, and if you go and ask for forgiveness, often they see the potential for a dramatic changing point in the relationship. There is always that hope of reconciliation.

I [Joe] had a patient who was very strict and very domineering in his family. He came to the point where he went to his son in tears and asked him to forgive him. This is a grown son who is married and has his own family. They started to develop a relationship like they never had before.

So we can model forgiveness and ask for forgiveness when it's called for. We can stop and say, "I sent some negative pulses through your love receptors, and I failed. That was wrong. Will you please forgive me?"

Yet these words of Anne Frank's father help keep things in perspective:

[Daddy] said: "All children must look after their own upbringing." Parents can only give good advice or put them on the right paths, but the final forming of a person's character lies in their own hands.[11]

We can only do so much to ensure our children's healthy growth in love. But we must do the best we can. If they choose to drink in our love, so be it. If they someday turn away, that must become acceptable too. For in either case, we will daily commit them into the care of the One who continues to call us all with unfettered, eternal affection:

I tell you the truth, unless you change and become like little children, you will never enter the kingdom of heaven.

Therefore, whoever humbles himself like this child is the greatest in the kingdom of heaven. *And whoever welcomes a little child like this in My name welcomes Me.*[12]

Out of the Shadows

As imagination bodies forth
the forms of things unknown,
the poet's pen turns them to shapes,
and gives to airy nothing
a local habitation and a name.
Such tricks hath strong imagination.

—William Shakespeare,

A Midsummer-Night's Dream

We began this book with a sweeping claim: that we were created for love. But is Shakespeare right? Is it possible that we too like imaginative poets have given "airy nothing" a name in hopes of making ourselves feel better? Anyone who makes a claim to "something more" in life than what we can see and touch is open to the legitimate charge of mere wish-fulfillment. Is love all that we claim it is? Does it meet our deepest need—because it is *real?*

Our Culture's Answer

We have referred to numerous works of art (literature and film) in this book because we believe art and the artist should be taken seriously; in art we discover a laudable search for life's meaning. One of the finest explorations of the workings of illusion and reality comes through in Dale Wasserman's play *Man of LaMancha*, which is based on Cervantes' sixteenth-century novel *Don Quixote*. In his book, Cervantes had developed his character, Don Quixote, as an incurable idealist, a man who believed he could redeem the ideals of chivalrous knighthood 300 years after its days of glory had faded. So Quixote wandered the countryside in rusty armor, riding an old,

213

slouching horse, seeing a castle for every roadside tavern, attacking windmills because he saw them as dragons.

The wandering knight saw beauty in everything. He searched far and wide for heroic deeds to perform, captives to free, ladies in distress to save. His view of the world was such that, in leaving reality behind, he became in the eyes of most a "crack brain," a mad dreamer.

Quixote's penchant for seeing only the good and beautiful comes through most powerfully in his relationship with Aldonza, a common kitchen maid who can't even read, who gives her body to any man who will "cross her palms with a coin." She is a woman filled with cynicism and bitterness. She hates life and she despises herself.

But what does Quixote see when he looks at Aldonza? Upon first glimpse he calls her by a new name: Dulcinea (which means "sweetness")—

> Quixote: Dear God . . . it is she! Sweet lady . . . fair virgin . . . I dare not gaze full upon thy countenance lest I be blinded by beauty. . . . Dulcinea . . . Dulcinea . . . I see heaven when I see thee, Dulcinea.
> . . . Most lovely sovereign and highborn lady—Oh, fairest of the fair, purest of the pure! Incomparable Dulcinea.
> Aldonza: Take the clouds from your eyes and see me as I really am! You have shown me the sky, but what good is the sky
> To a creature who'll never do better than crawl? . . .
> I am no one! I'm nothing!

Aldonza, of course, can't see in herself what Quixote sees. But later, toward the end of the play, when Quixote is on his deathbed and unable to comprehend anything but stark "reality," she begs him to remember what he once saw: "You spoke to me and everything was—different!"[1] So in the play, *illusion becomes reality*. Aldonza becomes beautiful Dulcinea because she has been beholden as such in the eyes of another.

There is an aspect of truth here—the transforming power of love and faith. Have you known it in your own life? Recall the look of delight from anyone you care about, especially from a parent. Did that look not reach into your soul and produce something new? Didn't you, as an object of delight, become a little bit more delightful? Yet everyone who sees *Man of LaMancha* leaves the theater knowing that Aldonza's transformation was *just* an illusion in the mind of a dreamer.

We believe the truth is fuller still. The theme of our book has been, not that illusion can become reality, but that *reality can become evident*.

When We Appear—in Reality

Can it be possible
    that joy flows through and, when the course is run

it leaves no change, no mark on us to tell its passing?
And as poor as we've begun
    we end the richest day?[2]

We believe the answer to this poetic question is no! Love and its joy do transform us. Being loved—delighted in—changes us to become what the Delighter has already declared us to be. Christian growth is about becoming who you already are. *Being the object of delight, you shall be revealed as delightful.* For if God exists, then He must be the absolute truth of existence, not a deluder or imaginative poet.

God *is* love, while Quixote was only *affected* with love—he needed it to survive—and was therefore a dreamer, for better or worse. God has no such need. He gives because He delights to do so. And as oil and water always remain separate, so there can be no mingling of illusion in what is the very essence and definition of reality itself.

When Christ, who is your life, appears,
    then you also will appear with Him in glory.[3]

So we will appear in the bright glory of truth—in our belovedness, in our complete acceptance—because all mere appearances will someday be stripped away. We shall know fully that love, and love's power, and love's source, are real because of the unquestionable change in us as having been delighted in by Truth itself. And our true condition of being delight-objects can become evident daily, as we let go of our love-blocks and learn to receive, to imbibe the truth of our having been accepted. To a great extent, what *shall be* already *is*, as we open to it.

The future enters into us,
    in order to transform itself in us,
    long before it happens.[4]

Can It Be Lived?

Opening to it is the key. For so many years I [Joe] tried to eke out my happiness from my work alone. What I did was so important to me. I submerged myself in workaholism until I came to the point of needing a reality check: to begin seeing that *my work is not who I am.* I came to realize that I could be successful, but it would not make a difference in who I was.

The trouble with the rat race is that even if you win,
    you're still a rat.[5]

So now rather than being satisfied with droplets of happiness that can come from achievement, I live into being loved simply for who I am.

And it *is* a way to live, every day. In my medical offices, love and joy now seem to flow. I've had people come to my offices not because they were sick but because they just wanted to be in an atmosphere of love and acceptance. Imagine: going to the doctor's even when you don't need to!

So keep the vision of reality, and move ahead. It's not what you do, it's who you are. It's connecting with God and others in the reality of love. I've found that the love-block offers us an amazing array of illusive false loves, tempting us to deny that we were created for love. But we can *break out of illusion into reality by living our lives as a daily assault on its unworthy vision.* Life is real, but our interpretations, so often, shimmer like mirages in the desert. They give us the illusion that love is not there for us, or that even if it is available it must be earned, or that our loneliness, fear, and other blocks are hopeless obstacles to joy. Such falsehoods can be confronted and challenged daily. Thus we move out of the dark, fearful shadows of the love-block . . . into the sunshine of truth.

The Enduring Call

We introduced our book with the story of Professor Borg in *Wild Strawberries*. Let us conclude, then, by following his story to its ending. Like any of our own lives, his could not be "all tied up neatly" at its end. The film leaves some questions lingering: Has Dr. Borg indeed responded to the tugging that tells him to relax his grip on pure self-interest? Will he be able to release his son from a burdensome loan, or accept a kiss on the cheek from his daughter-in-law, or offer a kind word to his housekeeper? Will he change, even now? Can his life be redeemed with a smile? an inward turning? a kiss?

It is possible! The turning to love requires only the smallest inner movement, a faint "yes" whispered in the inner recesses. In this respect it is not large, but it is majestic. What is required for your yes, this turning in your life? When? Where? With whom will it be?

For Borg, his hope lies in the recollection of what he has once known of love but covered up through the years. In the final scene of the film, he's in bed, but restless at the end of a long day in which he has considered being a different kind of man with his children and faithful housekeeper.

But he has trouble falling asleep. Only can he rest in the recollection of the most significant and powerful images from his childhood, when—beyond accomplishment, prestige, and financial success—he knew the blessing of acceptance.

> Whenever I felt restless or sad during the day, I'd try to relax by recalling memories of my childhood. So that is what I did this evening. . . .

In his mind's eye, before drifting off, he walks with his cousin Sara. They are looking for their parents, tramping through the woods to the other side of the small island where the family lived. And suddenly the imagery becomes surreal, as if Borg were stepping out of earth's boundaries and into a heavenly vista. As he comes to the end of the woods and steps up on the rocks at the water's edge, he looks across a small bay. And he sees Father and Mother in the distance, sitting on the shore, bathed in sunlight. They are waving, gently waving—to *him*—as if calling from the very heart of love.

And Dr. Borg can rest.

He can lay down his head in peace.

That one magnificent scene touches the core of all of us, for it is the behind-the-scenes tableau that defines the vast meaning of every life. Surely the Love-relationship in the Trinity is mirrored in the love that is possible within a human family. Though we struggle with different problems, the calling from that heart of love beckons in every unique life situation and invites a step forward out of the woods into a clearer vision. We may be in dire straits or feel mostly satisfied and content. But all of us are caught in the pull between the hope of love and the crush of our final earthly sleep. Like Dr. Borg, we are called to choose—in each act—to either strengthen our ties to the Giver of love (and His children) or gradually loosen them.

Will we wave back?

A P P E N D I X   A

Survey Your Own Relationship Patterns

Each person evolves a unique pattern, or style, of making, sustaining, and breaking major life relationships. Before probing for the factor that may have originally shaped this idiosyncratic pattern, and before embarking on corrective steps to reverse a flawed pattern, it is of vital importance to form a "map" of the apparent pattern that already characterizes your history of relationships.

Here is a survey that can help you begin to discern these patterns as you work your way through this book. Initially, it is best to focus primarily on the recurrent surface patterns without attempting to probe the underlying "why." A premature jump toward identifying the "magical key" to relationship failures or disappointments may simply reconfirm a previous false premise (such as, "I don't feel close to many people and the reason must be my inadequacy to offer anything meaningful to them").

Also, do not attempt to complete this survey all at once, in one or two sittings. Instead, come back to it after each chapter and do some additional reflecting and writing. Since writing can be a valuable therapeutic tool in the process of opening to love, we strongly recommend that you respond to this survey in a permanent journal (or at least use separate sheets of paper that you can refer back to over the coming weeks).

PHASE I

1. First, compile a list of all your major relationships throughout your history and including the present. Jot brief descriptions and dates, if possible:

Person(s):

Dates:

Nature of the Relationship:

Note: You may choose to divide this relationship survey into several broad categories such as: (a) relationships in the original family; (b)

219

relationships with the opposite sex (especially starting in the teen years); (c) relationships with authority figures; (d) relationships with colleagues at work; (e) relationships with my own children; and (f) my ongoing relationship with God.

2. Now begin reflecting on those relationships, recalling what it felt like (or feels like) to be in those relationships. For each one, ask yourself questions like these and spend plenty of time reflecting on (and writing down) your responses:

❑ How did this relationship begin?

❑ What was the apparent sense of "balance"—between giving and receiving—during the course of this relationship?

❑ What sense of trust and security came through during the relationship?

❑ To what extent did I fear that the other person(s) might leave, or otherwise disappoint me?

❑ In what ways was I critical or judgmental toward the other person(s) (perhaps as a means of masking my own insecurity)?

❑ Were there special compulsive or heroic efforts displayed to win and keep the approval of the other?

❑ What was my level of preoccupation with the other person's apparent rejection or acceptance of me?

❑ How did this relationship end? What part did my own dysfunction play? The other's dysfunction?

❑ Did I allow myself to adequately grieve the termination of this relationship? How? Or: Why not?

PHASE II

Although we caution you to avoid pushing for insights or conclusions about these relationships right away, this second phase of the survey is an effort to discern repeating patterns or major themes that have dominated the history of your "love economy." Only after completing Phase I of history recollection and journaling (which should cover several weeks) begin asking yourself the following kinds of overview questions:

❑ Are there specific types of persons (wounded birds, abusers, emotionally unaccessible, overly demanding, parasitic-dependent, etc.–which is discussed in chapter 2) that I am drawn to or that I draw to me on a recurrent basis?

❑ How is anger mediated in the relationships?

❑ Is there an invisible barrier or threshold of intimacy that I bump up against and seemingly cannot move beyond? Explain.

❑ What are the repetitious messages that bombard my thinking while in the midst of intense involvements?

❑ Am I genuinely sensitive to and responsive to the needs of the other? How?

❑ Is there a predominant sense that I am fundamentally better than—or worse than—those with whom I attempt to link up? Explain.

❑ Does there always seem to be something missing in these relationships? Describe.

The process of this survey journal and the answers to these questions create a map or topographical picture of what may be the underlying love-block. This surface picture points the way toward an understanding of the more subtle (even unconscious) love-block messages that may radiate from the core inability to receive love.

The key is to think these things through during the course of your reading—over time, with prayer, and perhaps in dialogue with a good friend or counselor. Go back to this survey again and again.

A P P E N D I X   B

The Bottom Line: Knowing the Source of Love

As you've read through this book, it should have become obvious: you cannot get to where we are talking about going without having a personal relationship with God through His Son. There is no other way. Since God is love, and all love comes from God, to have a personal relationship with the source of love is imperative in this process of learning to give and receive love.

If you do not have a personal relationship with Jesus Christ, consider opening your heart to Him today. He will not only provide the pathway for your walk in love, but your fellowship with Him will add to your life in every dimension—now and forever.

We have emphasized the unconditional nature of grace and love throughout this book, so it should be no surprise that beginning a personal relationship with Jesus is simply an act of acceptance. We admit our alienation and pure self-interest, ask God for forgiveness and help, and in an act of obedience, faith, and submission, turn away from our old life.

So ask Jesus Christ to come into your heart and live in you. Accept His presence and let Him guide you every day in deeper fellowship and discipleship.

If you have done this recently, or as a result of reading this book, let us be the first to welcome you into the family of Christ. Now begins the lifetime adventure of becoming more and more like Him as His Spirit works within you. We would love to hear from you:

Dr. Joseph Biuso
330 Turner McCall Blvd., Suite 304
Rome, GA 30165

Dr. Brian Newman
Minirth-Meier Clinic
2100 N. Collins Blvd.
Richardson, TX 75080

Now to Him who is able to keep you from falling and to present you before
His glorious presence without fault and with great joy—
To the only God our Savior be glory, majesty, power and authority,
through Jesus Christ our Lord, before all ages, now and forevermore! Amen.

N O T E S

Introduction

1. Ephesians 3:16-19.
2. John Powell, *Fully Human, Fully Alive* (Niles, Ill.: Argus Communications, 1976), 30.
3. Corrie ten Boom, *The Hiding Place* (Washington Depot, Conn.: Chosen Books, 1971), 47.
4. Matthew 11:29, italics added.

Chapter 1

1. Some of the ideas in this section come from the work of Dr. Robert Hemfelt.
2. In the Colorado Springs *Gazette-Telegraph,* August 2, 1995.
3. Thomas Campbell, from "Ode to the Memory of Burns."
4. Herbert Shipman, from "No Thoroughfare."
5. Song of Songs 8:7.

Chapter 2

1. Arthur Janov, *The New Primal Scream* (Wilmington, Del.: Enterprise Pub., 1991), 307.
2. Charles Whitfield, *Co-dependence: Healing the Human Condition* (Deerfield Beach, Fla.: Health Communications, Inc., 1991), 3–4.
3. Nathaniel Brandon, in Leo Buscaglia, *Born for Love* (Thorofare, N.J.: Random House, 1992), 139.
4. Ibid., 229.
5. Lewis Carroll, *Alice's Adventures in Wonderland* (New York: William Morrow, 1992), 60.
6. Arthur Janov, 308.
7. Leo Buscaglia, 55, 75.
8. Romans 8:35-37.
9. Romans 8:38-39.

Chapter 3

1. Norman Cousins, *Head First: The Biology of Hope* (New York: E.P. Dutton, 1989), 37–38.

2. Reported in an article by C. Ford, "The Somatization Disorders," 1983.

3. S.I. McMillen, *None of These Diseases* (Westwood, N.J.: Revell, 1963), 7.

4. Ibid., 108–9.

5. Frank Minirth and Paul Meier, et al., *Love Hunger: Recovery from Food Addiction* (New York: Fawcett Columbine, 1990), 24.

6. Norman Cousins, 35–36.

7. Bernie S. Siegel, *Peace, Love, and Healing* (New York: Harper and Row, 1989), 35.

8. Mickey Mantle, after admitting himself into the Betty Ford alcoholic rehabilitation center, in *Sports Illustrated*, April 18, 1994.

9. Adapted from material provided by Nancy Mickleson, at the Center for Psychotherapy, Geneva, Ill.

10. Pamela Pettler, *The Joy of Stress*, quoted in *Your Work Matters to God* (Colorado Springs, Colo.: NavPress, 1987), 37.

11. S.I. McMillen, 115.

12. 1 Corinthians 15:31.

Chapter 4

1. Psalms 6:6; 38:6, 8, 10.

2. William Styron, *Darkness Visible* (New York: Random House, 1990), 59.

3. Philip Yancey and Tim Stafford, *Unhappy Secrets of the Christian Life* (Grand Rapids: Zondervan, and Wheaton, Ill.: Campus Life Books, 1979), 63.

4. Josephine Hart, *Damage* (New York: Alfred A. Knopf, 1991), 9.

5. Ibid., 26–27.

6. Alfred Lord Tennyson, from *The Two Voices*, quoted in John Bartlett, *Bartlett's Familiar Quotations*, 16th Ed., Justin Kaplan, gen. ed., 453:18. (Note: *Bartlett's* will be designated as BFQ in references to follow.)

Chapter 5

1. Ephesians 4:22-24.

2. John 8:44.

3. Scott Peck, *People of the Lie* (New York: Simon and Schuster, 1983), 182–83.

4. Ibid., 206–7.

5. Frederick Buechner, *Wishful Thinking* (New York: HarperCollins, 1993), 22.

6. Chris Thurman, *The Lies We Believe* (Nashville: Thomas Nelson, 1989), 23.

7. Madame Guyon, in Richard J. Foster and James Bryan Smith, eds., *Devotional Classics* (San Francisco: Harper & Row, 1993), 322.

8. Larry Stephens, *Please Let Me Know You, God* (Nashville: Thomas Nelson, 1993), 58–59.

9. Eugene H. Peterson, *The Message* (Colorado Springs, Colo.: NavPress, 1994), 403.

10. Romans 8:29-30.

11. Romans 12:2.

12. John Powell, *Fully Human, Fully Alive* (Niles, Ill.: Argus Communications, 1976), 68.

13. Victor Frankl, *Man's Search for Meaning* (New York: Pocket Books, 1984), 33–34.

14. Ibid., 86–87.

15. Octavio Paz.

16. C.S. Lewis, *Mere Christianity* (New York: Macmillan, 1952), 190.

Chapter 6

1. Job 4:7-8.

2. Gerald May, from a Shalem Institute retreat at the Bon Secours Retreat Center, Marriotsville, Md., Dec. 6, 1993.

3. Larry Dossey, *Meaning and Medicine* (New York: Bantam Books, 1991), 212.

4. Lesley Hazleton, *The Right to Feel Bad* (New York: Doubleday, 1984), 13.

5. See Psalm 85:10.

6. Dylan Thomas, *Fern Hill.*

7. Madeleine L'Engle, *Two-part Invention: The Story of a Marriage* (New York: Farrar, Straus and Giroux, 1988), 124.

8. Oscar Wilde.

9. Victor Hugo.

10. Job 5:18.

11. C.S. Lewis, *The Lion, the Witch and the Wardrobe* (New York: Collier Books, 1950), 64, 74–75.

12. Psalm 81:10.

13. Romans 7:15-19.

14. Richard Purdy Wilbur, from *Someone Talking to Himself,* in BFQ, 750:4.

15. Maria Rainer Rilke, from *Letters to a Young Poet,* quoted in Walter Trobisch, *Love Yourself* (Downers Grove, Ill.: InterVarsity Press, 1976), 51.

16. John Steinbeck, *The Grapes of Wrath* (New York: The Viking Press, 1939).

Chapter 7

1. John A. Shedd.

2. Keith Miller, *The Scent of Love* (New York: Guideposts, 1983), 122.

3. Arthur Miller, *Death of a Salesman* (New York: Viking Press, 1949), 111.

4. David Augsburger, *Caring Enough to Confront* (Glendale, Calif.: GL / Regal Books, 1976), 100.

5. Psalm 51:6.

6. Genesis 50:15-21, italics added.

7. Matthew 6:14-15.

8. Lewis Smedes, *Forgive and Forget* (New York: Pocket Books, 1984), 45.

9. Philippians 3:13.

10. Walter Wangerin, *As for Me and My House* (Nashville: Thomas Nelson, 1987), 79.

11. Lewis Smedes, 111.

12. Dale Carnegie.

13. James E. Dittes, *The Male Predicament: On Being a Man Today* (San Francisco: Harper & Row, 1985), 58.

14. Henry Vaughan, from *The Retreat*, in BFQ, 270:5.

15. Thomas Merton, quoted in Daniel Moore, ed., *Warrior Wisdom* (Philadelphia: Running Press, 1993), 81.

16. Gerard Manley Hopkins, from *The Blessed Virgin Compared to the Air We Breathe*, in BFQ, 550:9.

17. Thomas Dreier, quoted in Lloyd Cory, ed., *Quote, Unquote* (Wheaton, Ill.: Scripture Press, 1977).

Chapter 8

1. Romans 8:34.

2. Christina Bucher, *Biblical Imagery for God* (Elgin, Ill.: Brethren Press, 1995), 1, 5.

3. Adapted from J.B. Phillips' book *Your God Is Too Small* (New York: Macmillan, 1971), Part I.

4. Eddie Ensley, *Prayer That Heals Our Emotions* (San Francisco: Harper and Row, 1988), 7.

5. Flannery O'Connor, "The Enduring Chill," in *Everything That Rises Must Converge* (New York: Signet, 1965).

6. C.S. Lewis, *Miracles* (New York: Macmillan, 1978), 94.

7. Anders Nygren, *Essence of Christianity* (Philadelphia: Muhlenberg Press, 1961), 111.

8. Max Lucado, *A Gentle Thunder* (Dallas: Word, 1995), 46–47.

9. Jeremiah 1:5.

10. John Bradshaw, *Healing the Shame That Binds You* (Deerfield Beach, Fla.: Health Communications, Inc., 1988), 11–12.

11. Elie Wiesel's story is paraphrased here, based on an interview he did in the '70s for the BBC film series, *The Long Search*, Vol. 7: *Judaism: The*

Chosen People, distributed by Ambrose Video Publishing Incorporated, New York, NY 10016.

12. Genesis 32:24-26.

13. Song of Songs 4:1-7.

14. Sallie McFague, *Models of God,* as quoted in Christina Bucher, 28.

15. Richard J. Foster, *Celebration of Discipline* (San Francisco: Harper & Row, 1978), 15.

16. James E. Dittes, *The Male Predicament: On Being a Man Today* (San Francisco: Harper & Row, 1958), 181–82.

17. Psalm 139:7, 9.

18. Gary Wilde, *Your Ministry of Prayer* (Elgin, Ill.: David C. Cook Pub. Co., 1990), 40.

19. Reported in Will Steger's *Crossing Antarctica* (New York: Knopf, 1991), 278–85.

20. Quoted in Richard Foster and James Bryan Smith, eds., *Devotional Classics* (New York: HarperCollins, 1993), 82–83.

21. A.W. Tozer, *The Pursuit of God* (Alberta, Canada: Horizon House, 1976), 80.

22. Eddie Ensley, *Prayer That Heals Our Emotions* (San Francisco: Harper & Row, 1988), 5.

23. C.S. Lewis, *Mere Christianity* (New York: Macmillan, 1952).

24. Gerard Manley Hopkins, from *Pied Beauty,* in BFQ 550:23 and 551:1.

25. Nathanael West, *Miss Lonelyhearts* (New York: New Directions Publishing Corp., 1962), 1–8.

26. Thomas Moore, *The Care of Souls,* excerpt in *Psychology Today,* May–June 1993, vol. 26, #3.

Chapter 9

1. Scott Peck, *The Road Less Traveled* (New York: Simon and Schuster, 1978), 120.

2. Jerry Seinfeld, *SeinLanguage* (New York: Bantam Books, 1993), 22.

3. The basic idea here, of reframing mistakes, draws heavily from John Bradshaw, *Healing the Shame That Binds You* (Deerfield Beach, Fla.: Health Communications, Inc., 1988), 162–65.

4. Manuel J. Smith, *When I Say "No" I Feel Guilty* (New York: Bantam Books, 1975).

5. Wayne Dyer, *Pulling Your Own Strings* (New York: Avon Books, 1978), 9–11.

6. Augustine, from *The City of God,* in BFQ 115:3.

7. Erwin Rudolph, ed., *The John Wesley Treasury* (Wheaton, Ill.: Victor Books, 1979), 68–69.

8. Emily Dickinson, in BFQ 511:13.

9. Source unknown.

10. Pat Conroy, in Joanna Powell's *Things I Should Have Said to My Father* (New York: Avon Books, 1994), 59.

11. Philip Yancey and Tim Stafford, *Unhappy Secrets of the Christian Life* (Grand Rapids: Zondervan, and Wheaton, Ill.: Campus Books, 1979), 75.

12. Eric Fromm, *The Art of Loving* (New York: Harper & Row, 1956).

Chapter 10

1. Albert Schweitzer, upon receiving the Nobel Prize, 1952, in BFQ 630:19.

2. Molly Haskell, "Can You Be Too Independent?" *Self* magazine, September 1995.

3. Matthew 25:40, 45, italics added.

4. John 1:9, italics added.

5. Romans 2:14-15.

6. C.S. Lewis, *The Weight of Glory and Other Addresses* (New York: Macmillan, 1980), 18–19.

7. Luke 12:27.

8. 1 Corinthians 13:4-8, in Eugene H. Peterson, *The Message*, 359.

9. Charles Colson, *Dare to Be Different* (Wheaton, Ill.: Victor Books, 1986), 20–21.

10. Frederick Buechner, *Wishful Thinking* (New York: HarperCollins, 1993), 65.

11. In Craig Brian Larson, ed., *Illustrations for Preaching and Teaching* (Grand Rapids: Baker Books, 1993), 139.

12. Ephesians 2:19-22; 4:15-16.

13. Bernie S. Siegel, *Peace, Love, and Healing* (New York: Harper & Row, 1989), 46.

14. See *The Journals of Jim Elliot* (Old Tappan, N.J.: Revell, 1978) and Elisabeth Elliot's book *Through Gates of Splendour* (Wheaton, Ill.: Tyndale, 1981) for a full account.

Chapter 11

1. Ephesians 3:18-19, in Eugene H. Peterson, *The Message*, 405.

2. The ideas presented in this paragraph adapted from Dr. Larry Crabb, according to Brian Newman's class notes.

3. Vanessa Ochs, *Safe and Sound: Protecting Your Child in an Unpredictable World* (New York: Penguin, 1995).

4. Chart content adapted from Vanessa Ochs, *Safe and Sound: Protecting Your Child in an Unpredictable World* (New York: Penguin, 1995), as reported

in "Overprotective Parents Build Walls of Fear Around Kids," by Karen S. Peterson, in the Colorado Springs *Gazette-Telegraph*, Sunday, October 29, 1995. Article originally written for *USA Today*.

5. Carl Jung, from *The Integration of the Personality*, in BFQ 628:13.

6. Benjamin Spock, from *The Common Sense Book of Baby and Child Care*, in BFQ 711:22.

7. Graham Greene, from *the Power and the Glory*, in BFQ 713:5.

8. Gary Smalley and John Trent, *The Blessing* (Nashville: Thomas Nelson, 1986), 35.

9. Marlon Brando, in *Chicago Tribune Magazine*, Nov. 20, 1994.

10. John Powell, *Fully Human, Fully Alive* (Niles, Ill.: Argus Communications), 71.

11. Anne Frank, from *The Diary of a Young Girl*, in BFQ 760:12.

12. Matthew 18:3-5, italics added.

Epilogue

1. Dale Wasserman, *Man of LaMancha* (New York: Dell Pub. Co., 1968). The three quotes here are taken from pages 54–55, 119.

2. C.S. Lewis, in *The Quotable Lewis*, Wayne Martindale and Jerry Root, eds. (Wheaton, Ill.: Tyndale House Publishers, 1989), 349.

3. Colossians 3:4.

4. Rainer Maria Rilke.

5. Lily Tomlin.